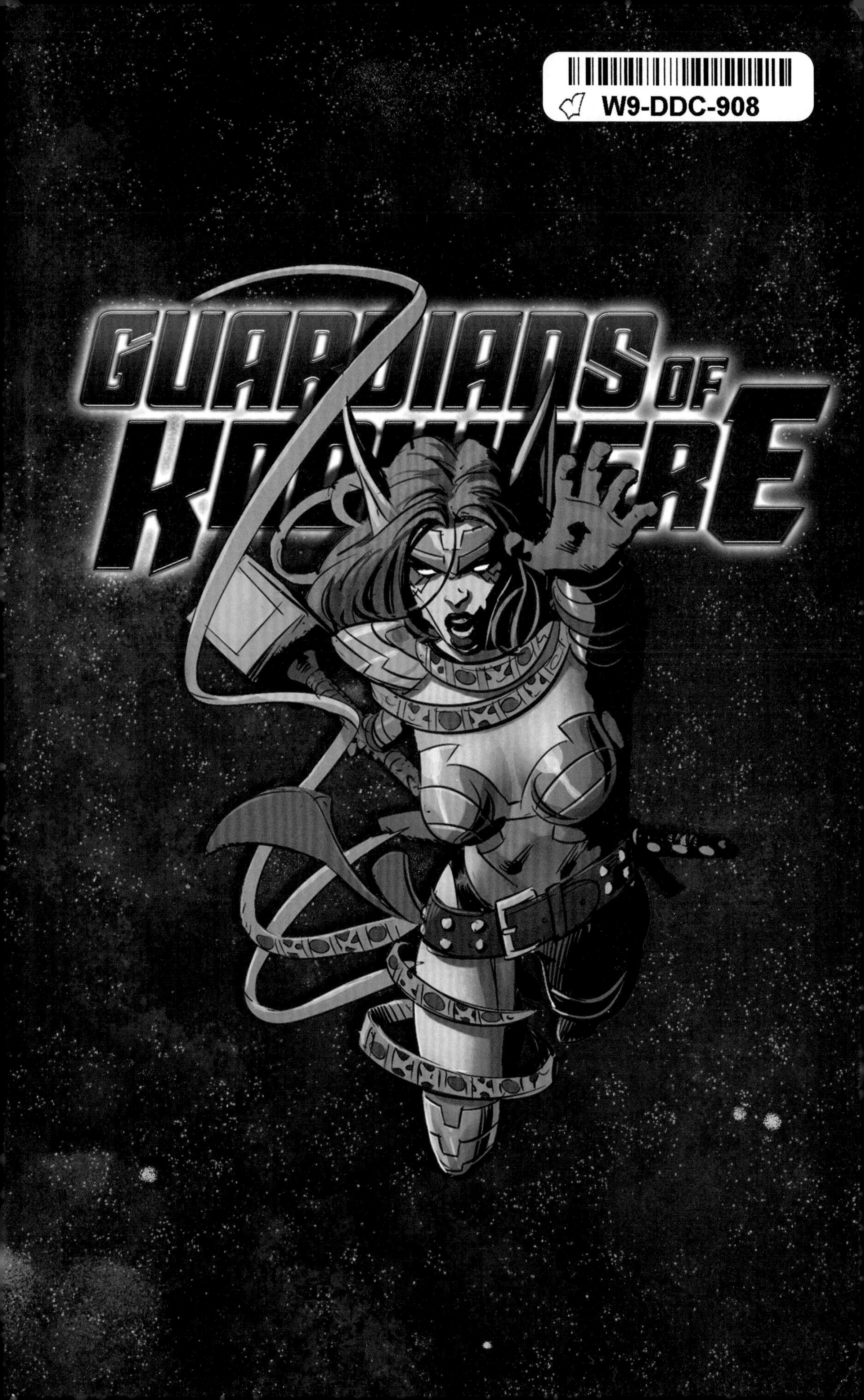
GUARDIANS OF

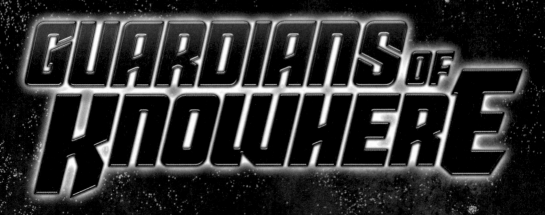

GUARDIANS OF KNOWHERE

WRITER
BRIAN MICHAEL BENDIS

ARTIST
MIKE DEODATO

COLOR ARTIST
FRANK MARTIN

LETTERER
VC's CORY PETIT

COVER ART
MIKE DEODATO & FRANK MARTIN

ASSOCIATE EDITOR
JAKE THOMAS

EDITOR
NICK LOWE

COLLECTION EDITOR **JENNIFER GRÜNWALD**
ASSISTANT EDITOR **SARAH BRUNSTAD**
ASSOCIATE MANAGING EDITOR **ALEX STARBUCK**
EDITOR, SPECIAL PROJECTS **MARK D. BEAZLEY**
SENIOR EDITOR, SPECIAL PROJECTS **JEFF YOUNGQUIST**
SVP PRINT, SALES & MARKETING **DAVID GABRIEL**
BOOK DESIGNER **ADAM DEL RE**

EDITOR IN CHIEF **AXEL ALONSO**
CHIEF CREATIVE OFFICER **JOE QUESADA**
PUBLISHER **DAN BUCKLEY**
EXECUTIVE PRODUCER **ALAN FINE**

GUARDIANS OF KNOWHERE. Contains material originally published in magazine form as GUARDIANS OF KNOWHERE #1-4 and NEW AVENGERS: ILLUMINATI #3. First printing 2015. ISBN# 978-0-7851-9844-4. Published by MARVEL WORLDWIDE, INC., a subsidiary of MARVEL ENTERTAINMENT, LLC. OFFICE OF PUBLICATION: 135 West 50th Street, New York, NY 10020. **Printed in Canada.** ALAN FINE, President, Marvel Entertainment; DAN BUCKLEY, President, TV, Publishing and Brand Management; JOE QUESADA, Chief Creative Officer; TOM BREVOORT, SVP of Publishing; DAVID BOGART, SVP of Operations & Procurement, Publishing; C.B. CEBULSKI, VP of International Development & Brand Management; DAVID GABRIEL, SVP Print, Sales & Marketing; JIM O'KEEFE, VP of Operations & Logistics; DAN CARR, Executive Director of Publishing Technology; SUSAN CRESPI, Editorial Operations Manager; ALEX MORALES, Publishing Operations Manager; STAN LEE, Chairman Emeritus. For information regarding advertising in Marvel Comics or on Marvel.com, please contact Jonathan Rheingold, VP of Custom Solutions & Ad Sales, at jrheingold@marvel.com. For Marvel subscription inquiries, please call 800-217-9158. **Manufactured between 9/25/2015 and 11/2/2015 by SOLISCO PRINTERS, SCOTT, QC, CANADA.**

10 9 8 7 6 5 4 3 2 1

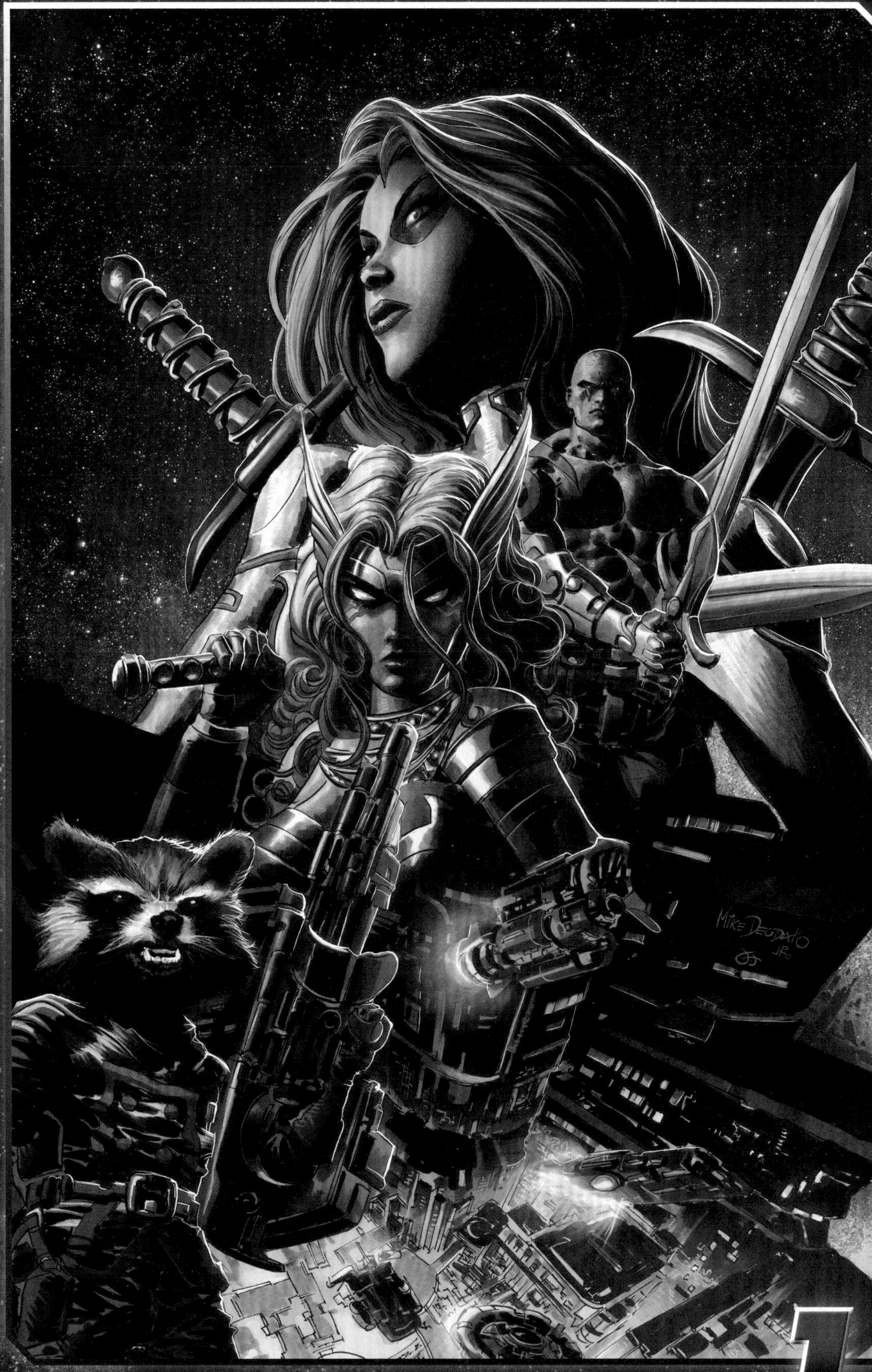
MIKE DEODATO JR.
1

SECRET WARS

THE MULTIVERSE WAS DESTROYED!

•

THE HEROES OF EARTH-616 AND EARTH-1610
WERE POWERLESS TO SAVE IT!

•

NOW, ALL THAT REMAINS...IS **BATTLEWORLD**!

•

A MASSIVE, PATCHWORK PLANET COMPOSED OF THE FRAGMENTS OF
WORLDS THAT NO LONGER EXIST, MAINTAINED BY THE IRON WILL OF ITS
GOD AND MASTER, VICTOR VON DOOM!

•

EACH REGION IS A DOMAIN UNTO ITSELF!

GUARDIANS OF KNOWHERE

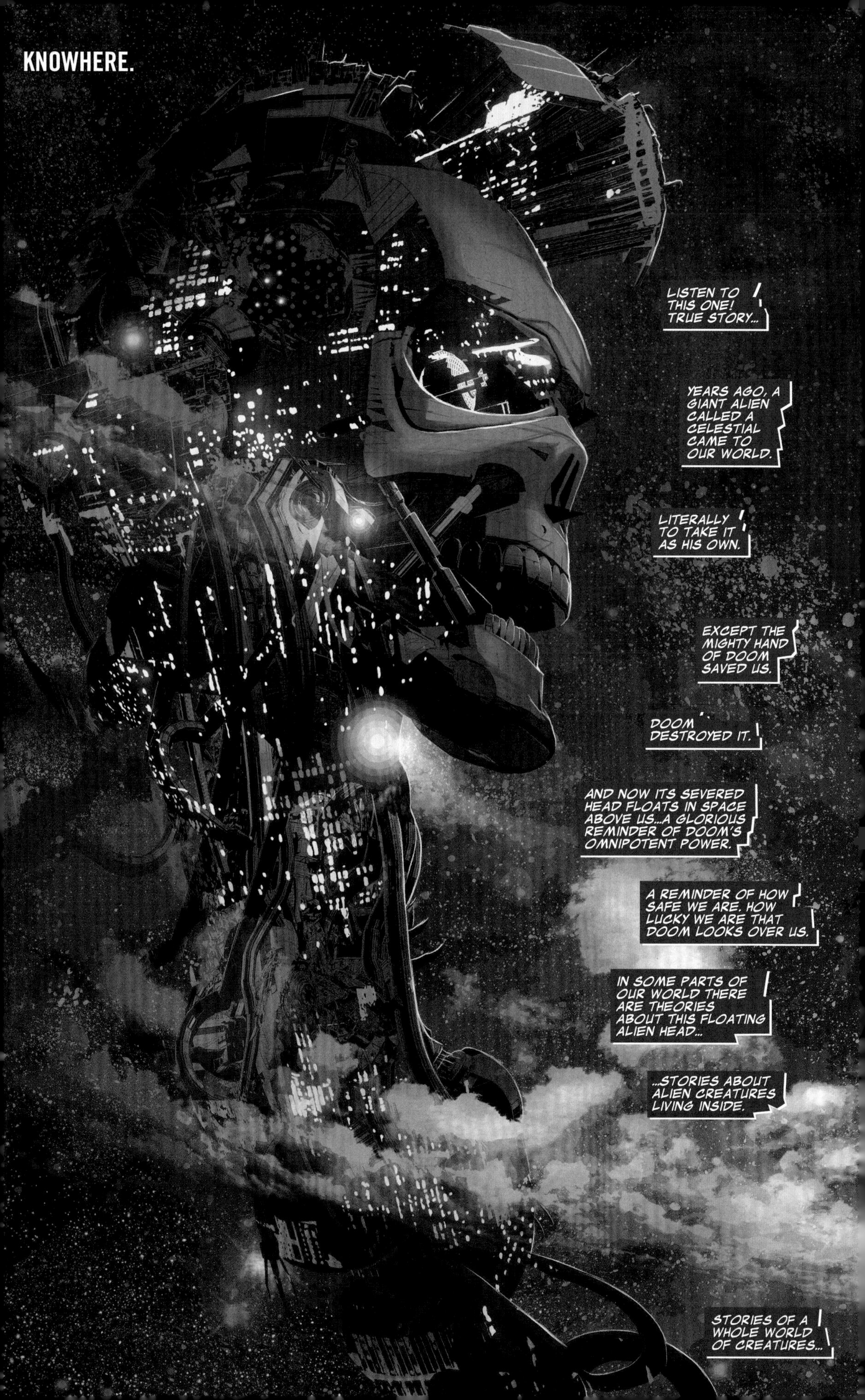
KNOWHERE.
LISTEN TO THIS ONE! TRUE STORY...
YEARS AGO, A GIANT ALIEN CALLED A CELESTIAL CAME TO OUR WORLD.
LITERALLY TO TAKE IT AS HIS OWN.
EXCEPT THE MIGHTY HAND OF DOOM SAVED US.
DOOM DESTROYED IT.
AND NOW ITS SEVERED HEAD FLOATS IN SPACE ABOVE US...A GLORIOUS REMINDER OF DOOM'S OMNIPOTENT POWER.
A REMINDER OF HOW SAFE WE ARE. HOW LUCKY WE ARE THAT DOOM LOOKS OVER US.
IN SOME PARTS OF OUR WORLD THERE ARE THEORIES ABOUT THIS FLOATING ALIEN HEAD...
...STORIES ABOUT ALIEN CREATURES LIVING INSIDE.
STORIES OF A WHOLE WORLD OF CREATURES...

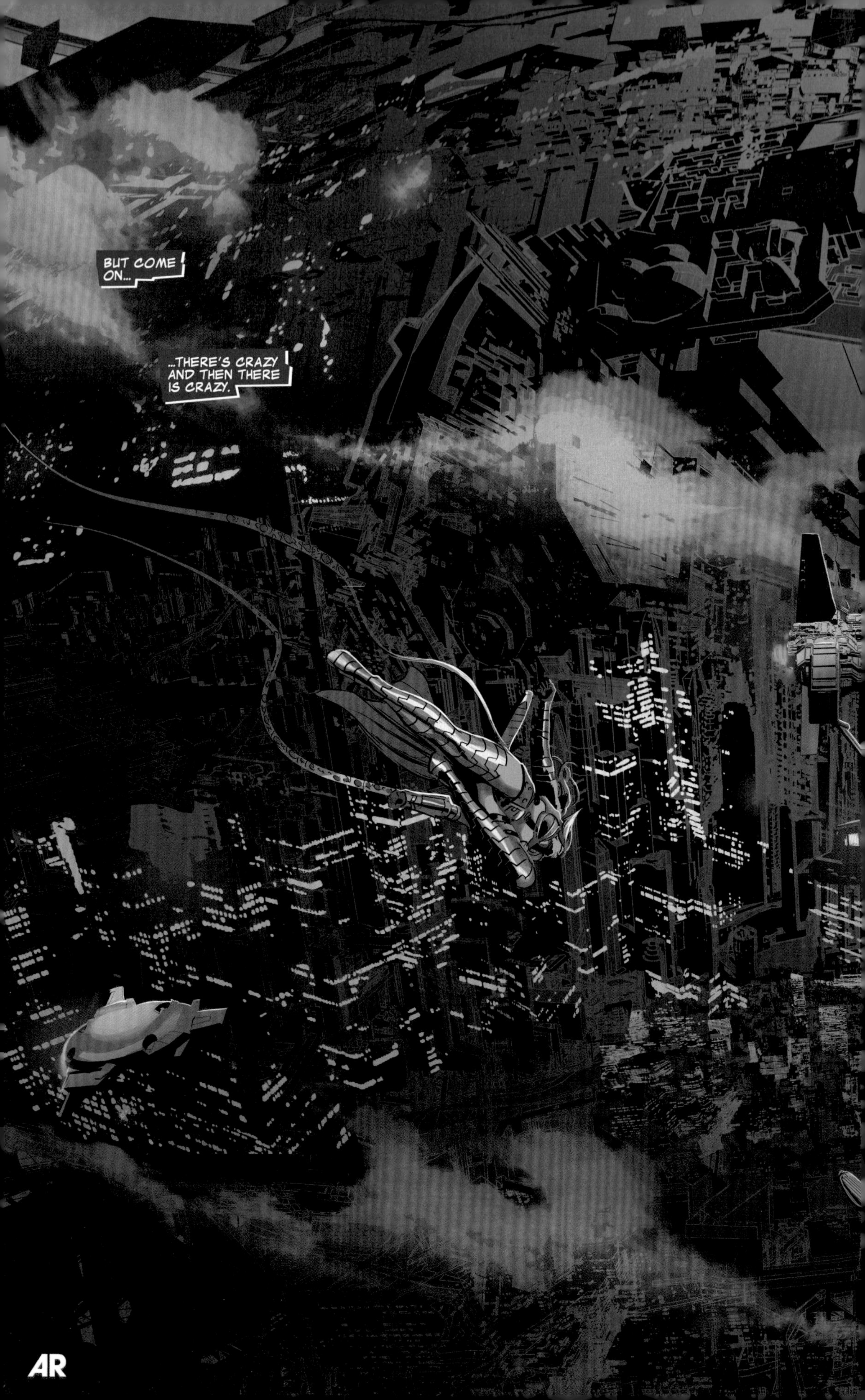
BUT COME ON...
...THERE'S CRAZY AND THEN THERE IS CRAZY.

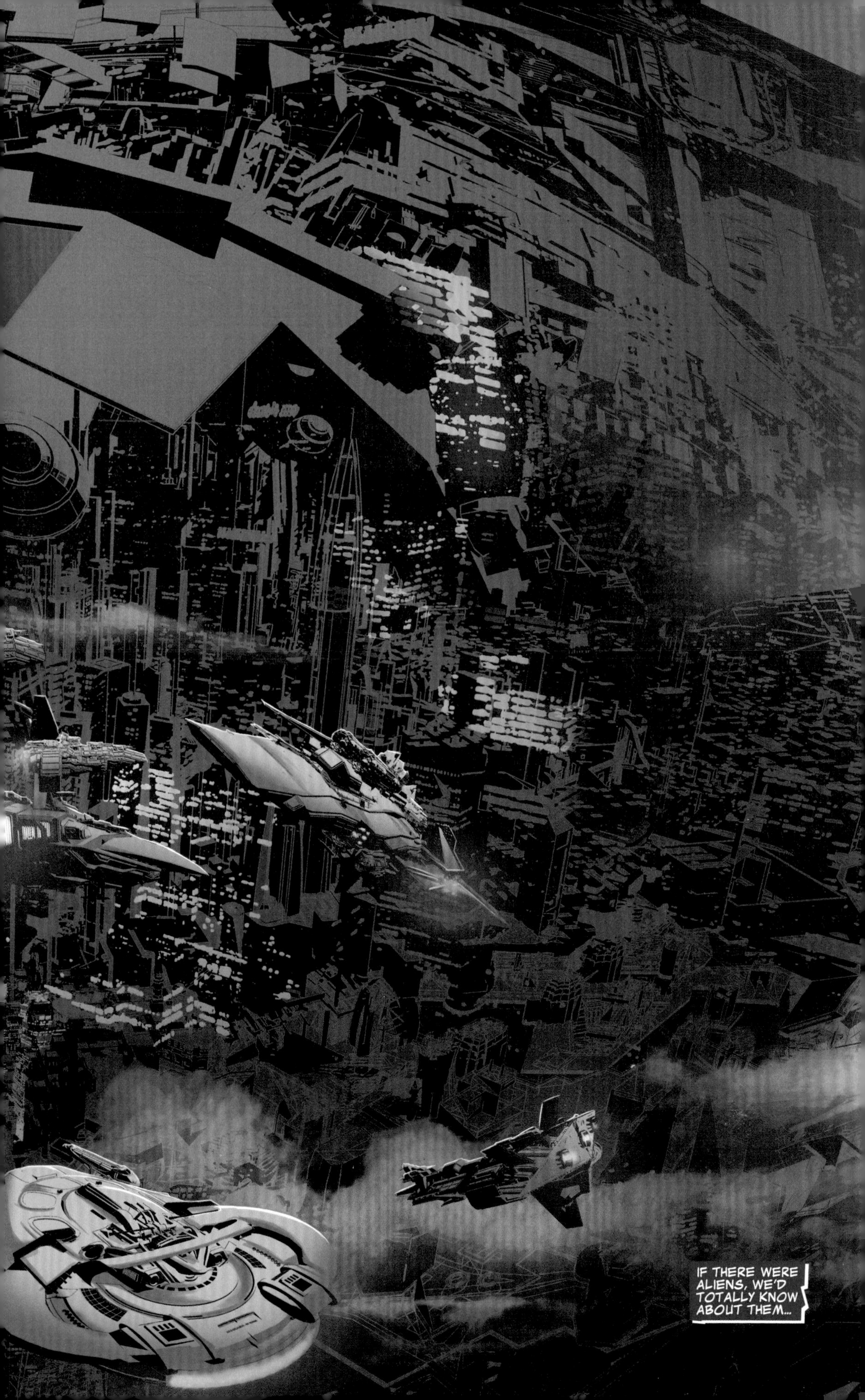
IF THERE WERE ALIENS, WE'D TOTALLY KNOW ABOUT THEM...

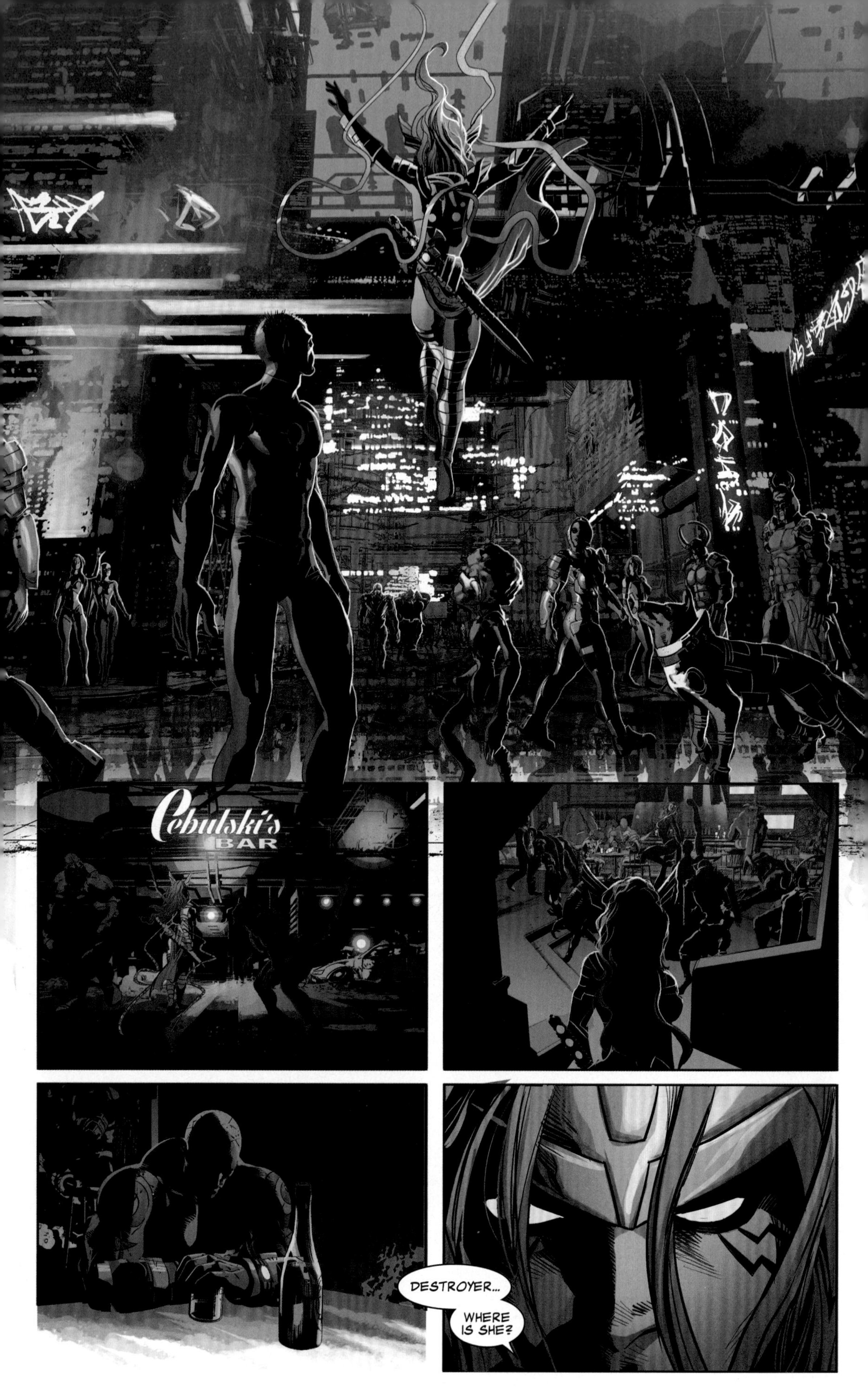
Cebulski's
BAR
DESTROYER...
WHERE IS SHE?

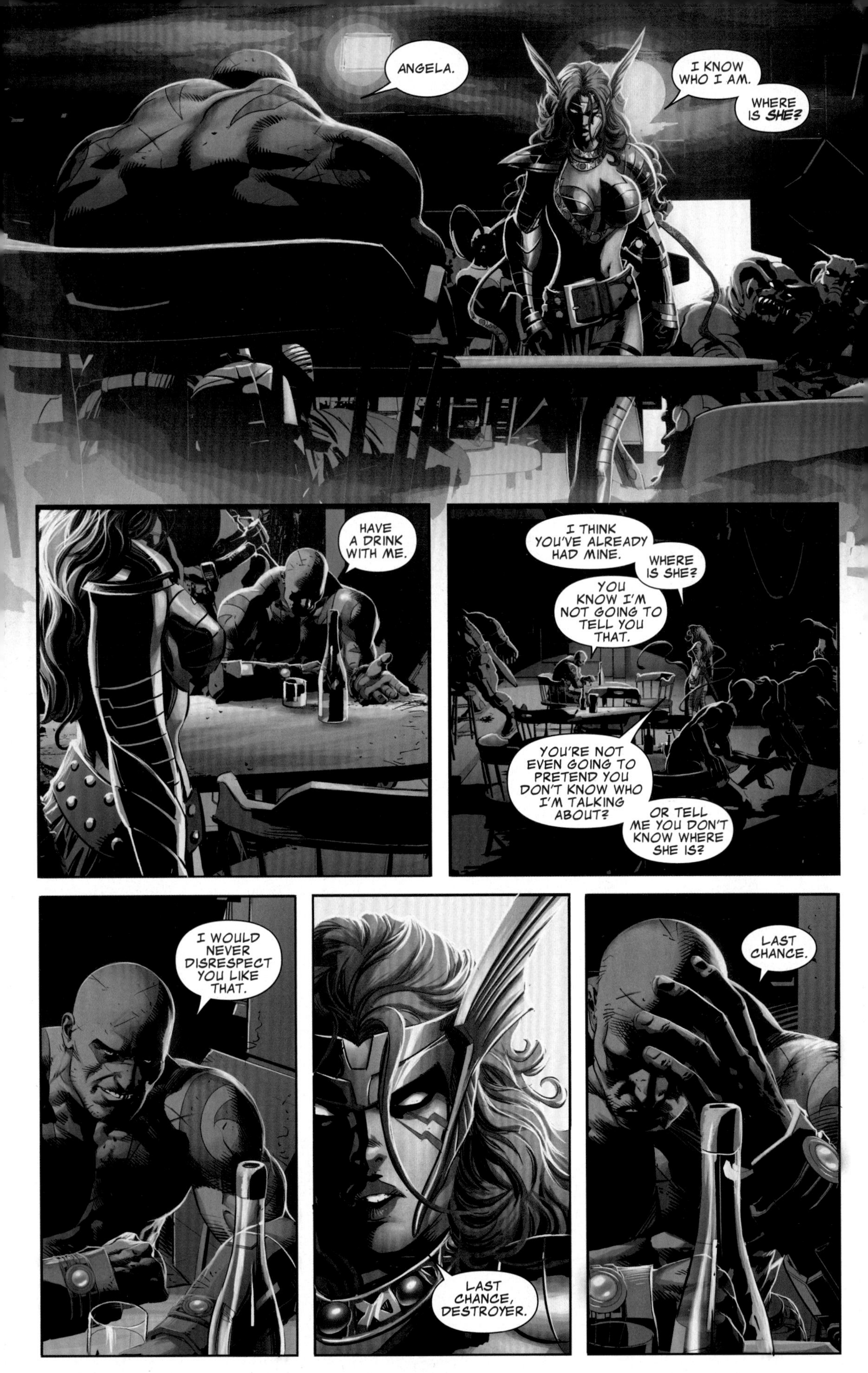
ANGELA.
I KNOW WHO I AM.
WHERE IS SHE?
HAVE A DRINK WITH ME.
I THINK YOU'VE ALREADY HAD MINE.
WHERE IS SHE?
YOU KNOW I'M NOT GOING TO TELL YOU THAT.
YOU'RE NOT EVEN GOING TO PRETEND YOU DON'T KNOW WHO I'M TALKING ABOUT?
OR TELL ME YOU DON'T KNOW WHERE SHE IS?
I WOULD NEVER DISRESPECT YOU LIKE THAT.
LAST CHANCE, DESTROYER.
LAST CHANCE.

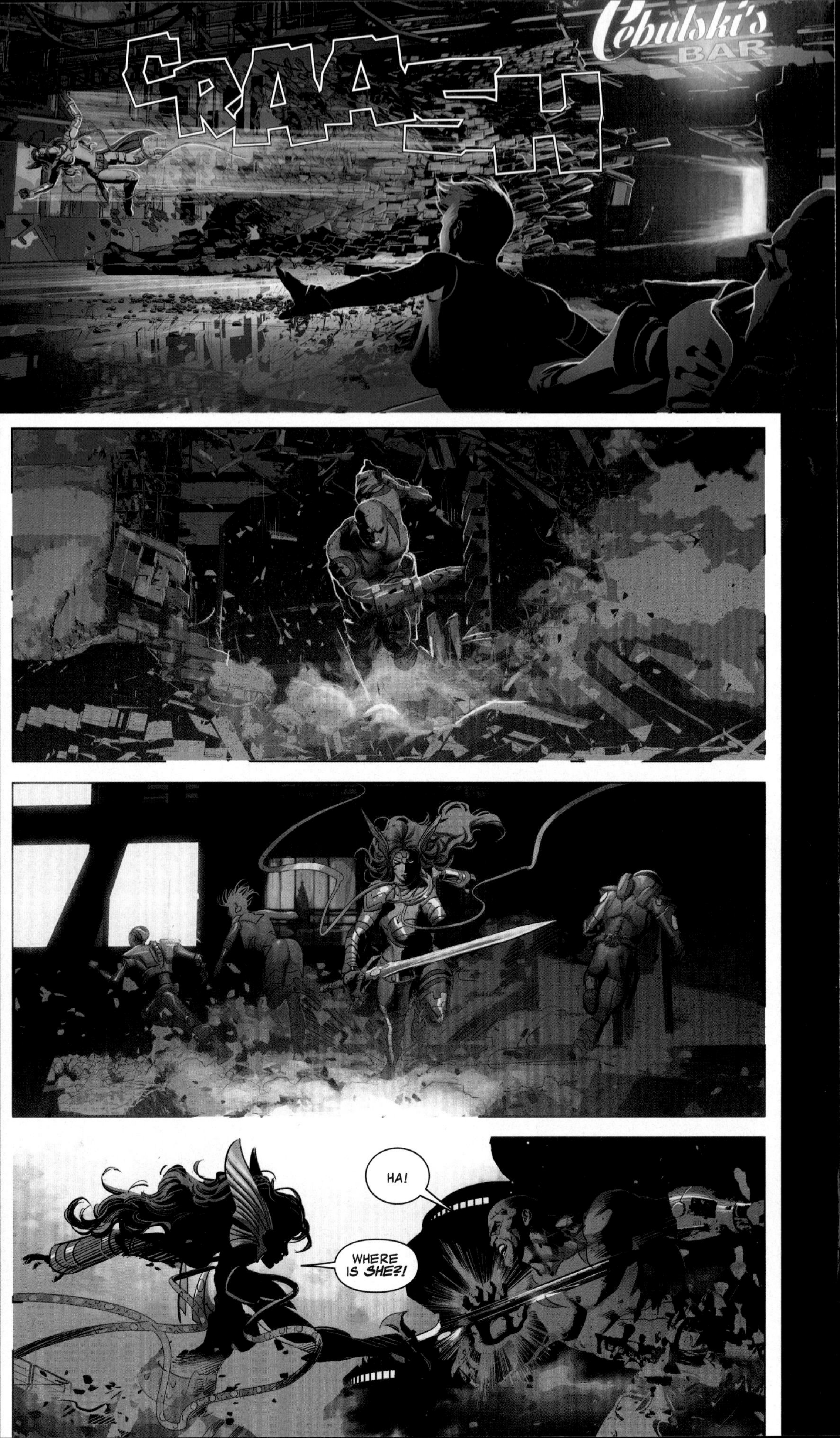

CRAA-H
Cebulski's BAR
HA!
WHERE IS SHE?!

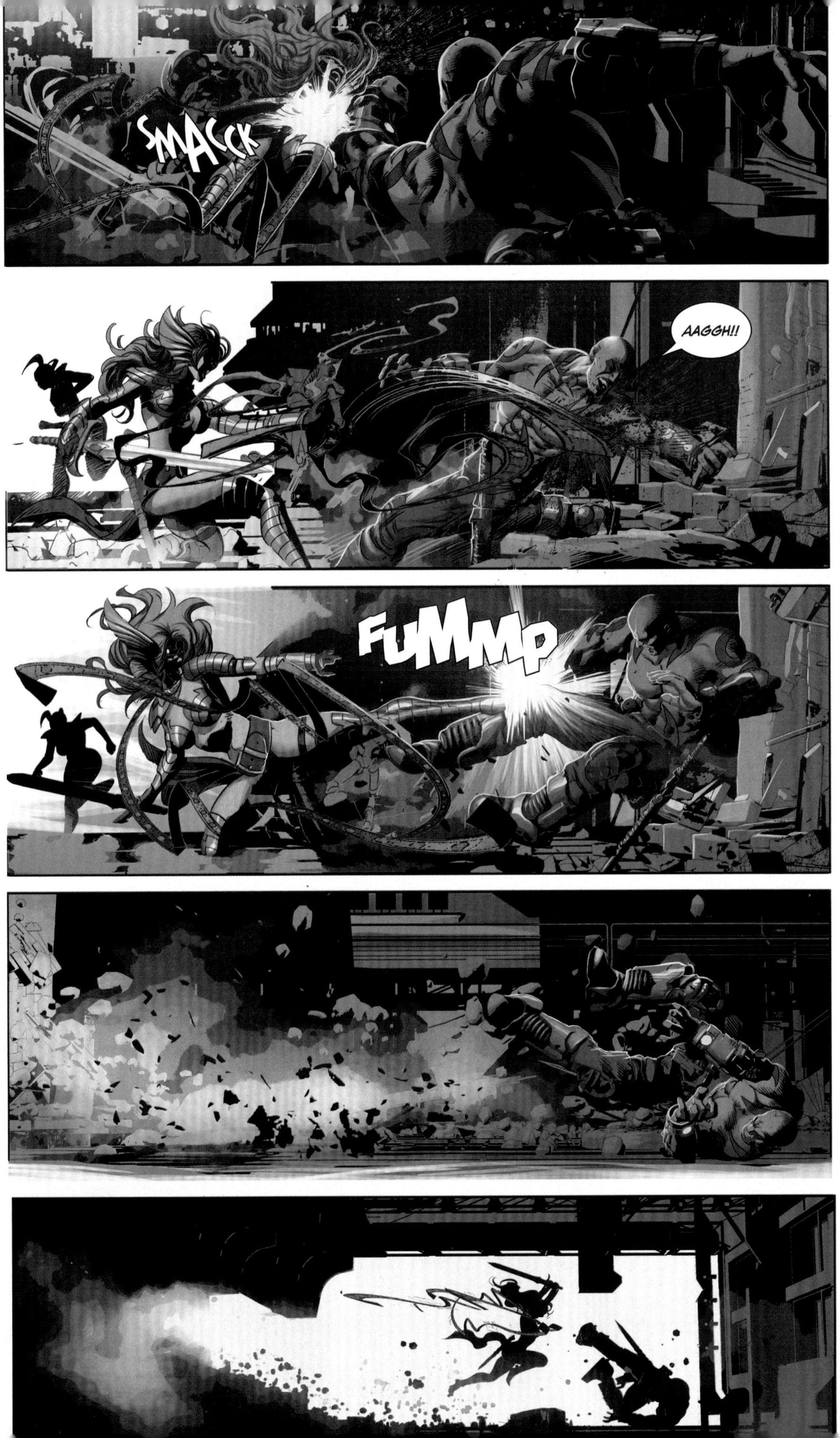
SMACCK
AAGGH!!
FUMMP

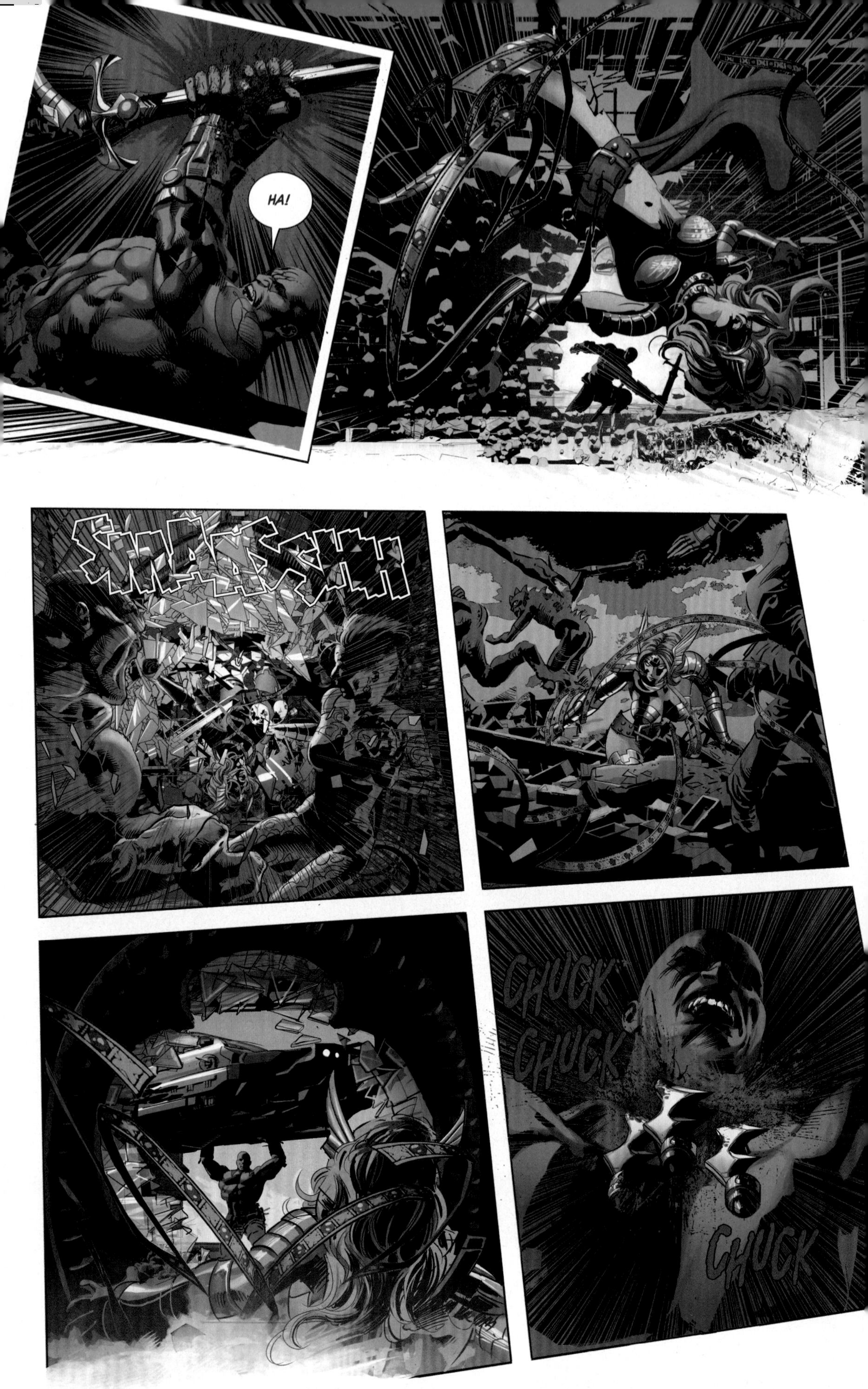
HA!
SMAASHH
CHUCK
CHUCK
CHUCK

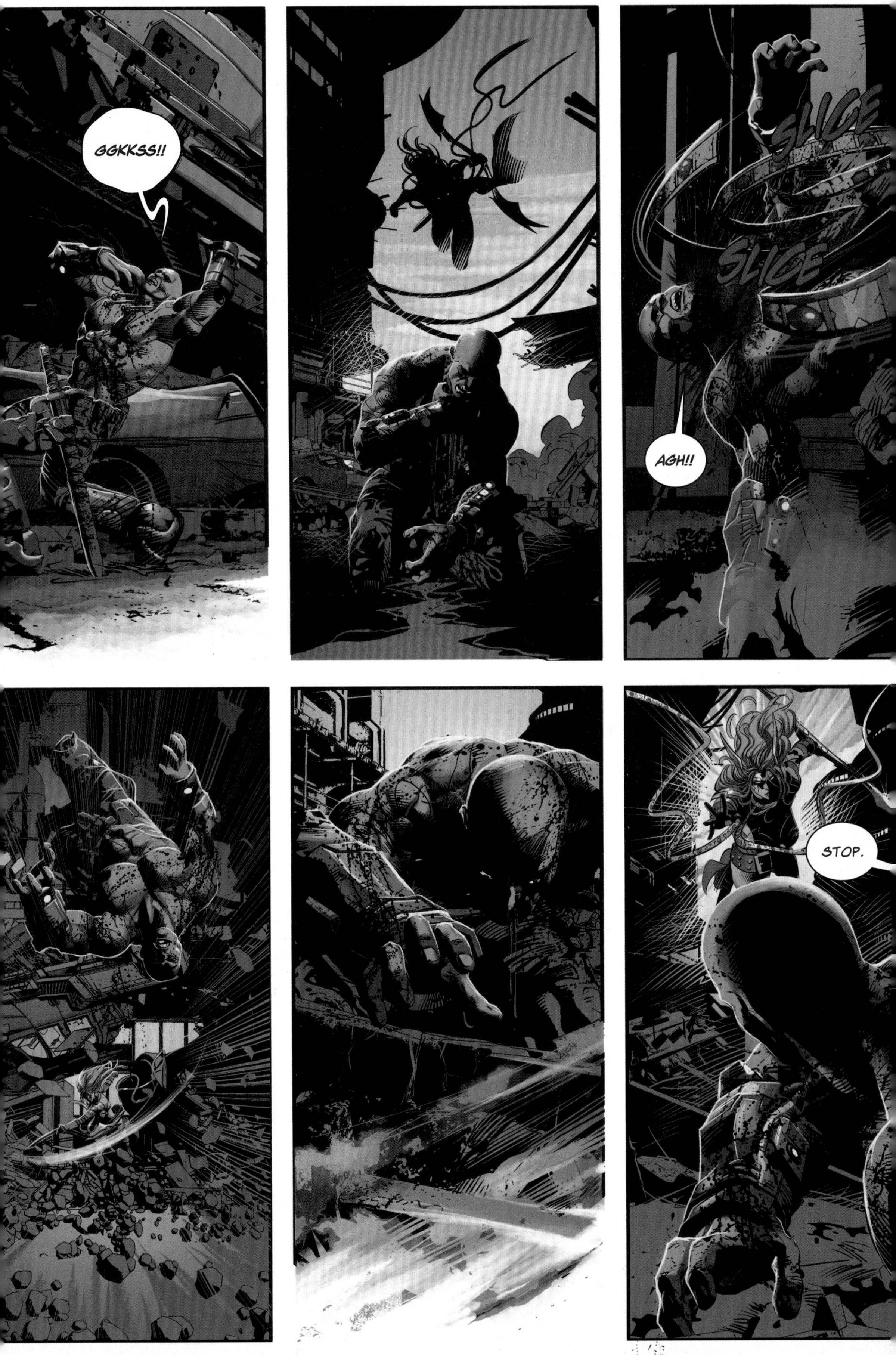
GGKKSS!!
SLICE
SLICE
AGH!!
STOP.

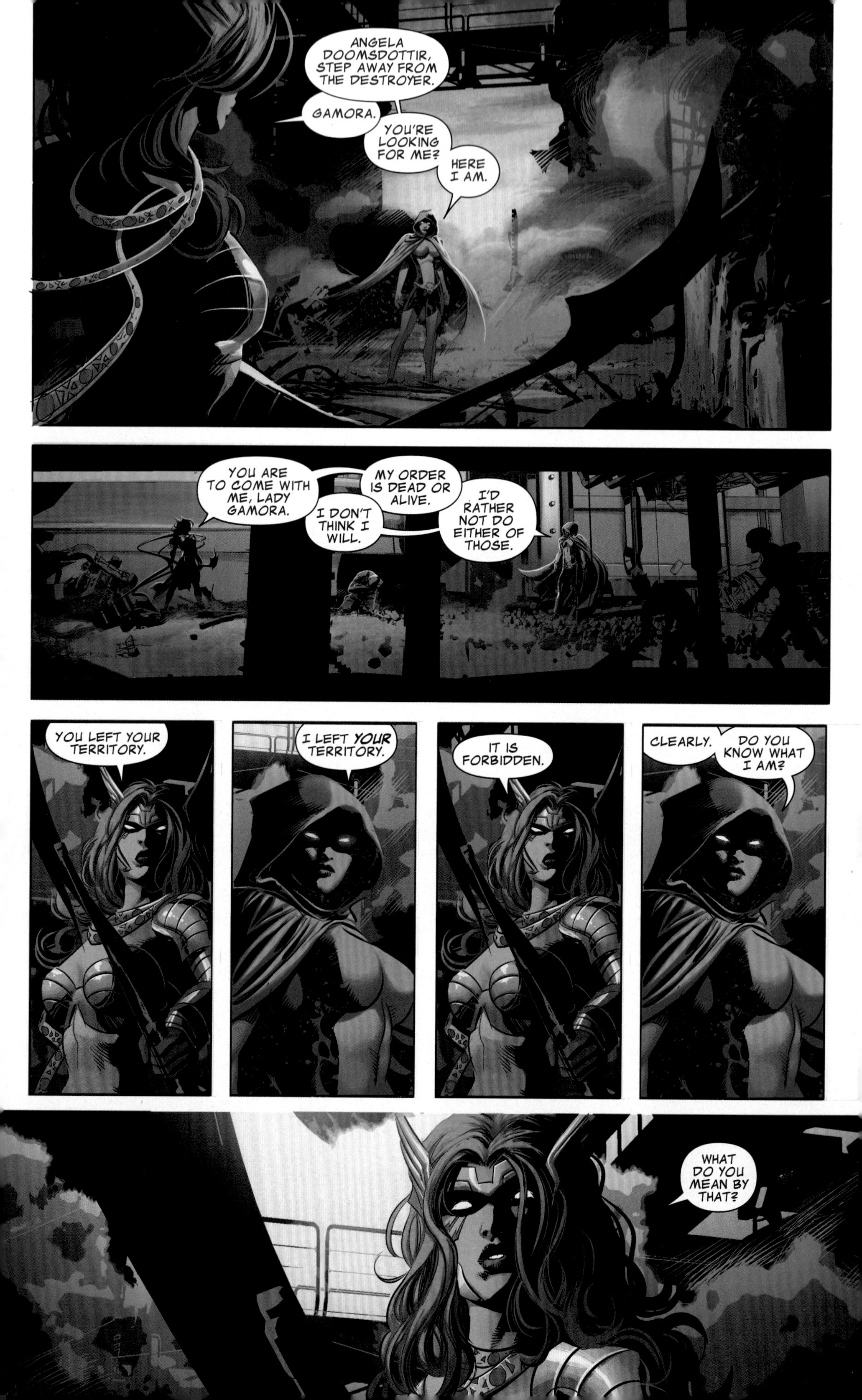
ANGELA DOOMSDOTTIR, STEP AWAY FROM THE DESTROYER.
GAMORA.
YOU'RE LOOKING FOR ME?
HERE I AM.
YOU ARE TO COME WITH ME, LADY GAMORA.
I DON'T THINK I WILL.
MY ORDER IS DEAD OR ALIVE.
I'D RATHER NOT DO EITHER OF THOSE.
YOU LEFT YOUR TERRITORY.
I LEFT *YOUR* TERRITORY.
IT IS FORBIDDEN.
CLEARLY.
DO YOU KNOW WHAT I AM?
WHAT DO YOU MEAN BY THAT?

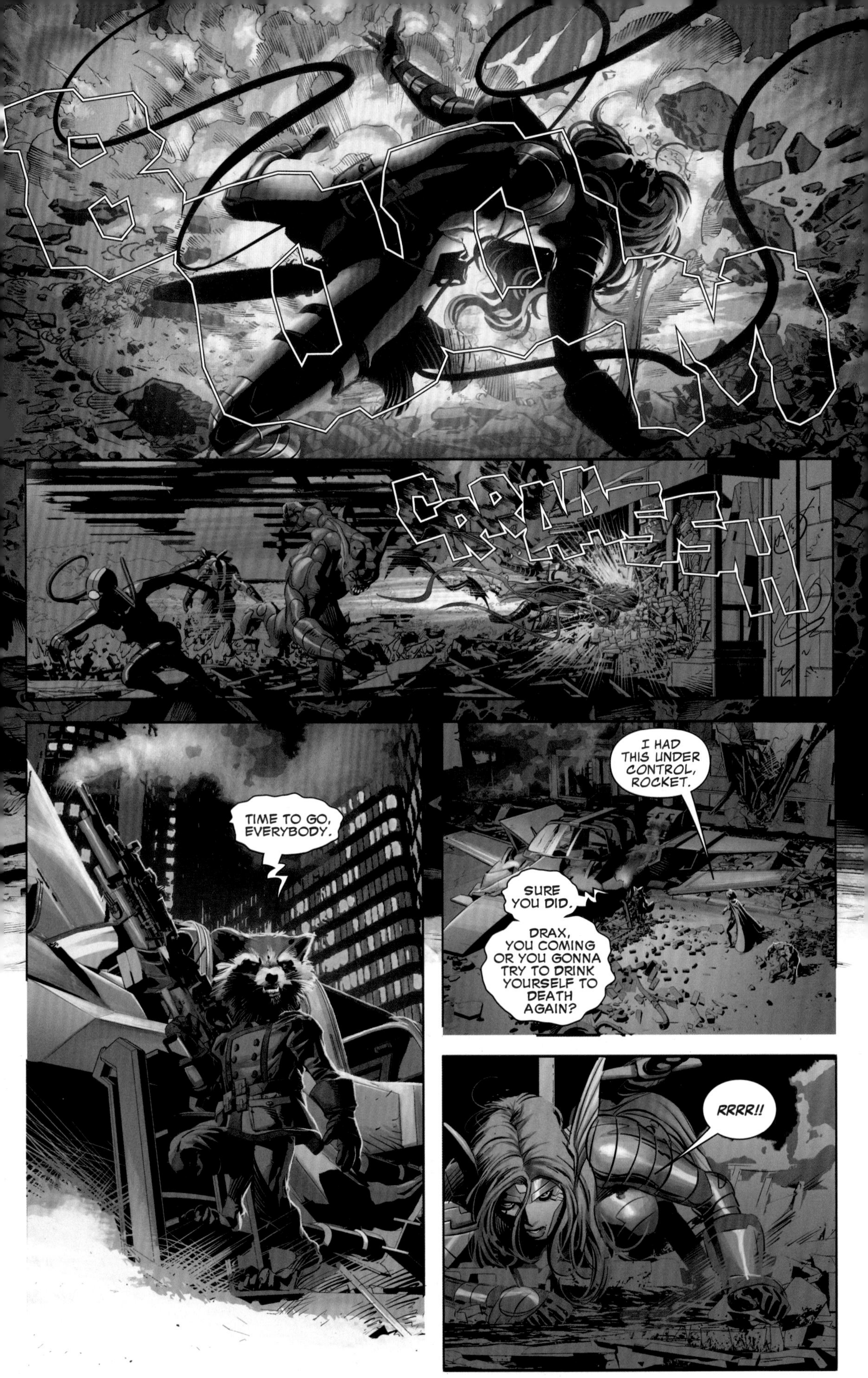
TIME TO GO, EVERYBODY.
I HAD THIS UNDER CONTROL, ROCKET.
SURE YOU DID.
DRAX, YOU COMING OR YOU GONNA TRY TO DRINK YOURSELF TO DEATH AGAIN?
RRRR!!

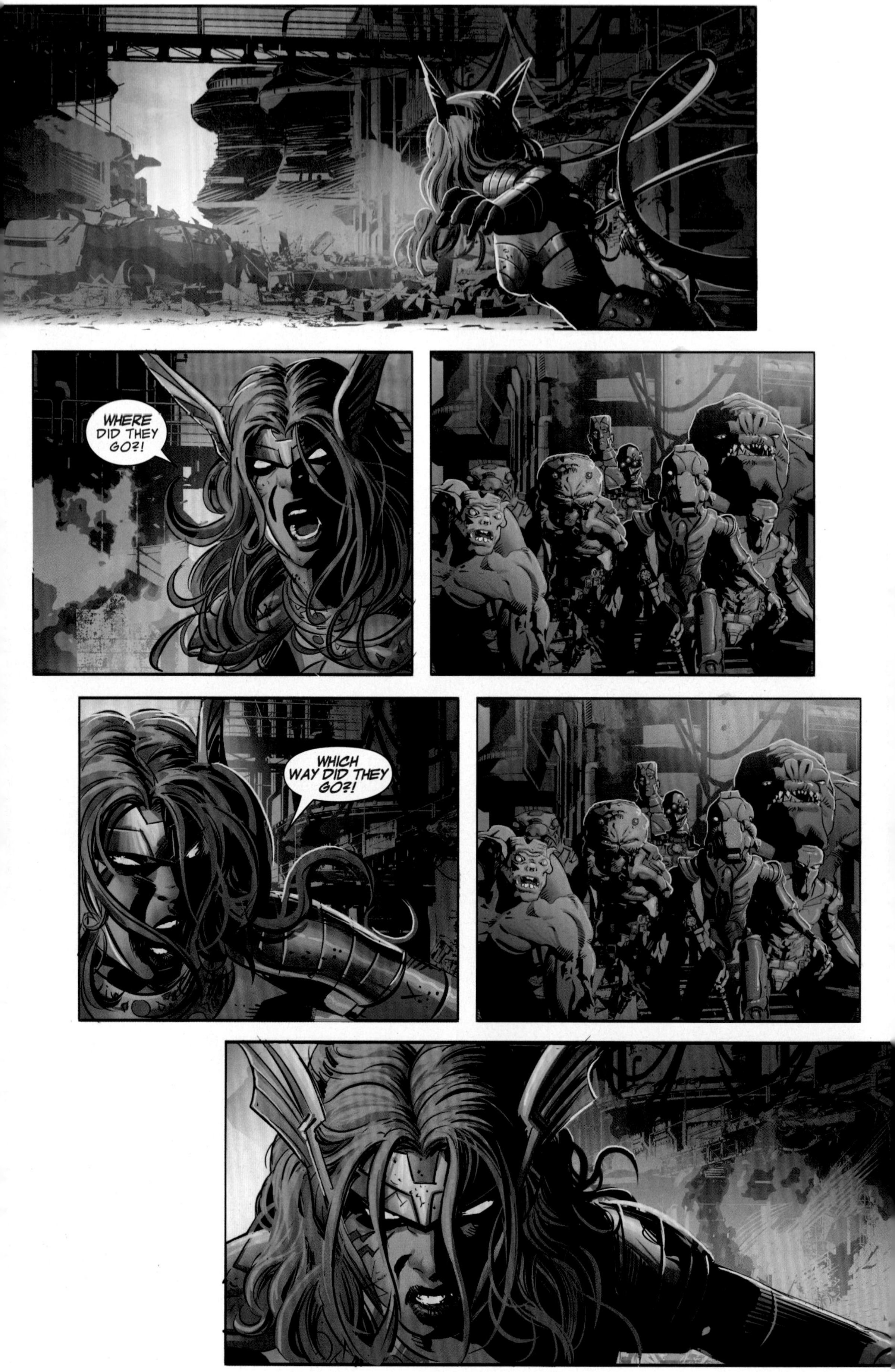
WHERE DID THEY GO?!
WHICH WAY DID THEY GO?!

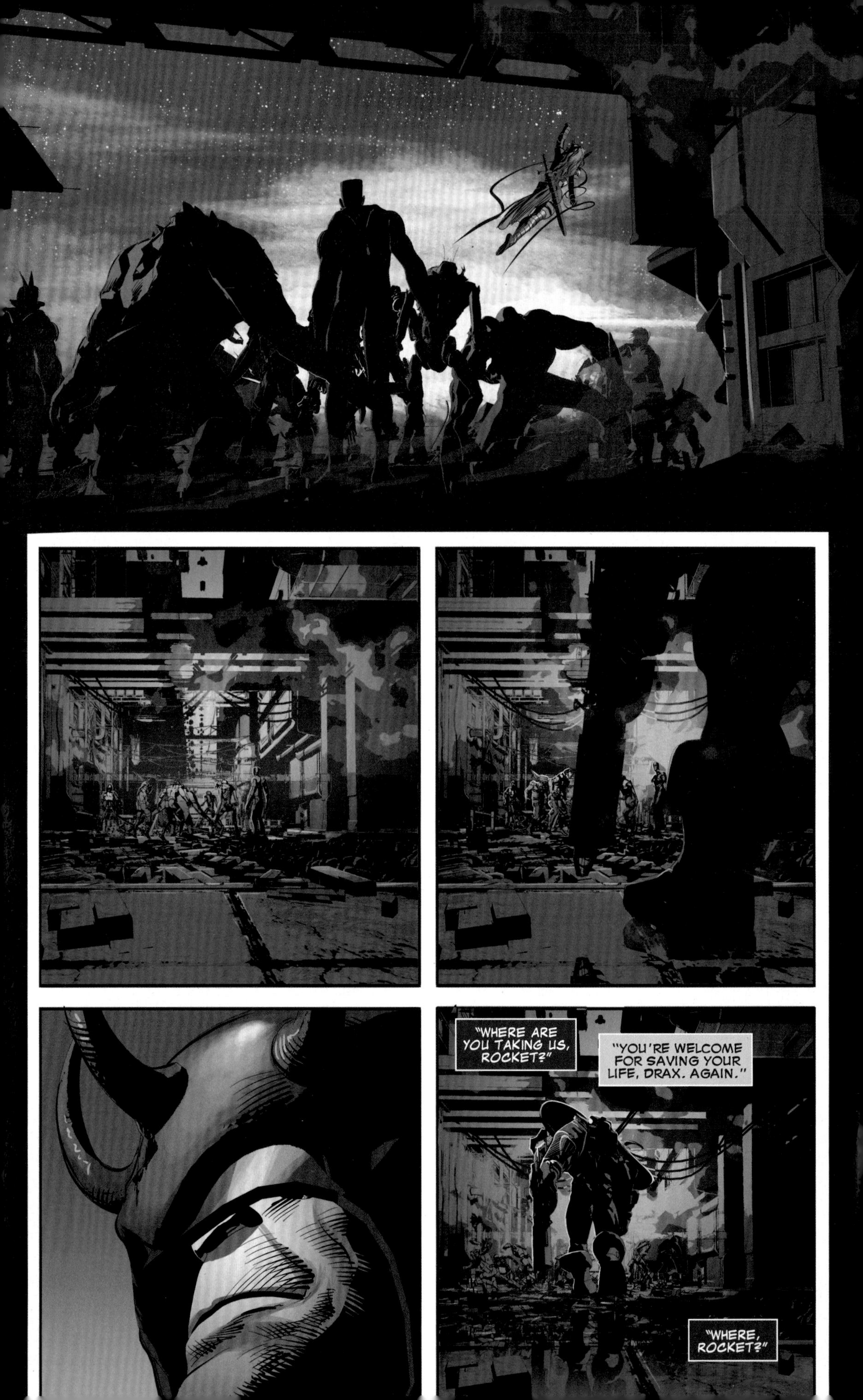
"WHERE ARE YOU TAKING US, ROCKET?"
"YOU'RE WELCOME FOR SAVING YOUR LIFE, DRAX. AGAIN."
"WHERE, ROCKET?"

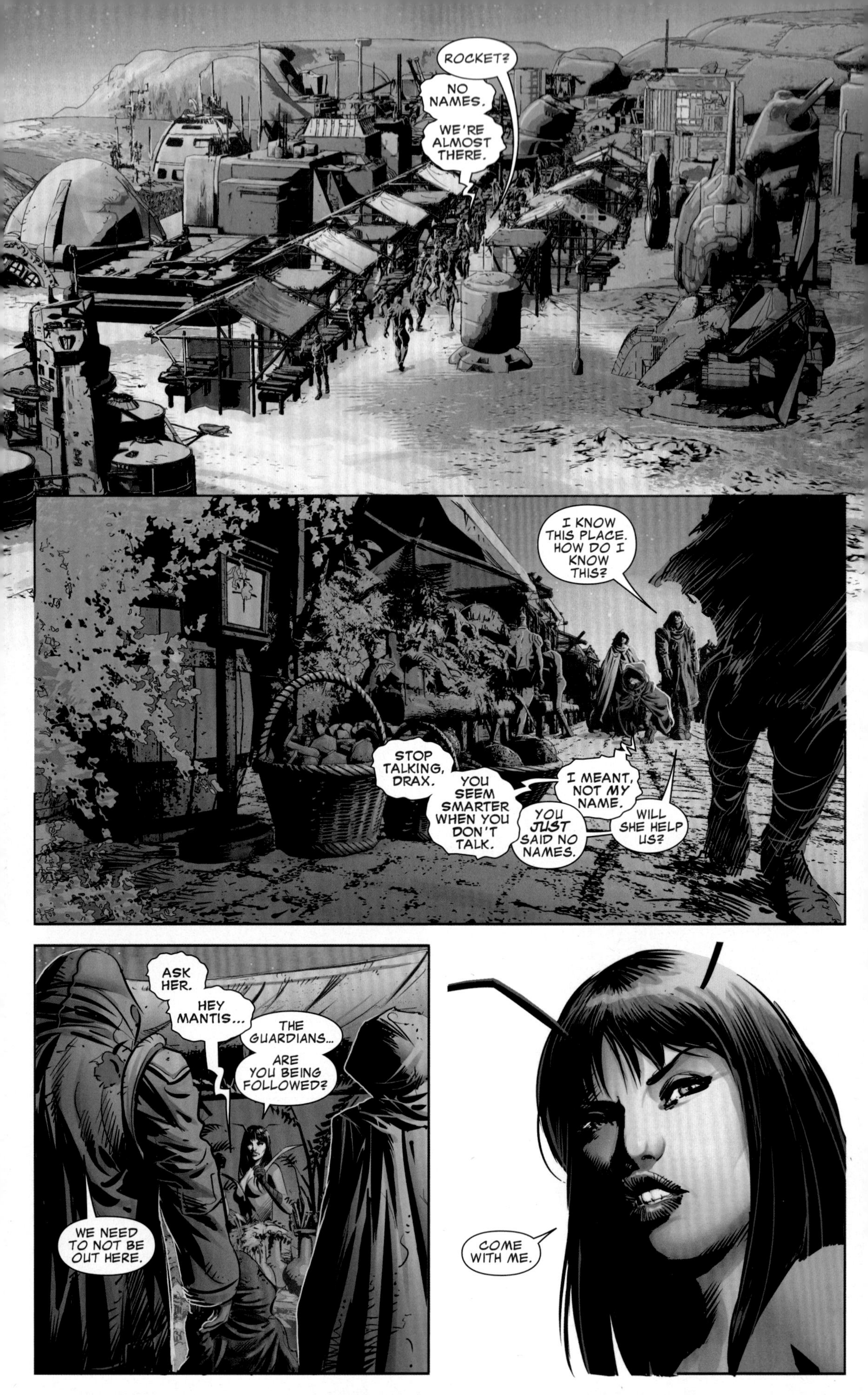
ROCKET?
NO NAMES.
WE'RE ALMOST THERE.
I KNOW THIS PLACE. HOW DO I KNOW THIS?
STOP TALKING, DRAX.
YOU SEEM SMARTER WHEN YOU DON'T TALK.
I MEANT, NOT MY NAME.
YOU JUST SAID NO NAMES.
WILL SHE HELP US?
ASK HER.
HEY MANTIS...
THE GUARDIANS...
ARE YOU BEING FOLLOWED?
WE NEED TO NOT BE OUT HERE.
COME WITH ME.

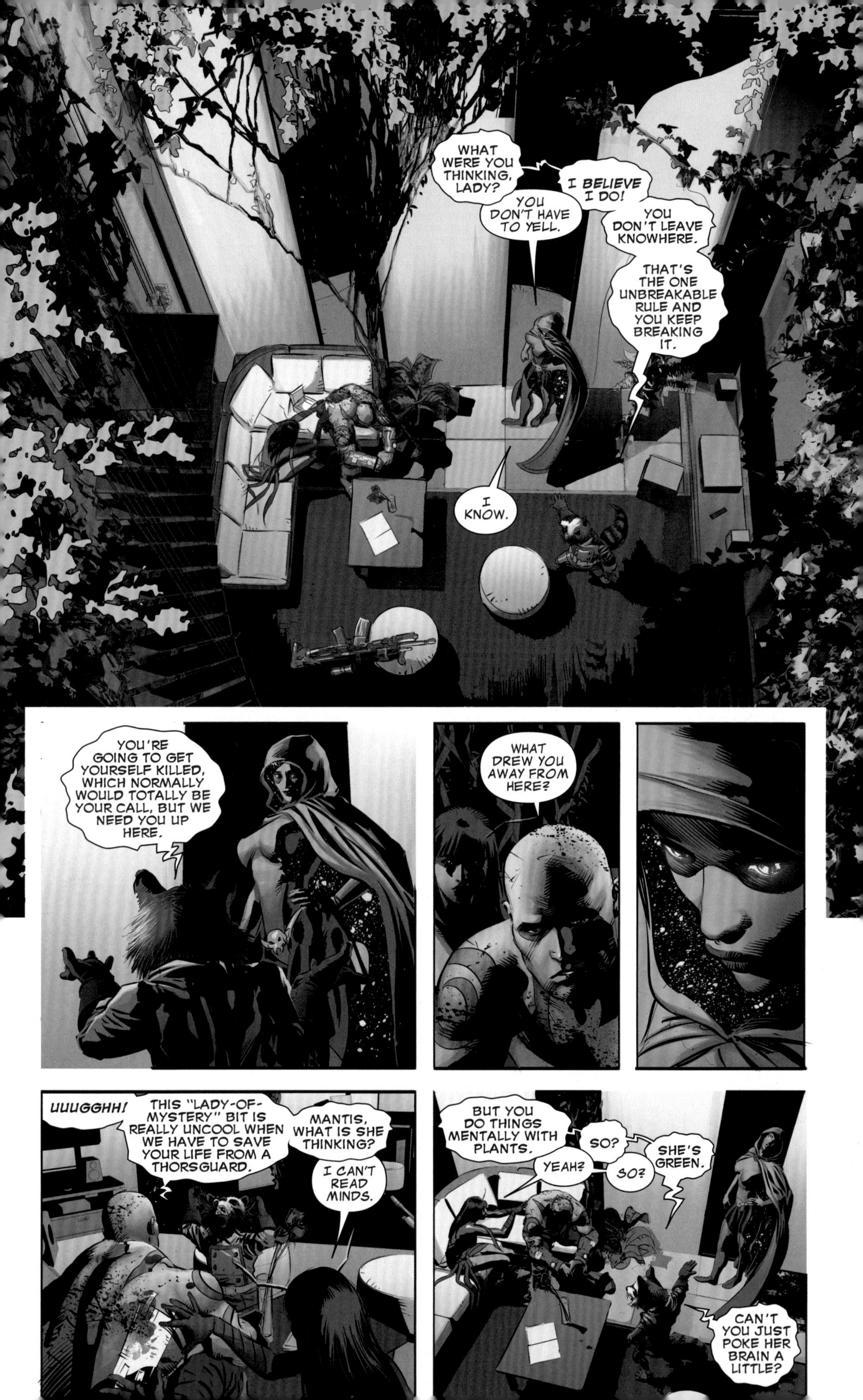
WHAT WERE YOU THINKING, LADY?
I BELIEVE I DO!
YOU DON'T HAVE TO YELL.
YOU DON'T LEAVE KNOWHERE.
THAT'S THE ONE UNBREAKABLE RULE AND YOU KEEP BREAKING IT.
I KNOW.
YOU'RE GOING TO GET YOURSELF KILLED, WHICH NORMALLY WOULD TOTALLY BE YOUR CALL, BUT WE NEED YOU UP HERE.
WHAT DREW YOU AWAY FROM HERE?
UUUGGHH!
THIS "LADY-OF-MYSTERY" BIT IS REALLY UNCOOL WHEN WE HAVE TO SAVE YOUR LIFE FROM A THORSGUARD.
MANTIS, WHAT IS SHE THINKING?
I CAN'T READ MINDS.
BUT YOU DO THINGS MENTALLY WITH PLANTS.
SO?
YEAH?
SO?
SHE'S GREEN.
CAN'T YOU JUST POKE HER BRAIN A LITTLE?

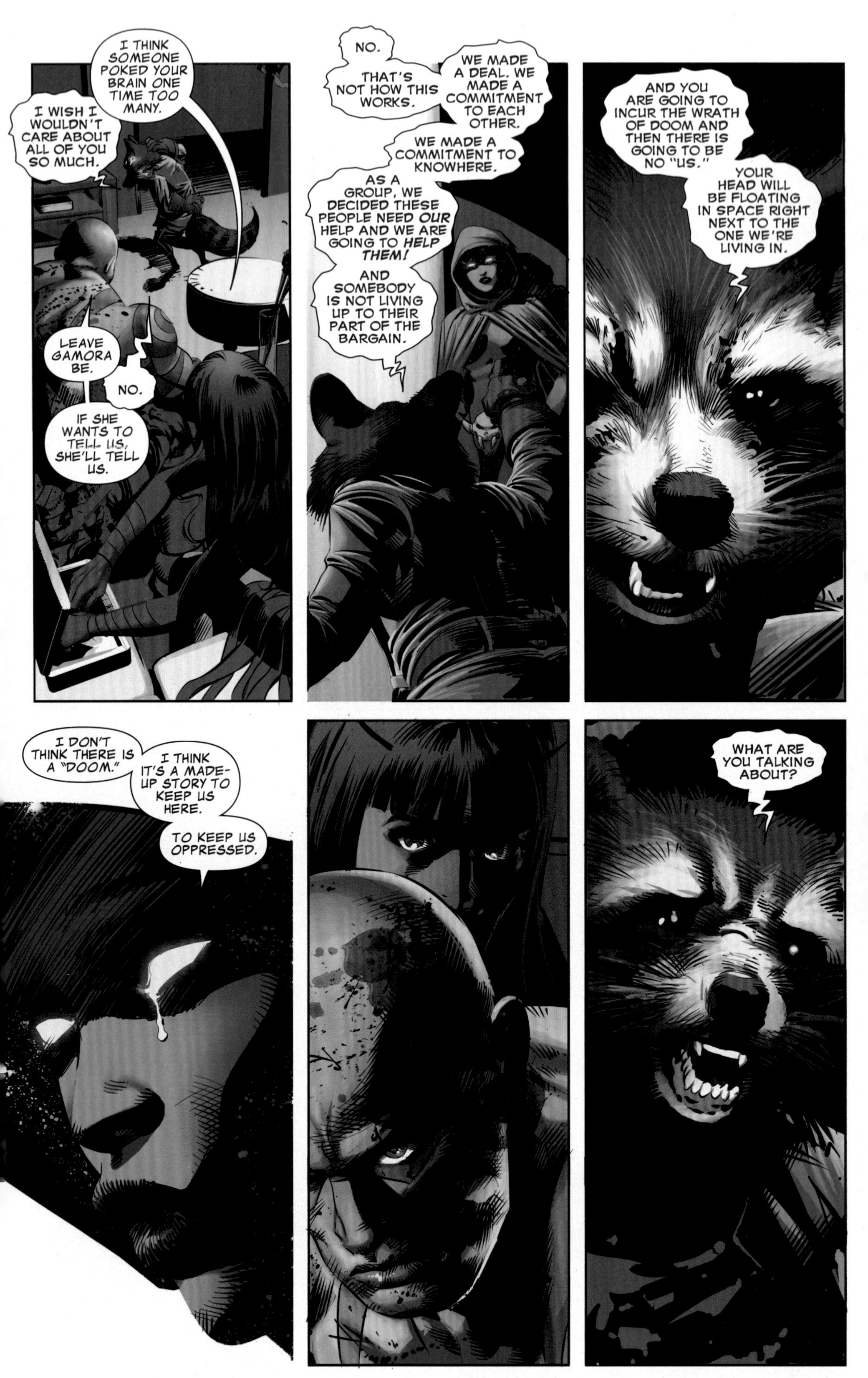
I THINK SOMEONE POKED YOUR BRAIN ONE TIME TOO MANY.
I WISH I WOULDN'T CARE ABOUT ALL OF YOU SO MUCH.
LEAVE GAMORA BE.
NO.
IF SHE WANTS TO TELL US, SHE'LL TELL US.
NO.
THAT'S NOT HOW THIS WORKS.
WE MADE A DEAL. WE MADE A COMMITMENT TO EACH OTHER.
WE MADE A COMMITMENT TO KNOWHERE.
AS A GROUP, WE DECIDED THESE PEOPLE NEED OUR HELP AND WE ARE GOING TO HELP THEM!
AND SOMEBODY IS NOT LIVING UP TO THEIR PART OF THE BARGAIN.
AND YOU ARE GOING TO INCUR THE WRATH OF DOOM AND THEN THERE IS GOING TO BE NO "US."
YOUR HEAD WILL BE FLOATING IN SPACE RIGHT NEXT TO THE ONE WE'RE LIVING IN.
I DON'T THINK THERE IS A "DOOM."
I THINK IT'S A MADE-UP STORY TO KEEP US HERE.
TO KEEP US OPPRESSED.
WHAT ARE YOU TALKING ABOUT?

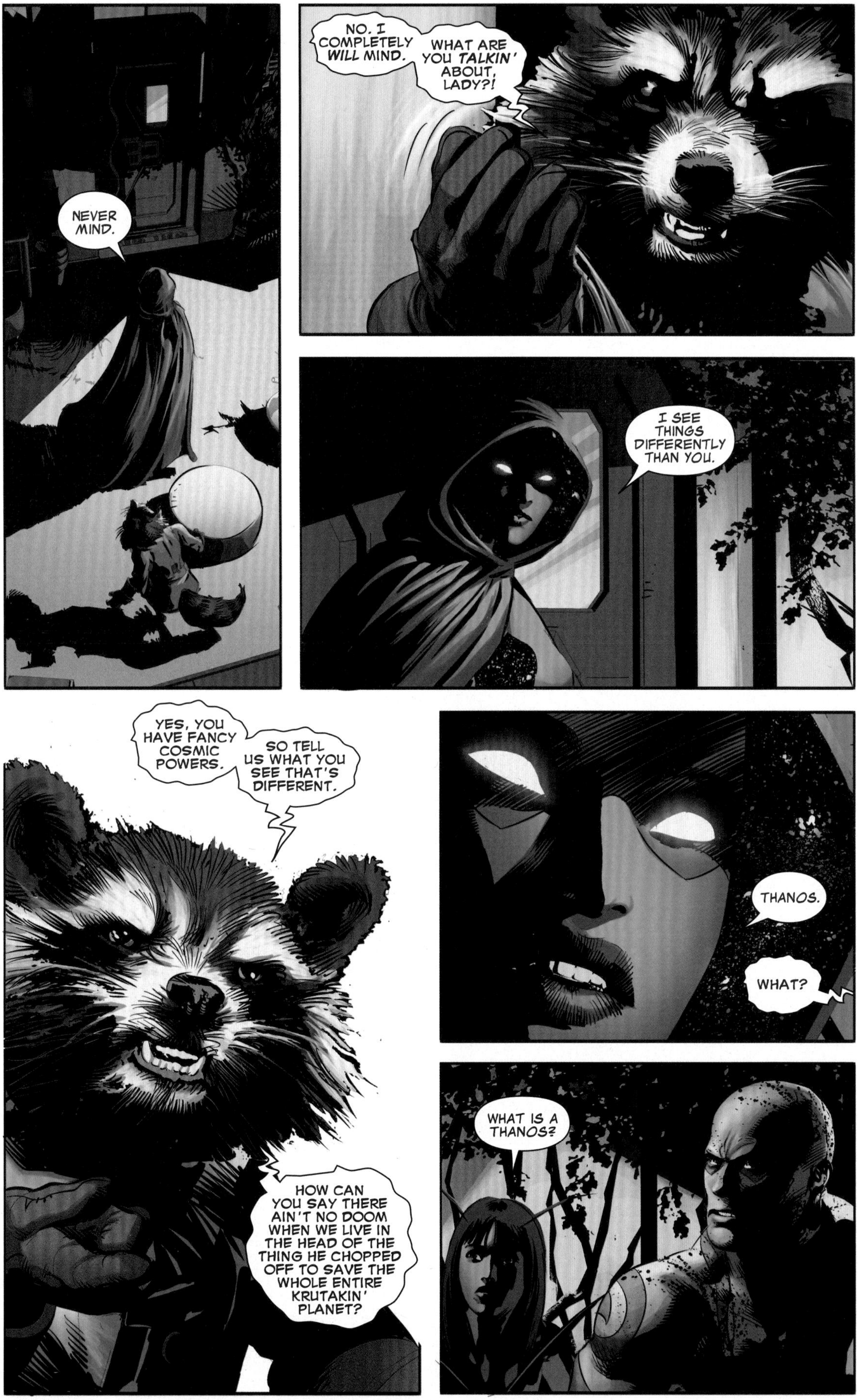
NEVER MIND.
NO. I COMPLETELY *WILL* MIND.
WHAT ARE YOU *TALKIN'* ABOUT, LADY?!
I SEE THINGS DIFFERENTLY THAN YOU.
YES, YOU HAVE FANCY COSMIC POWERS.
SO TELL US WHAT YOU SEE THAT'S DIFFERENT.
HOW CAN YOU SAY THERE AIN'T NO DOOM WHEN WE LIVE IN THE HEAD OF THE THING HE CHOPPED OFF TO SAVE THE WHOLE ENTIRE KRUTAKIN' PLANET?
THANOS.
WHAT?
WHAT IS A THANOS?

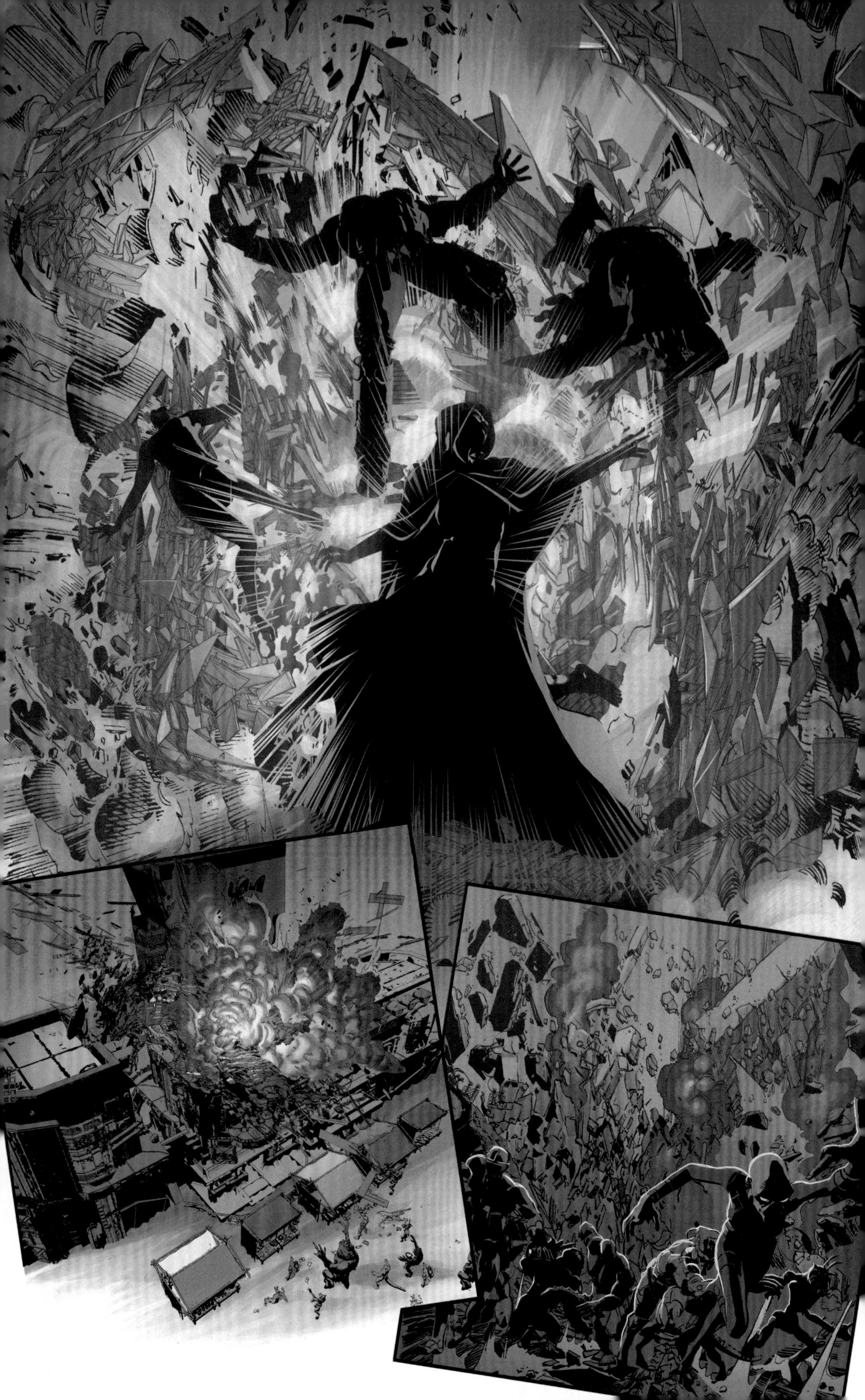

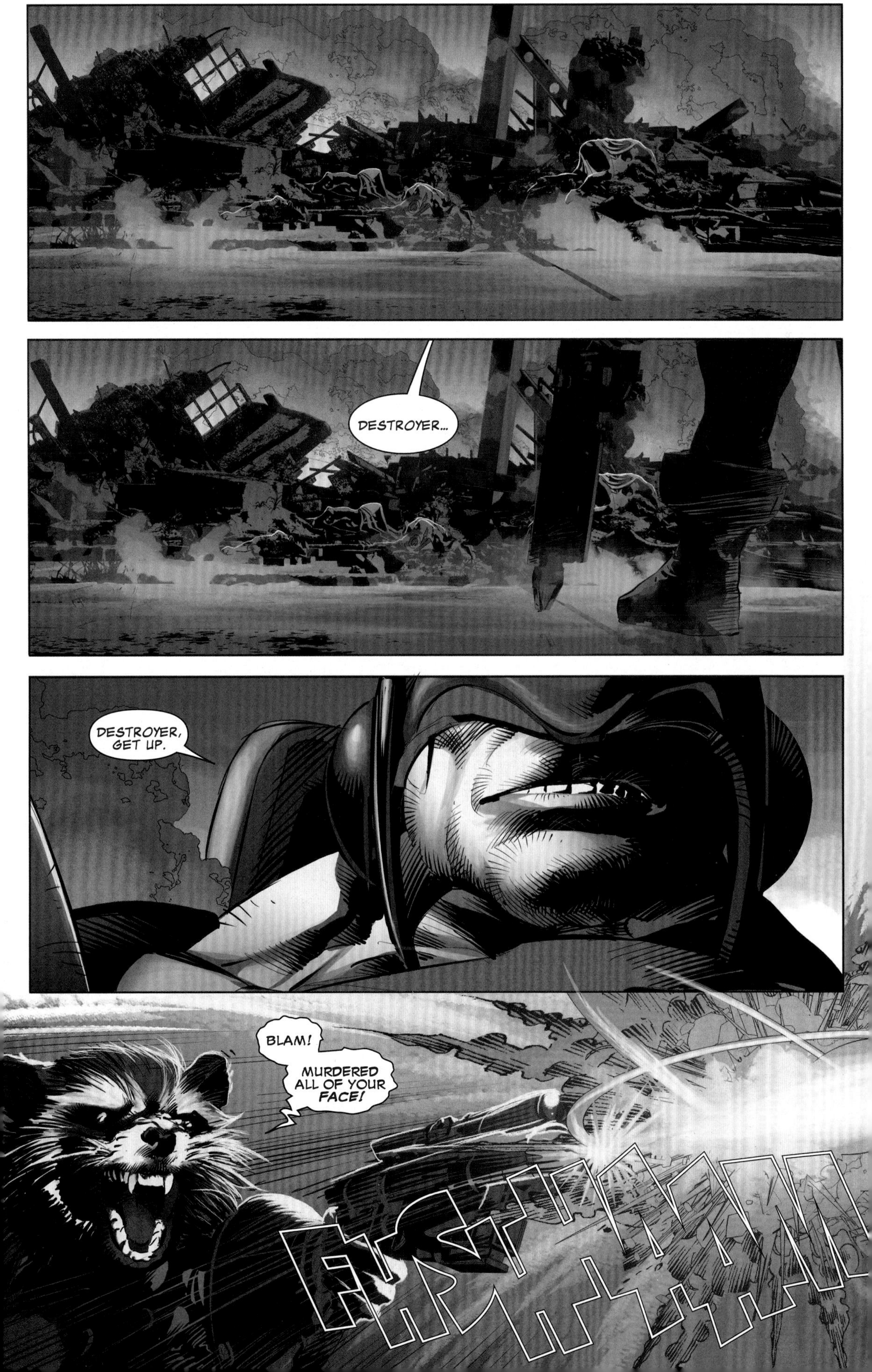
DESTROYER...
DESTROYER, GET UP.
BLAM!
MURDERED ALL OF YOUR FACE!

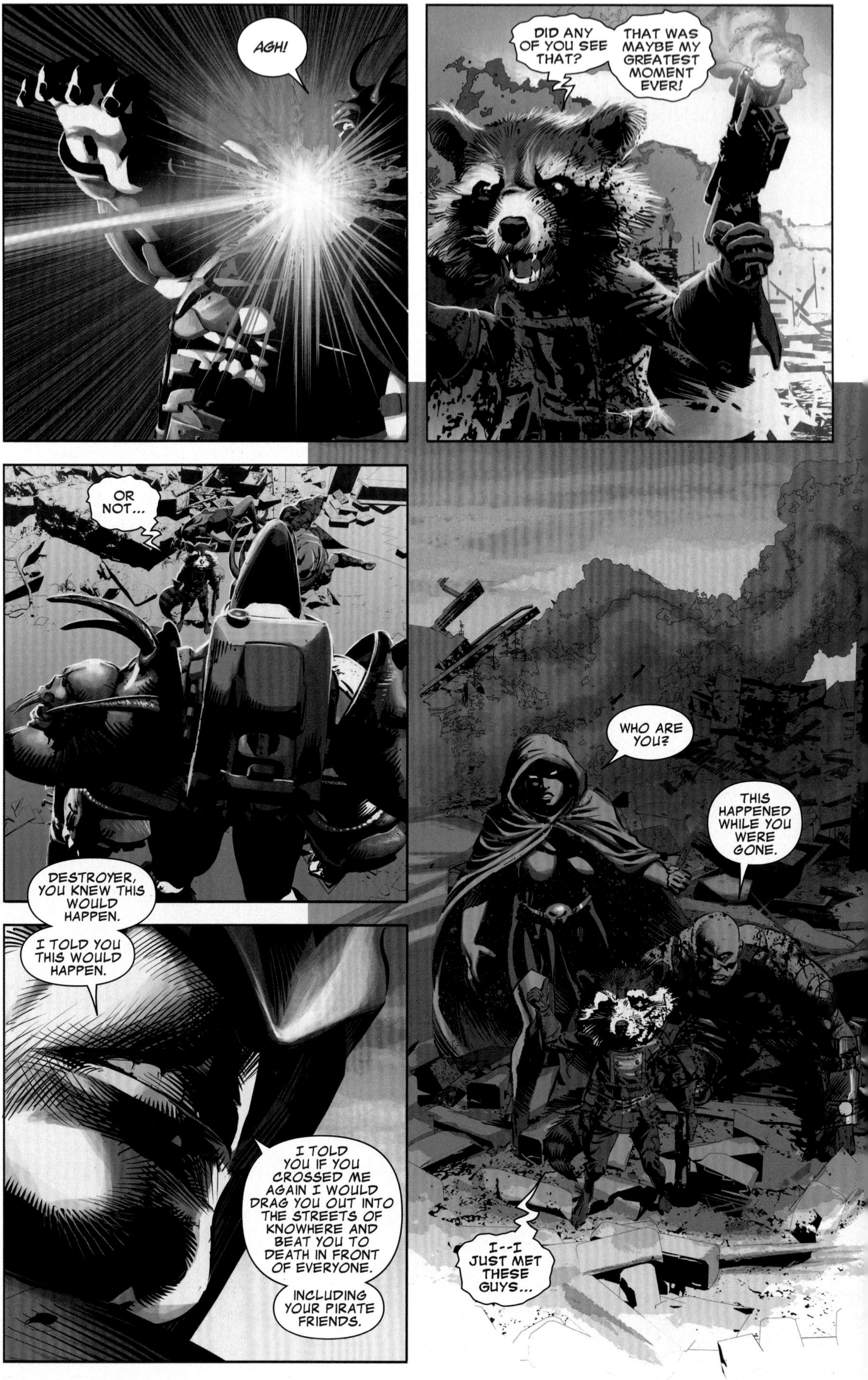
AGH!
DID ANY OF YOU SEE THAT?
THAT WAS MAYBE MY GREATEST MOMENT EVER!
OR NOT...
WHO ARE YOU?
THIS HAPPENED WHILE YOU WERE GONE.
DESTROYER, YOU KNEW THIS WOULD HAPPEN.
I TOLD YOU THIS WOULD HAPPEN.
I TOLD YOU IF YOU CROSSED ME AGAIN I WOULD DRAG YOU OUT INTO THE STREETS OF KNOWHERE AND BEAT YOU TO DEATH IN FRONT OF EVERYONE.
INCLUDING YOUR PIRATE FRIENDS.
I--I JUST MET THESE GUYS...

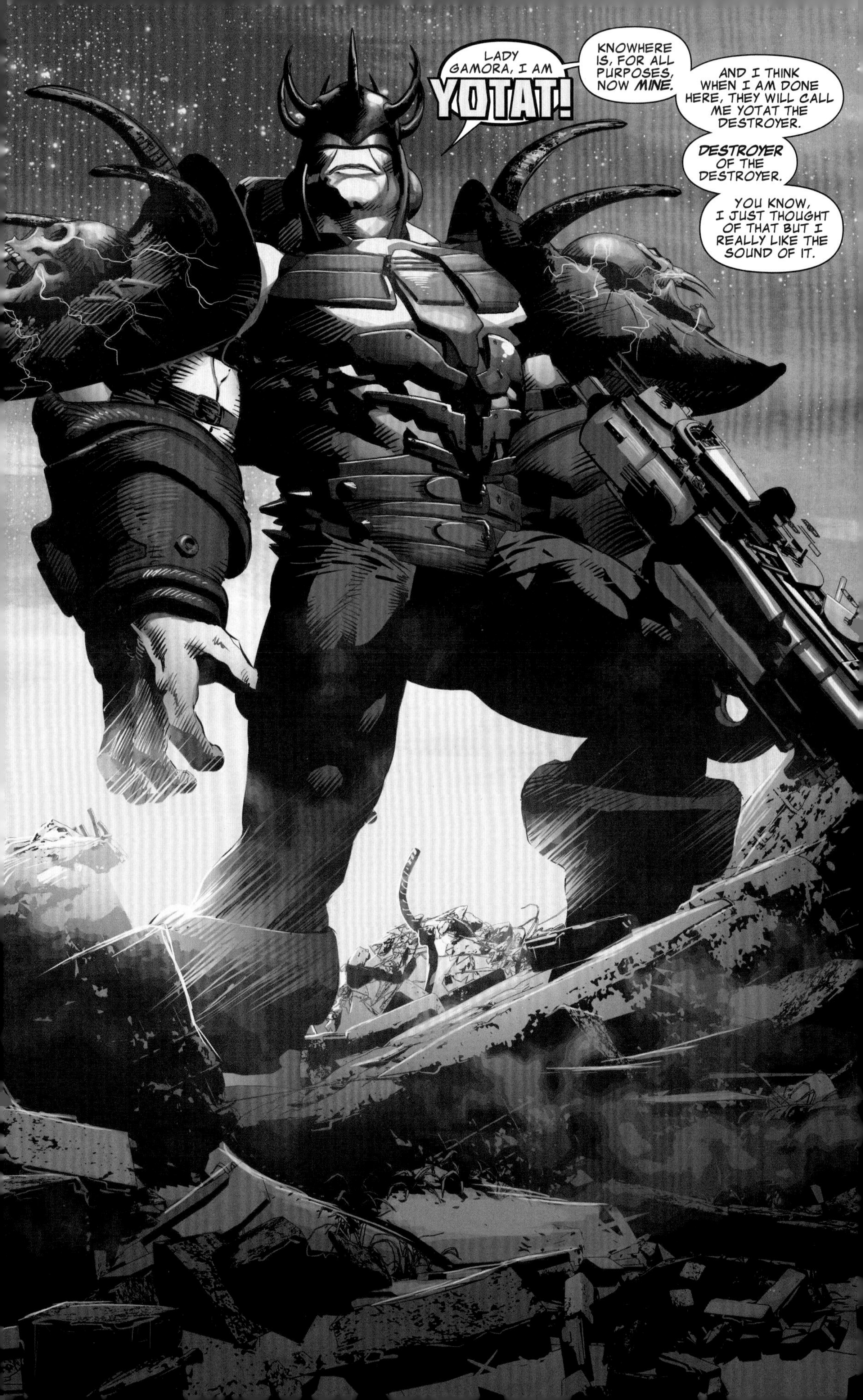
LADY GAMORA, I AM
YOTAT!
KNOWHERE IS, FOR ALL PURPOSES, NOW *MINE*.
AND I THINK WHEN I AM DONE HERE, THEY WILL CALL ME YOTAT THE DESTROYER.
DESTROYER OF THE DESTROYER.
YOU KNOW, I JUST THOUGHT OF THAT BUT I REALLY LIKE THE SOUND OF IT.

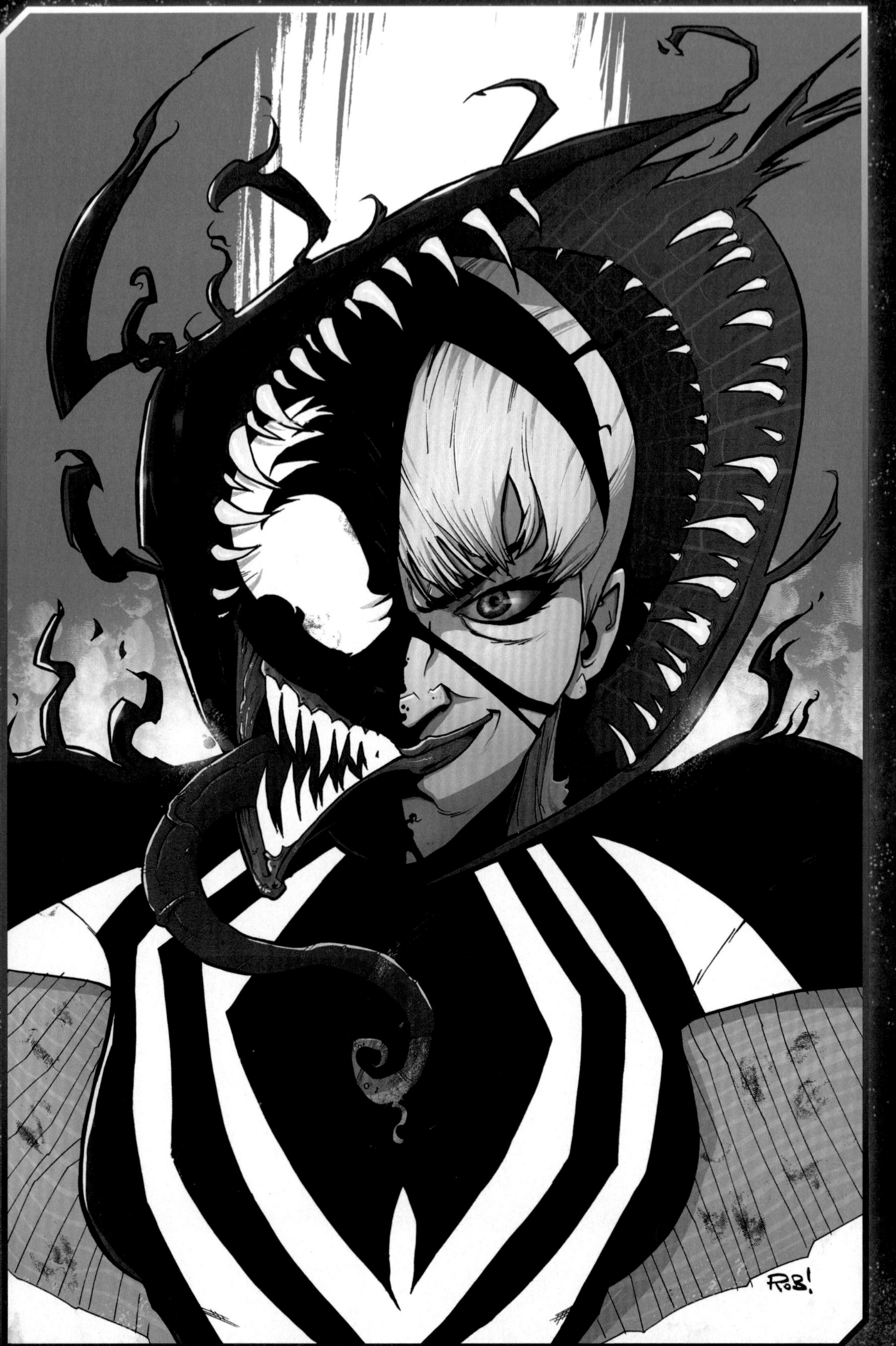
ROB!

GUARDIANS OF KNOWHERE #1
GWENOM VARIANT BY ROB GUILLORY

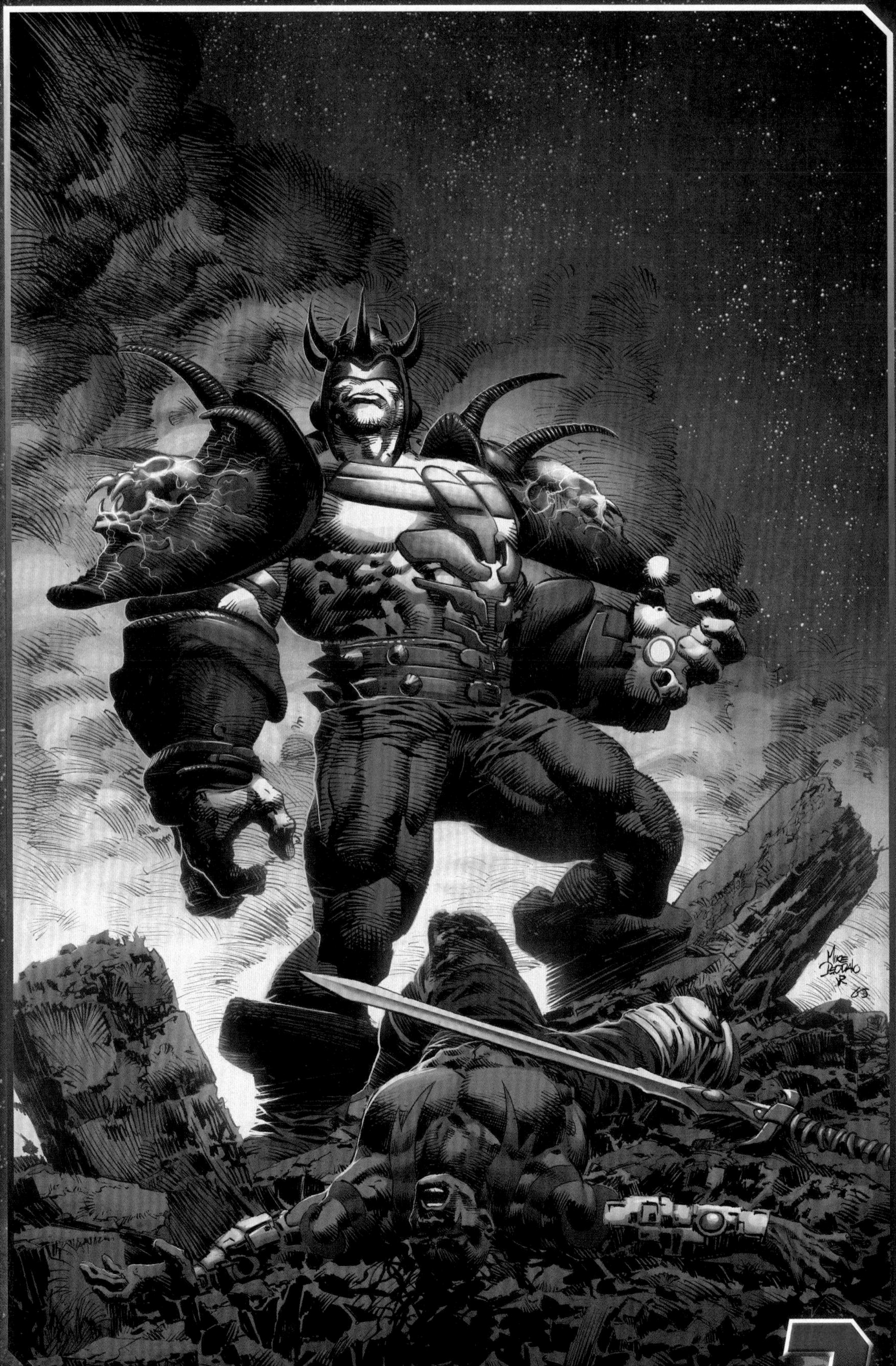

2

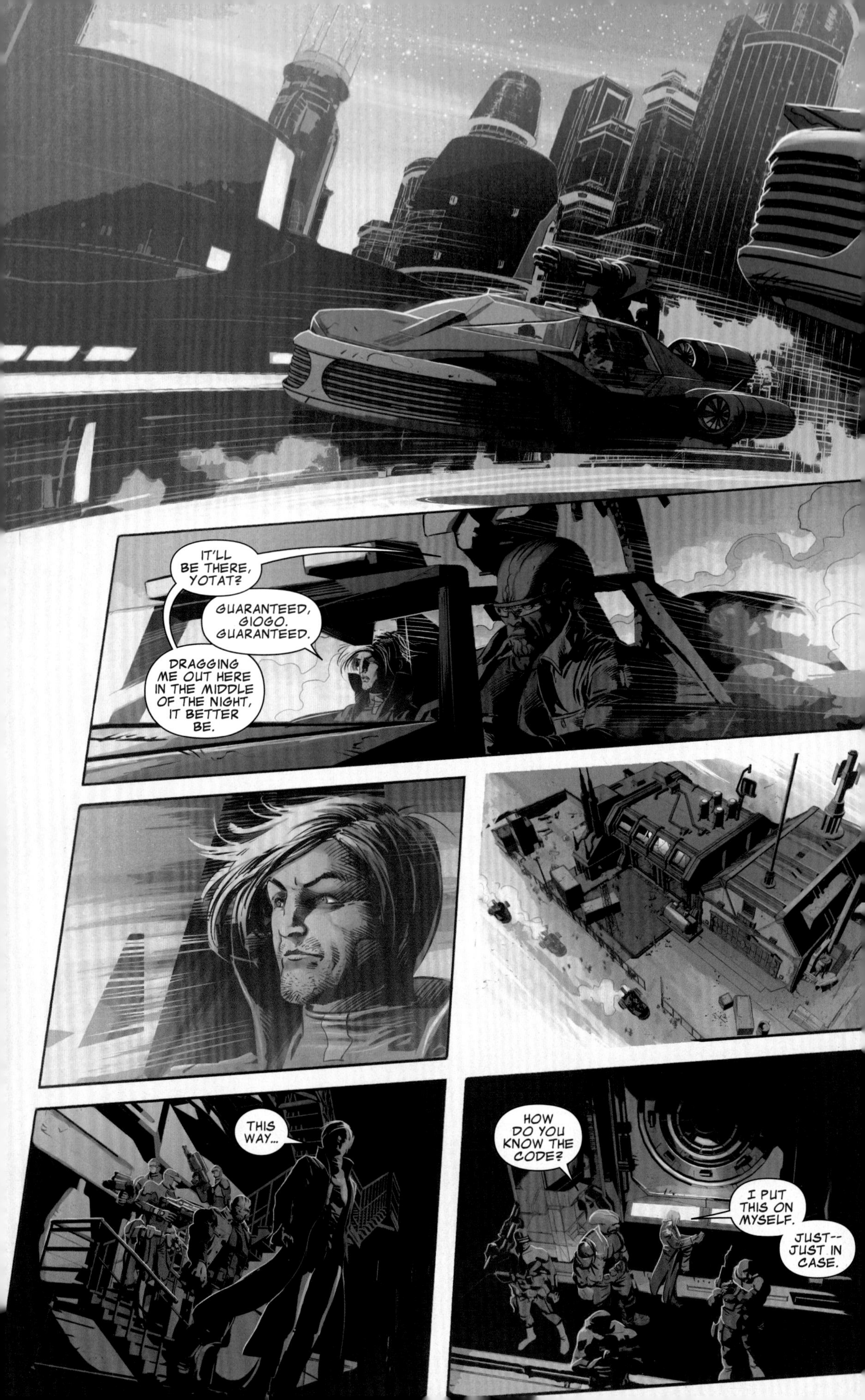
IT'LL BE THERE, YOTAT?
GUARANTEED, GIOGO. GUARANTEED.
DRAGGING ME OUT HERE IN THE MIDDLE OF THE NIGHT, IT BETTER BE.
THIS WAY...
HOW DO YOU KNOW THE CODE?
I PUT THIS ON MYSELF.
JUST-- JUST IN CASE.

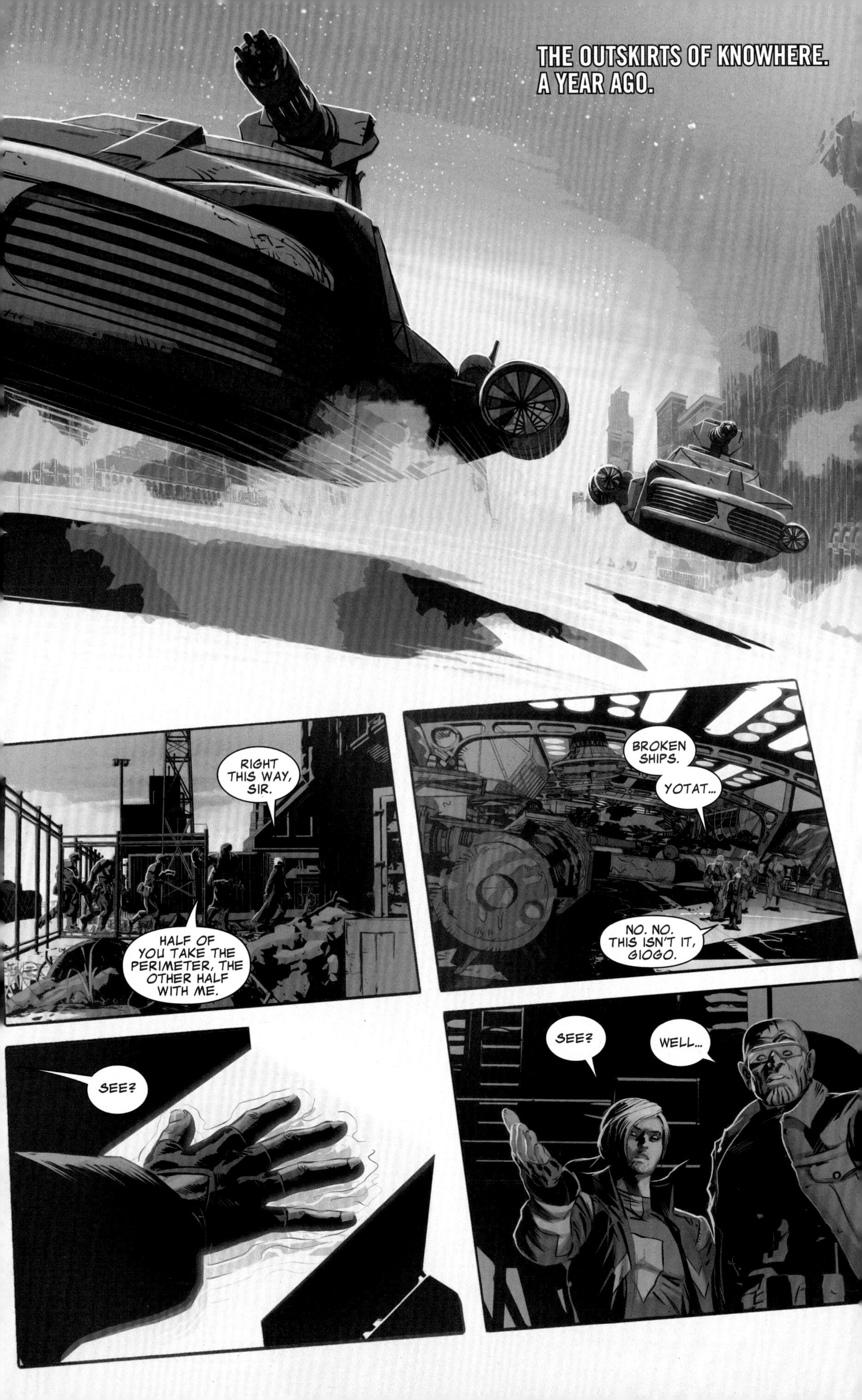
THE OUTSKIRTS OF KNOWHERE.
A YEAR AGO.
RIGHT THIS WAY, SIR.
HALF OF YOU TAKE THE PERIMETER, THE OTHER HALF WITH ME.
BROKEN SHIPS.
YOTAT...
NO. NO. THIS ISN'T IT, GIOGO.
SEE?
SEE?
WELL...

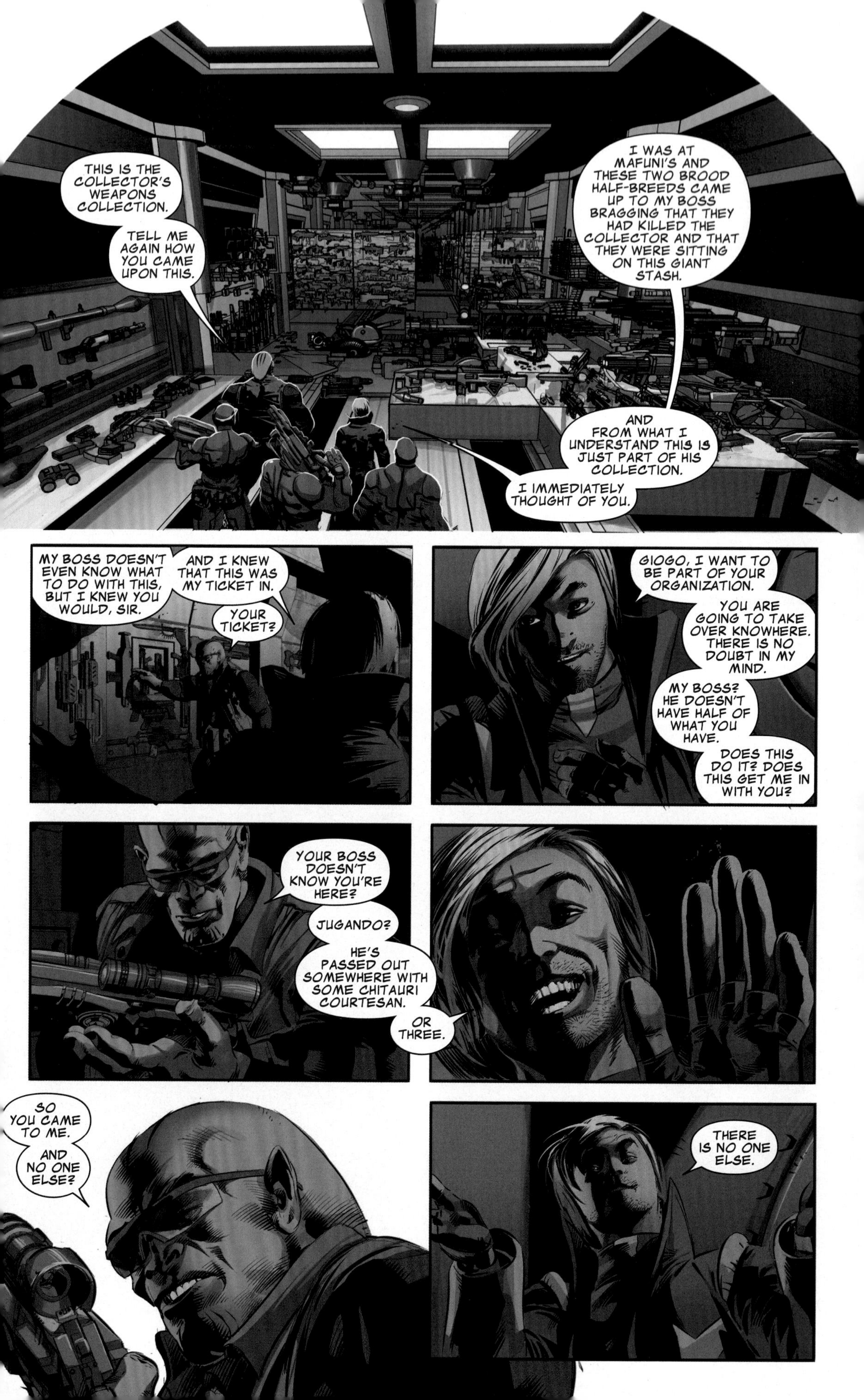
THIS IS THE COLLECTOR'S WEAPONS COLLECTION.
TELL ME AGAIN HOW YOU CAME UPON THIS.
I WAS AT MAFUNI'S AND THESE TWO BROOD HALF-BREEDS CAME UP TO MY BOSS BRAGGING THAT THEY HAD KILLED THE COLLECTOR AND THAT THEY WERE SITTING ON THIS GIANT STASH.
AND FROM WHAT I UNDERSTAND THIS IS JUST PART OF HIS COLLECTION.
I IMMEDIATELY THOUGHT OF YOU.
MY BOSS DOESN'T EVEN KNOW WHAT TO DO WITH THIS, BUT I KNEW YOU WOULD, SIR.
AND I KNEW THAT THIS WAS MY TICKET IN.
YOUR TICKET?
GIOGO, I WANT TO BE PART OF YOUR ORGANIZATION.
YOU ARE GOING TO TAKE OVER KNOWHERE. THERE IS NO DOUBT IN MY MIND.
MY BOSS? HE DOESN'T HAVE HALF OF WHAT YOU HAVE.
DOES THIS DO IT? DOES THIS GET ME IN WITH YOU?
YOUR BOSS DOESN'T KNOW YOU'RE HERE?
JUGANDO?
HE'S PASSED OUT SOMEWHERE WITH SOME CHITAURI COURTESAN.
OR THREE.
SO YOU CAME TO ME.
AND NO ONE ELSE?
THERE IS NO ONE ELSE.

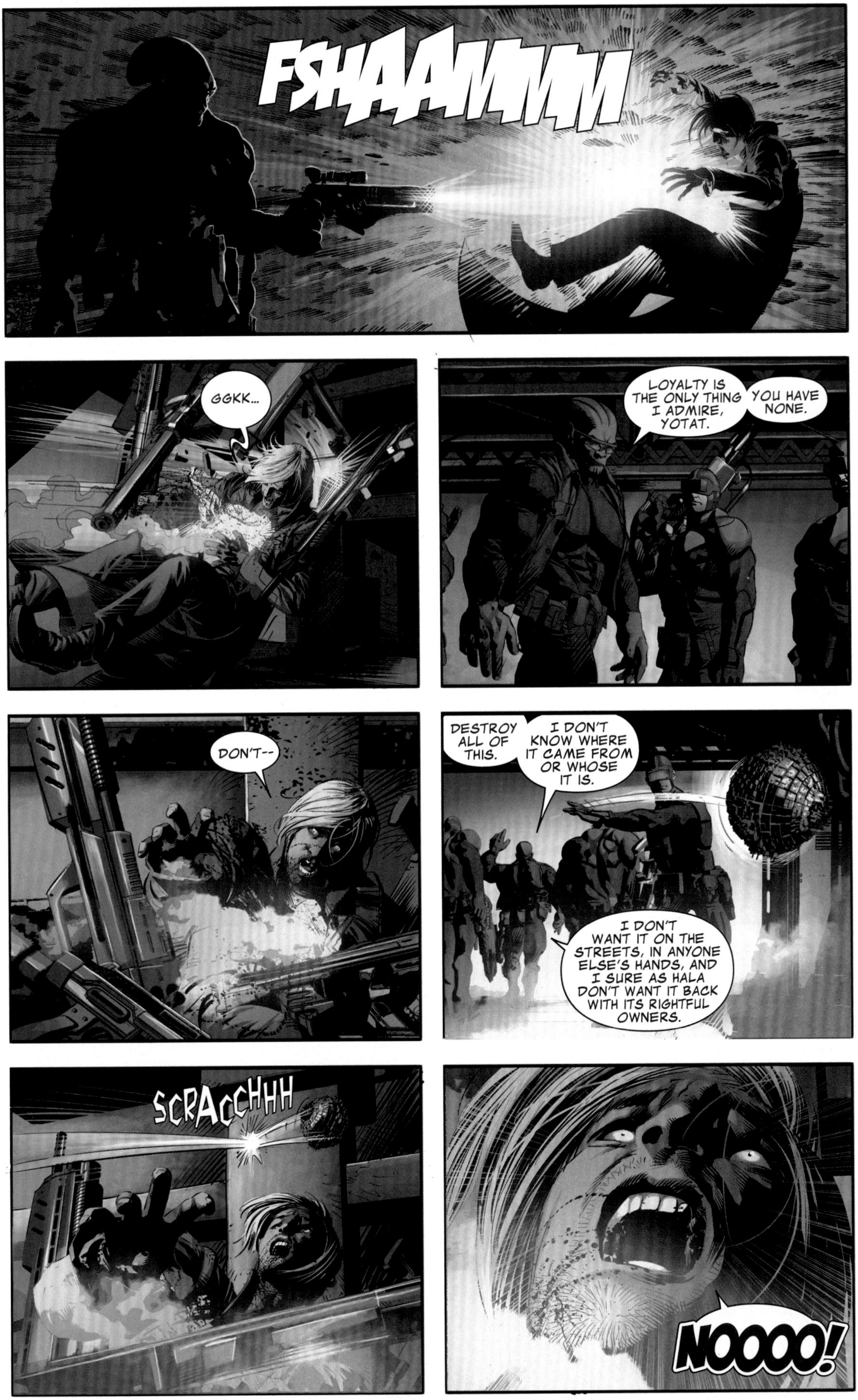
FSHAAMMMM
GGKK...
LOYALTY IS THE ONLY THING I ADMIRE, YOTAT.
YOU HAVE NONE.
DON'T--
DESTROY ALL OF THIS.
I DON'T KNOW WHERE IT CAME FROM OR WHOSE IT IS.
I DON'T WANT IT ON THE STREETS, IN ANYONE ELSE'S HANDS, AND I SURE AS HALA DON'T WANT IT BACK WITH ITS RIGHTFUL OWNERS.
SCRACCHHH
NOOOO!

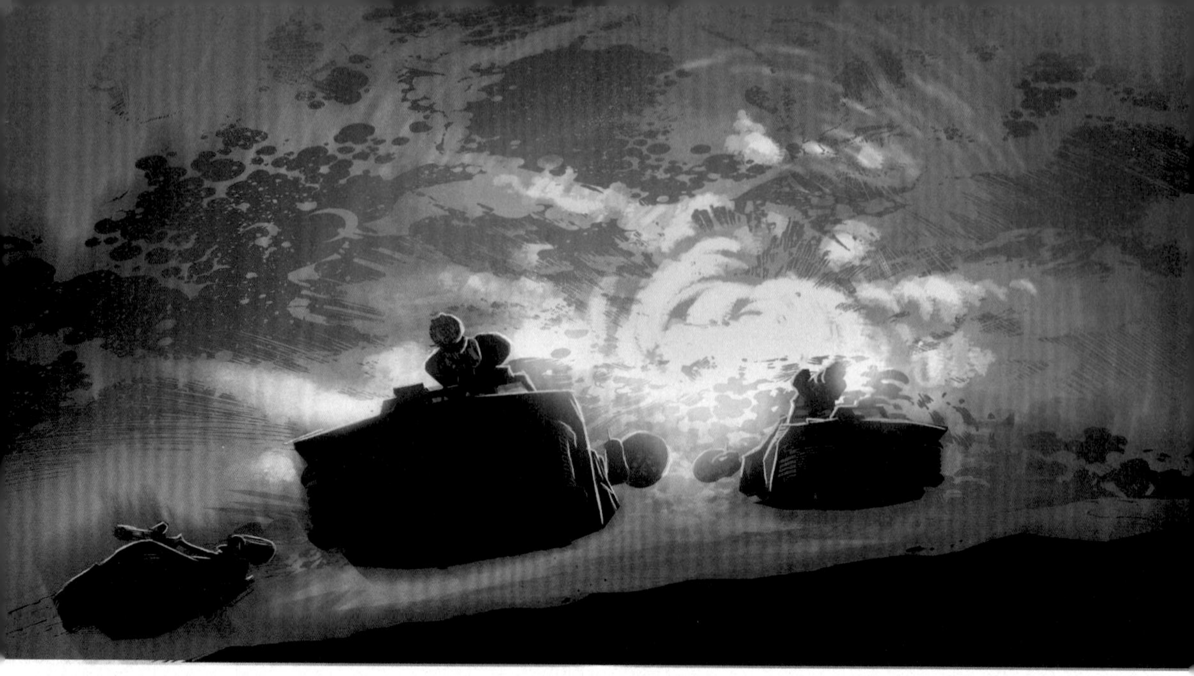

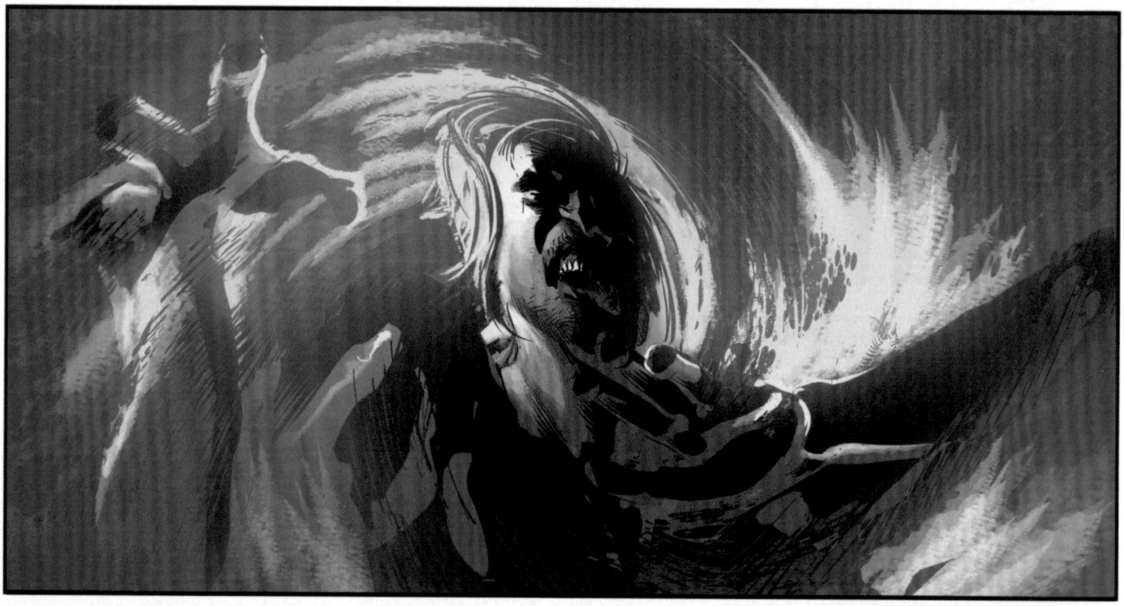

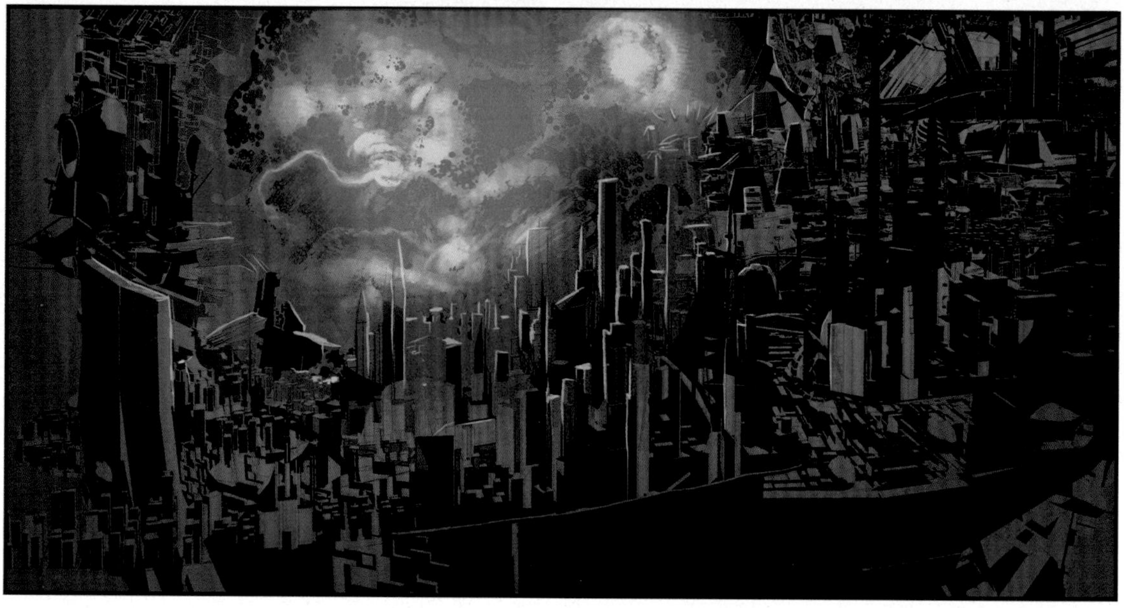

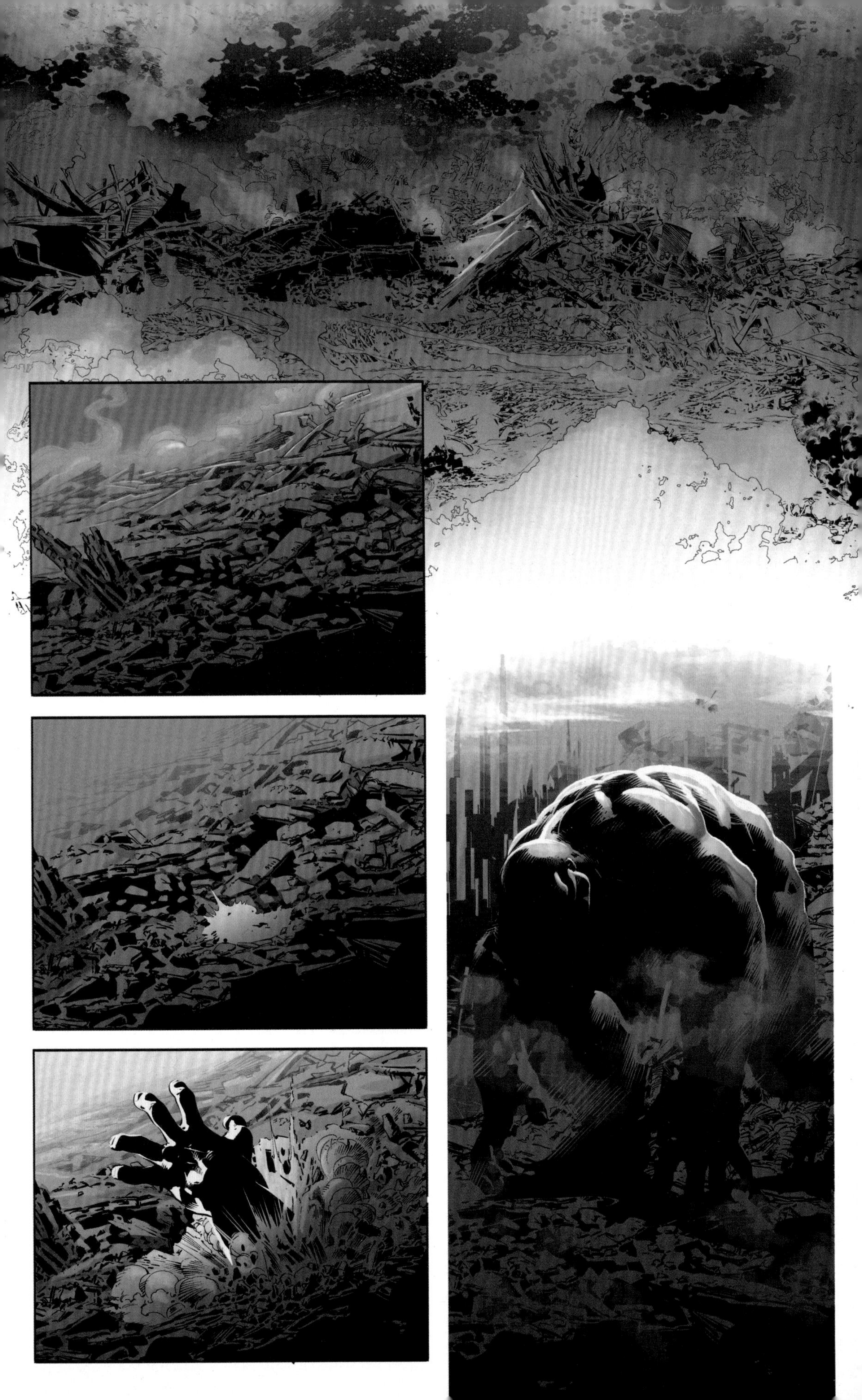

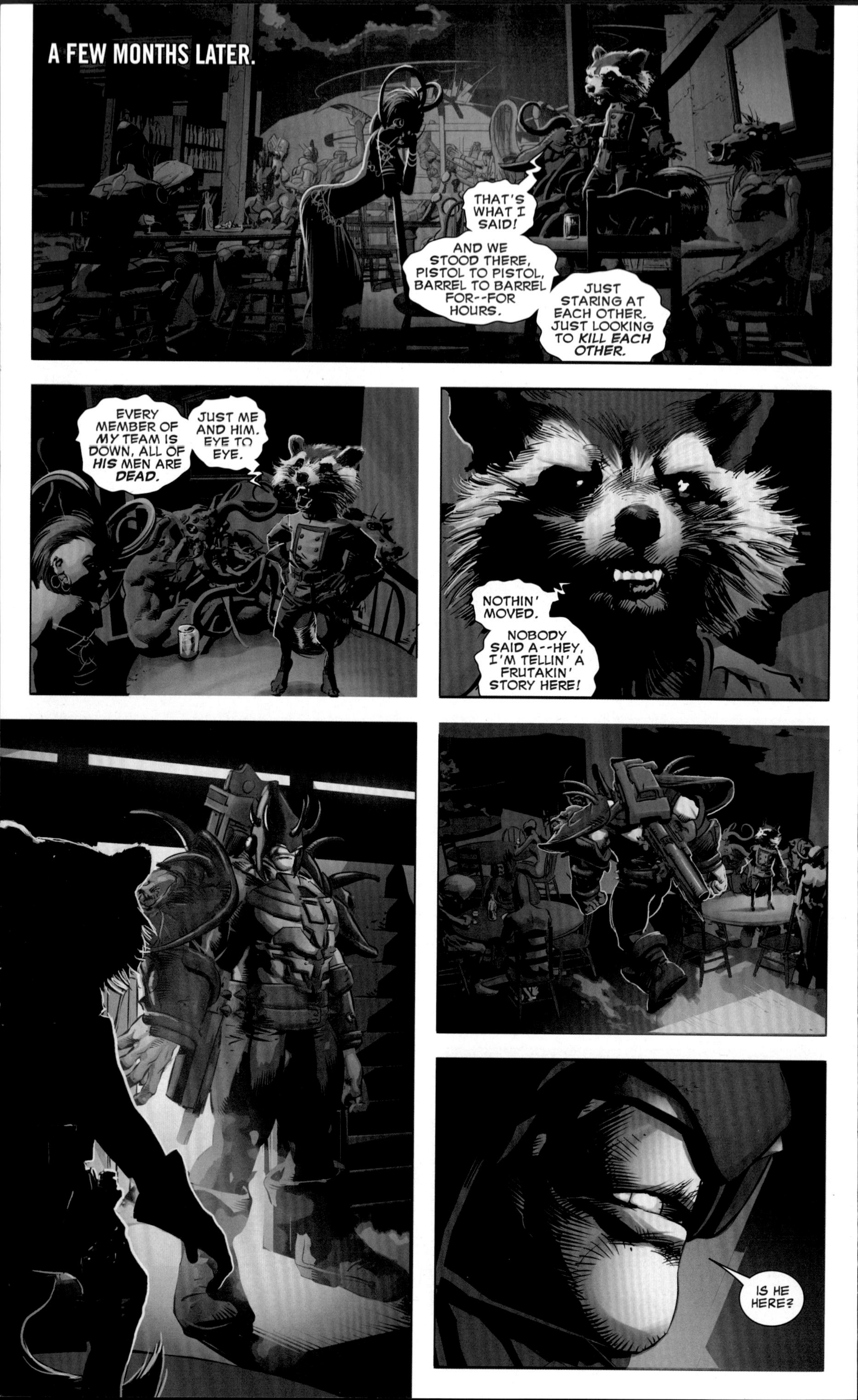
A FEW MONTHS LATER.
THAT'S WHAT I SAID!
AND WE STOOD THERE, PISTOL TO PISTOL, BARREL TO BARREL FOR--FOR HOURS.
JUST STARING AT EACH OTHER. JUST LOOKING TO KILL EACH OTHER.
EVERY MEMBER OF MY TEAM IS DOWN, ALL OF HIS MEN ARE DEAD.
JUST ME AND HIM. EYE TO EYE.
NOTHIN' MOVED.
NOBODY SAID A--HEY, I'M TELLIN' A FRUTAKIN' STORY HERE!
IS HE HERE?

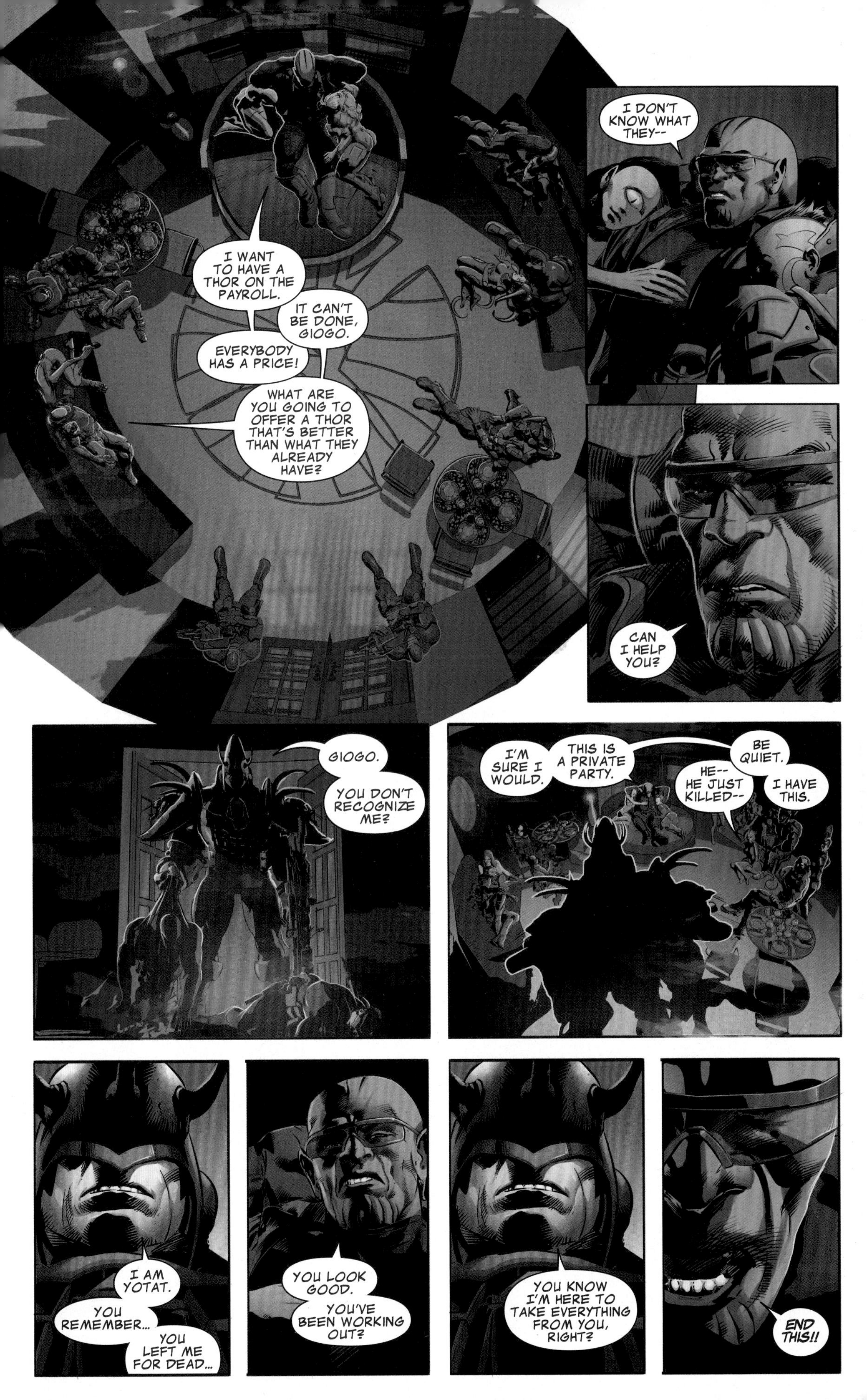
I WANT TO HAVE A THOR ON THE PAYROLL.
IT CAN'T BE DONE, GIOGO.
EVERYBODY HAS A PRICE!
WHAT ARE YOU GOING TO OFFER A THOR THAT'S BETTER THAN WHAT THEY ALREADY HAVE?
I DON'T KNOW WHAT THEY--
CAN I HELP YOU?
GIOGO.
YOU DON'T RECOGNIZE ME?
I'M SURE I WOULD.
THIS IS A PRIVATE PARTY.
BE QUIET.
HE-- HE JUST KILLED--
I HAVE THIS.
I AM YOTAT.
YOU REMEMBER...
YOU LEFT ME FOR DEAD...
YOU LOOK GOOD.
YOU'VE BEEN WORKING OUT?
YOU KNOW I'M HERE TO TAKE EVERYTHING FROM YOU, RIGHT?
END THIS!!

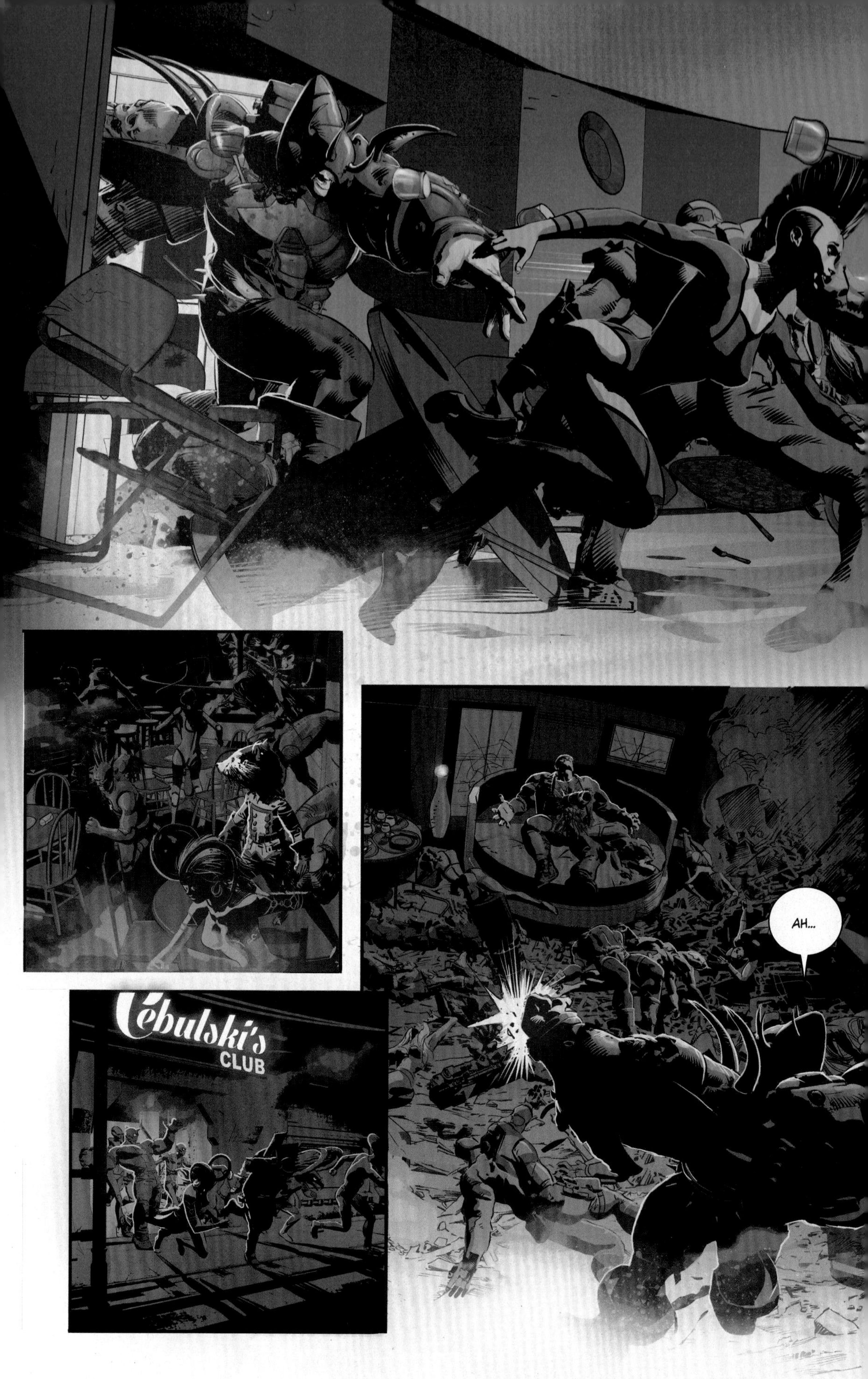
Cebulski's
CLUB
AH...

SO, UM, WHAT'S YOUR DEAL EXACTLY?

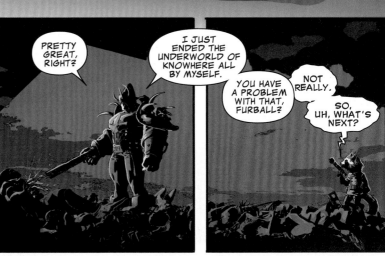

PRETTY GREAT, RIGHT?

I JUST ENDED THE UNDERWORLD OF KNOWHERE ALL BY MYSELF.

YOU HAVE A PROBLEM WITH THAT, FURBALL?

NOT REALLY.

SO, UH, WHAT'S NEXT?

NOW I TAKE CONTROL.

YOU NEED A JOB?

I'VE SEEN YOU AROUND. YOU'RE A LITTLE SCRAPPER.

YOU TAKE CONTROL?

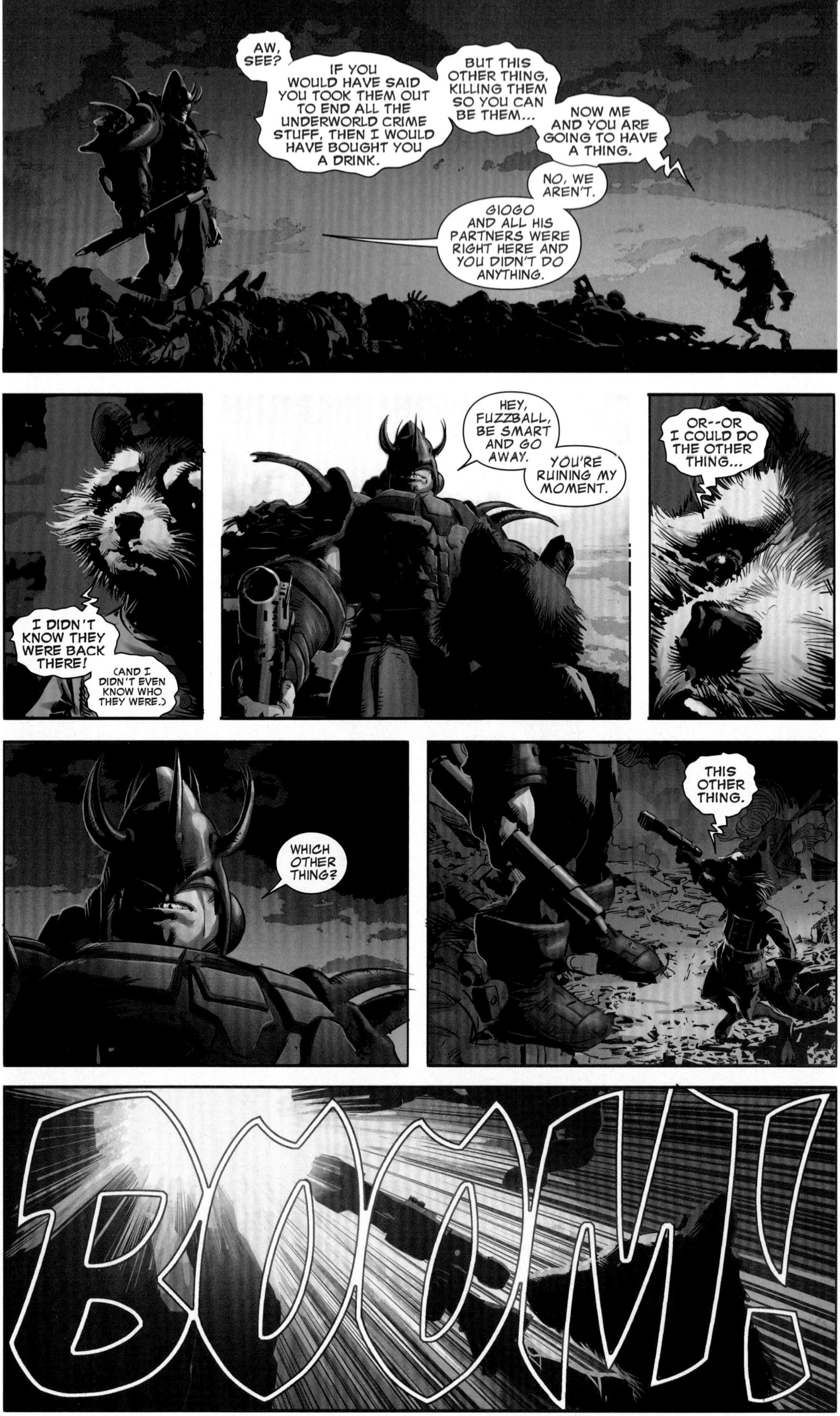
AW, SEE?
IF YOU WOULD HAVE SAID YOU TOOK THEM OUT TO END ALL THE UNDERWORLD CRIME STUFF, THEN I WOULD HAVE BOUGHT YOU A DRINK.
BUT THIS OTHER THING, KILLING THEM SO YOU CAN BE THEM...
NOW ME AND YOU ARE GOING TO HAVE A THING.
NO, WE AREN'T.
GIOGO AND ALL HIS PARTNERS WERE RIGHT HERE AND YOU DIDN'T DO ANYTHING.
I DIDN'T KNOW THEY WERE BACK THERE!
(AND I DIDN'T EVEN KNOW WHO THEY WERE.)
HEY, FUZZBALL, BE SMART AND GO AWAY.
YOU'RE RUINING MY MOMENT.
OR--OR I COULD DO THE OTHER THING...
WHICH OTHER THING?
THIS OTHER THING.
BOOM!

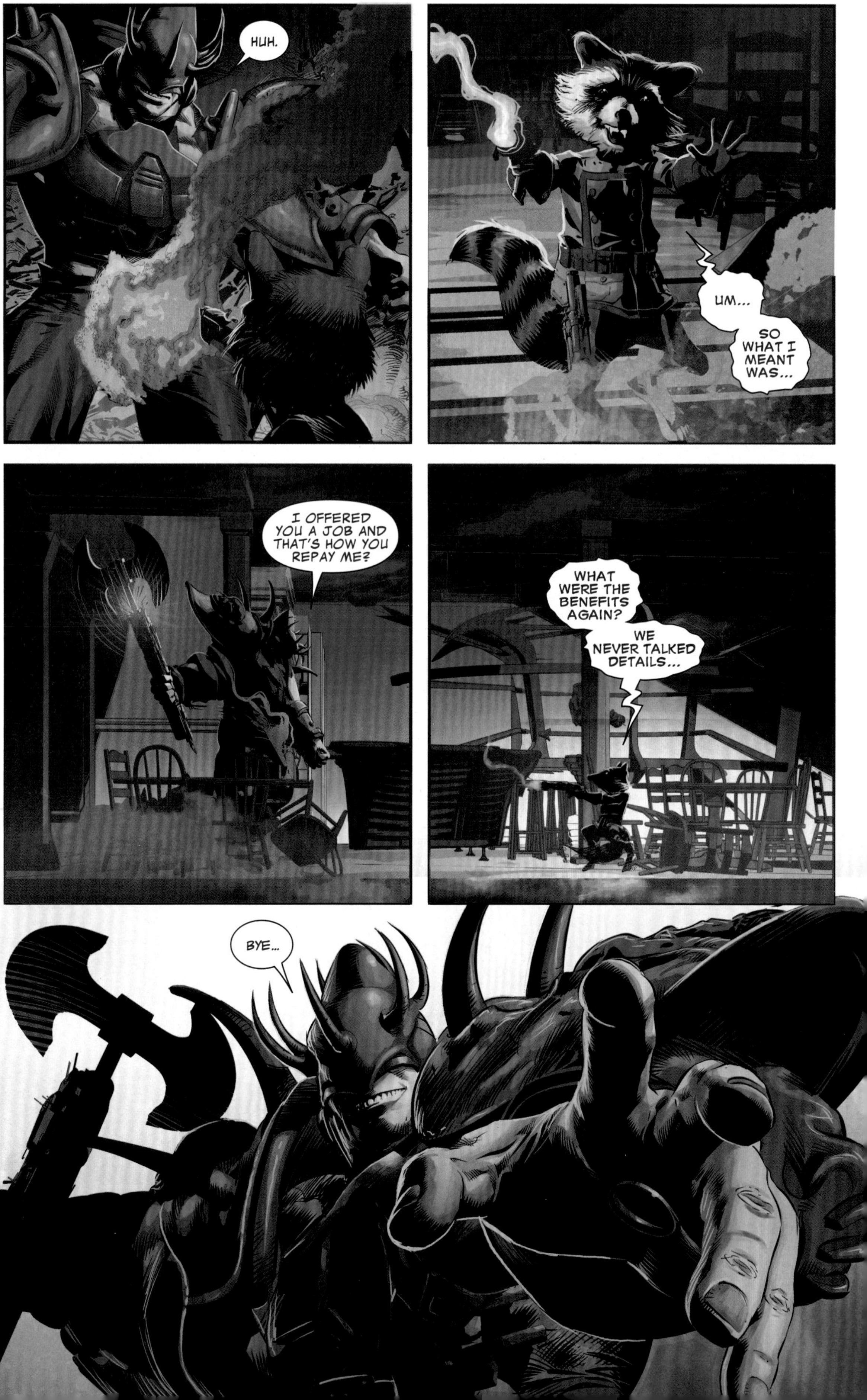
HUH.
UM...
SO WHAT I MEANT WAS...
I OFFERED YOU A JOB AND THAT'S HOW YOU REPAY ME?
WHAT WERE THE BENEFITS AGAIN?
WE NEVER TALKED DETAILS...
BYE...

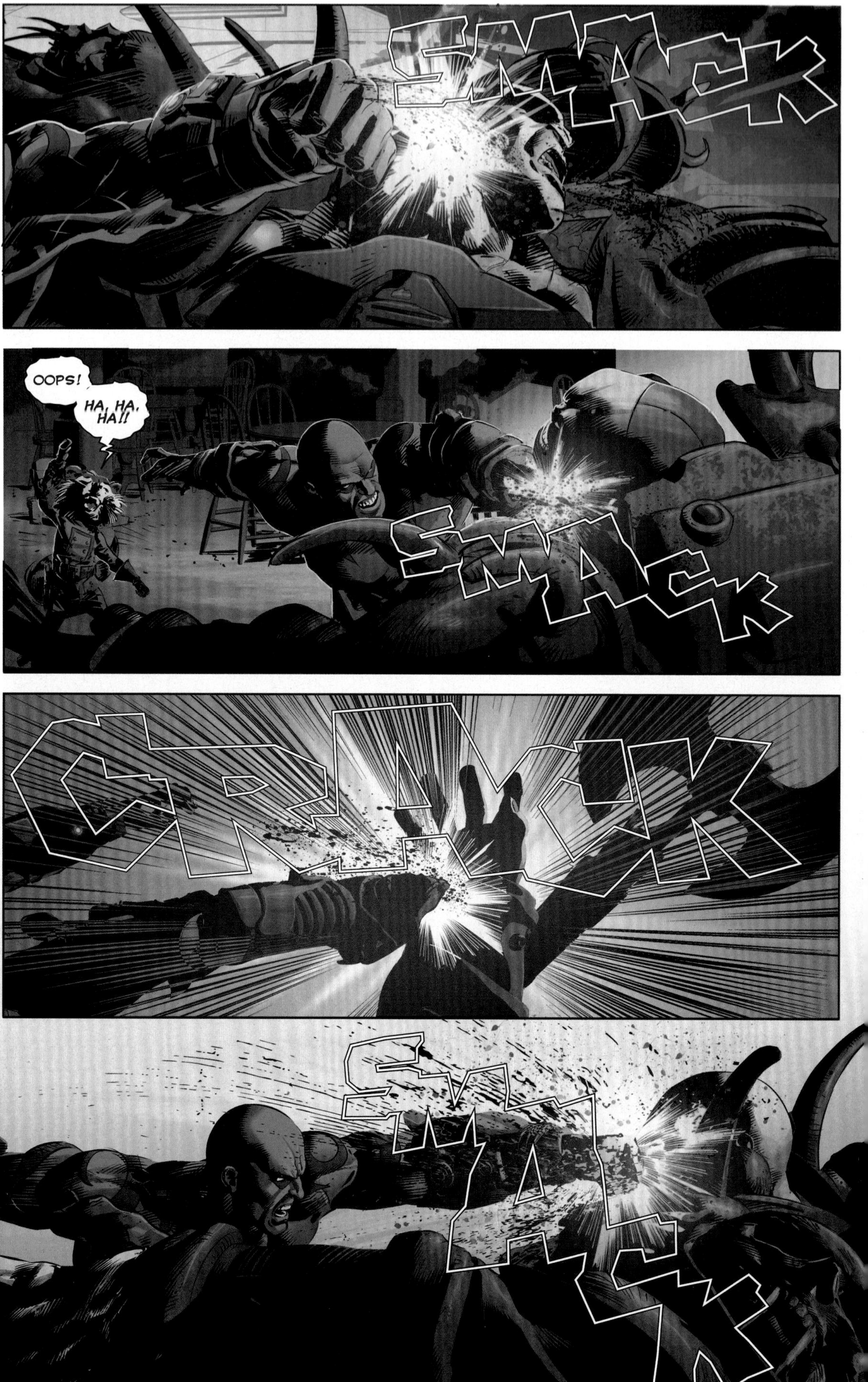
SMACK
OOPS!
HA, HA, HA!!
SMACK
CRACK
SMACK

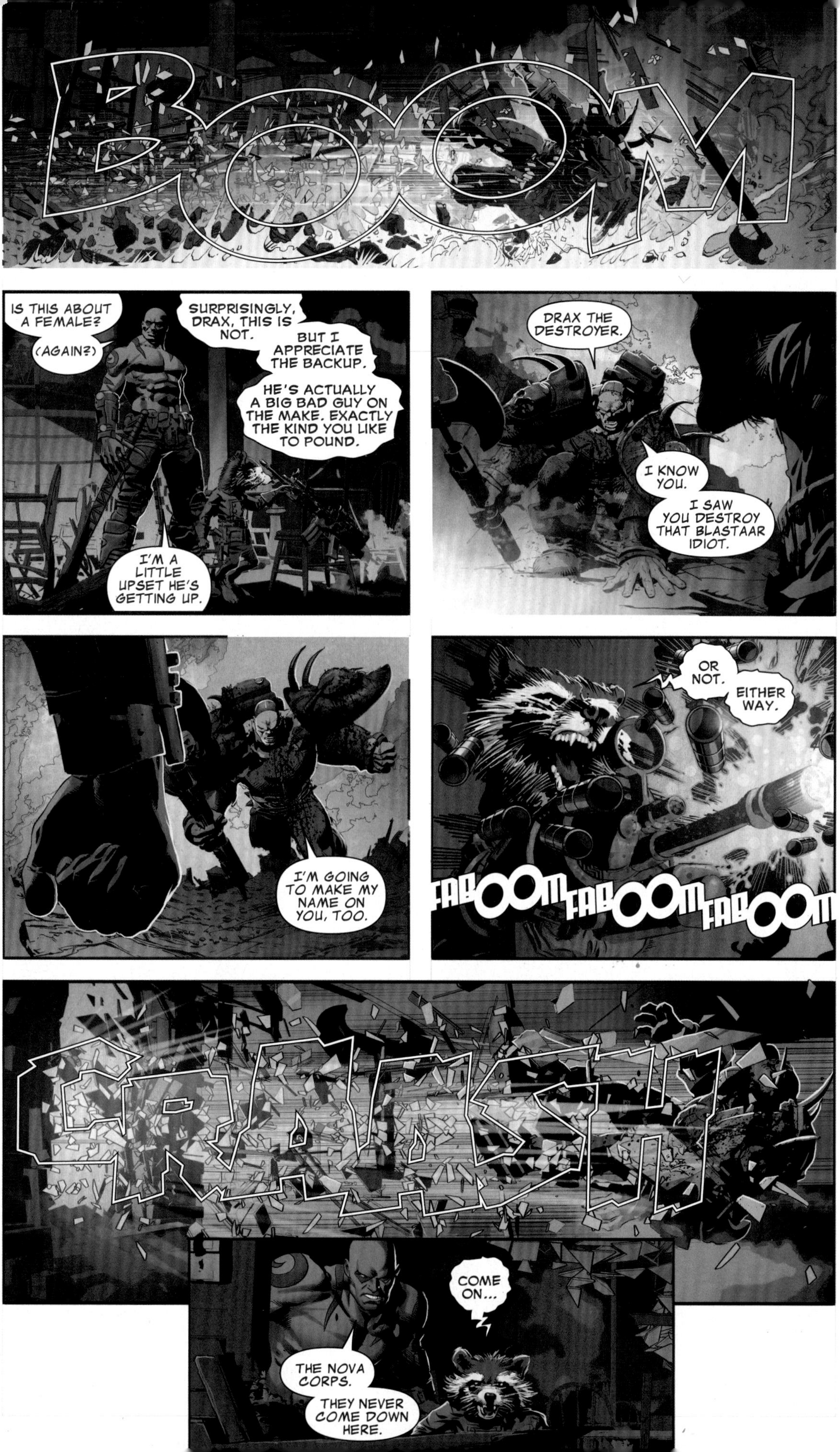
BOOM
IS THIS ABOUT A FEMALE?
(AGAIN?)
SURPRISINGLY, DRAX, THIS IS NOT.
BUT I APPRECIATE THE BACKUP.
HE'S ACTUALLY A BIG BAD GUY ON THE MAKE. EXACTLY THE KIND YOU LIKE TO POUND.
I'M A LITTLE UPSET HE'S GETTING UP.
DRAX THE DESTROYER.
I KNOW YOU.
I SAW YOU DESTROY THAT BLASTAAR IDIOT.
I'M GOING TO MAKE MY NAME ON YOU, TOO.
OR NOT.
EITHER WAY.
FABOOM FABOOM FABOOM
CRAKSH
COME ON...
THE NOVA CORPS.
THEY NEVER COME DOWN HERE.

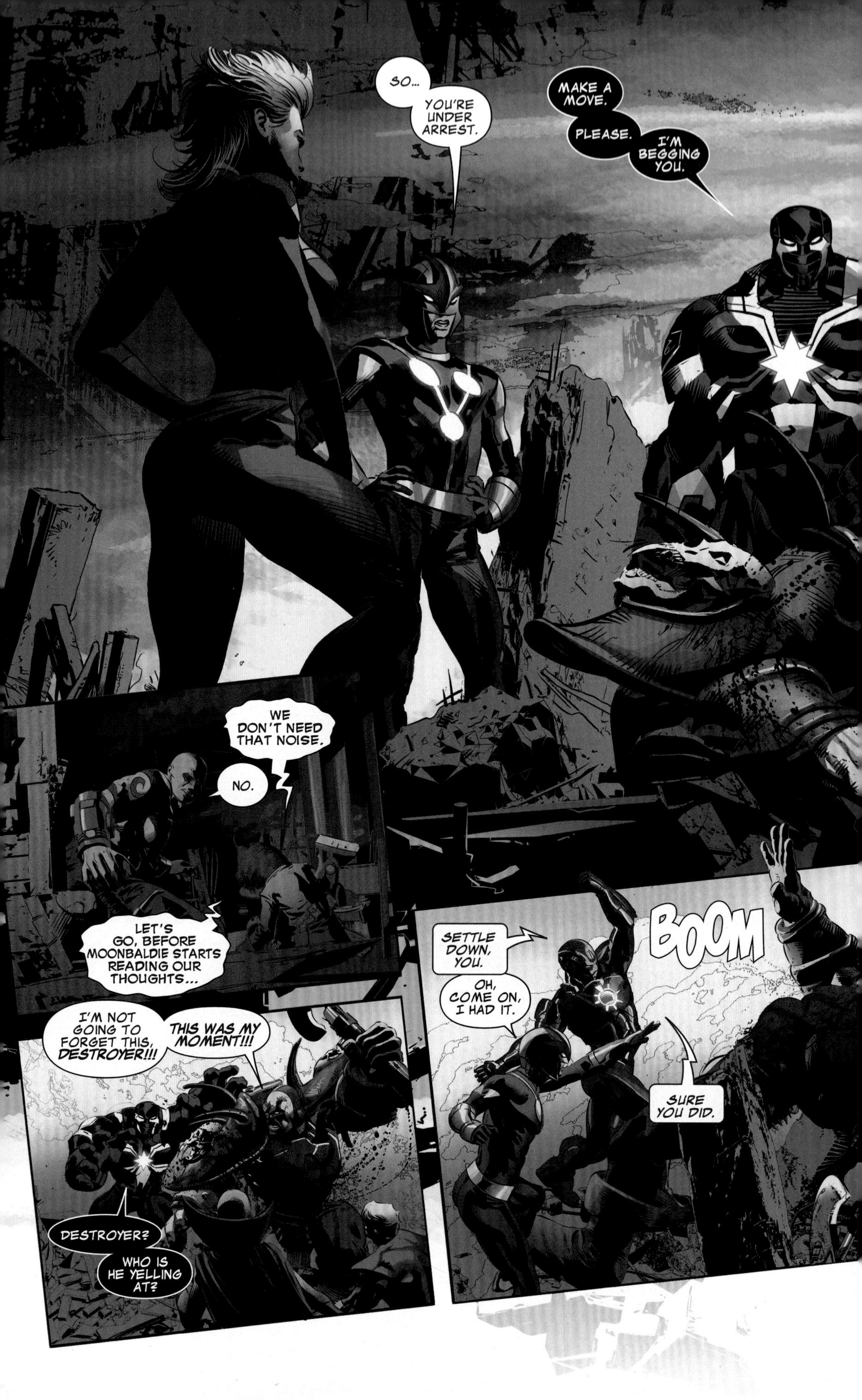
SO...
YOU'RE UNDER ARREST.
MAKE A MOVE.
PLEASE.
I'M BEGGING YOU.
WE DON'T NEED THAT NOISE.
NO.
LET'S GO, BEFORE MOONBALDIE STARTS READING OUR THOUGHTS...
SETTLE DOWN, YOU.
OH, COME ON, I HAD IT.
BOOM
SURE YOU DID.
I'M NOT GOING TO FORGET THIS, DESTROYER!!!
THIS WAS MY MOMENT!!!
DESTROYER?
WHO IS HE YELLING AT?

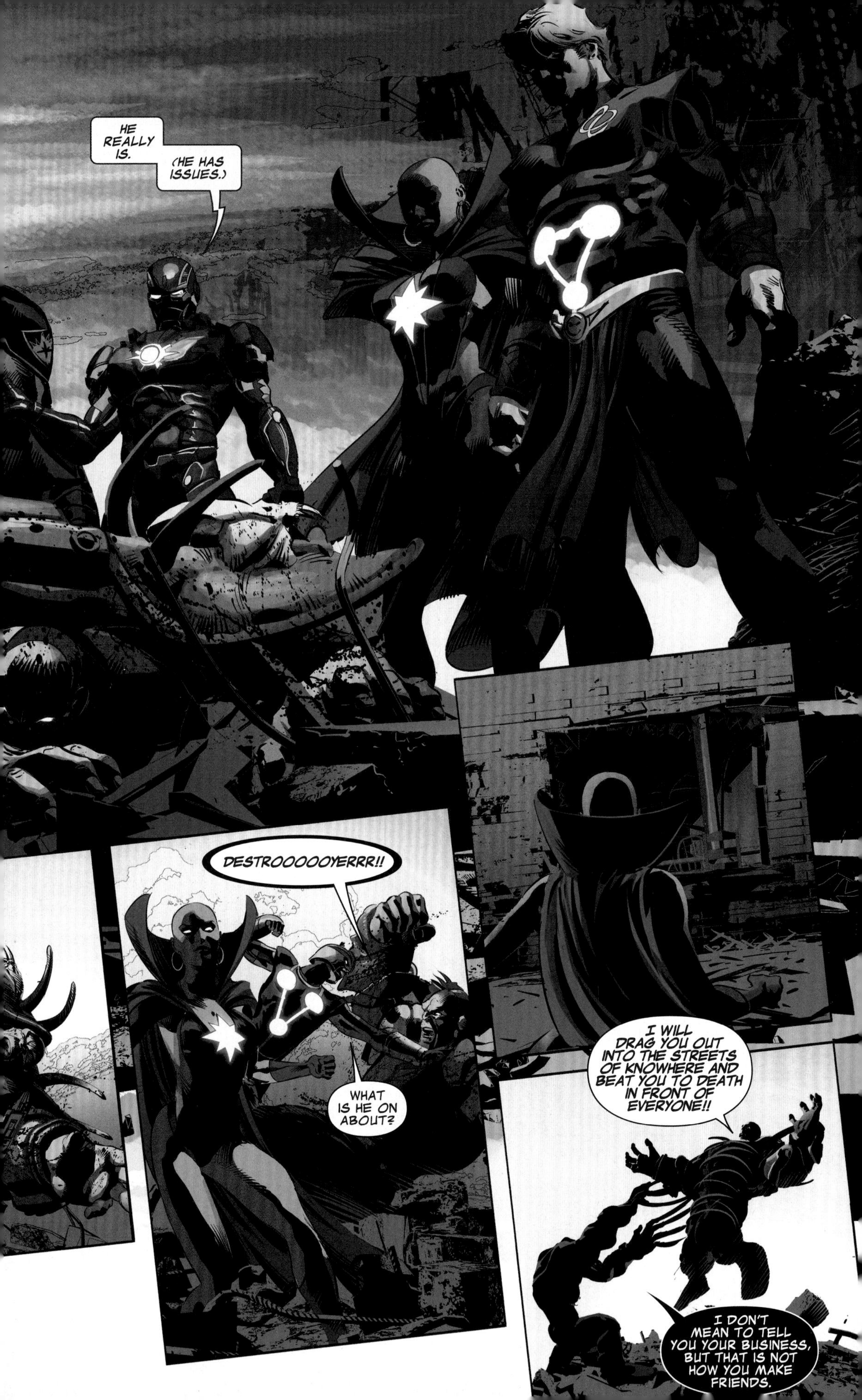
HE REALLY IS.
(HE HAS ISSUES.)
DESTROOOOOYERRR!!
WHAT IS HE ON ABOUT?
I WILL DRAG YOU OUT INTO THE STREETS OF KNOWHERE AND BEAT YOU TO DEATH IN FRONT OF EVERYONE!!
I DON'T MEAN TO TELL YOU YOUR BUSINESS, BUT THAT IS NOT HOW YOU MAKE FRIENDS.

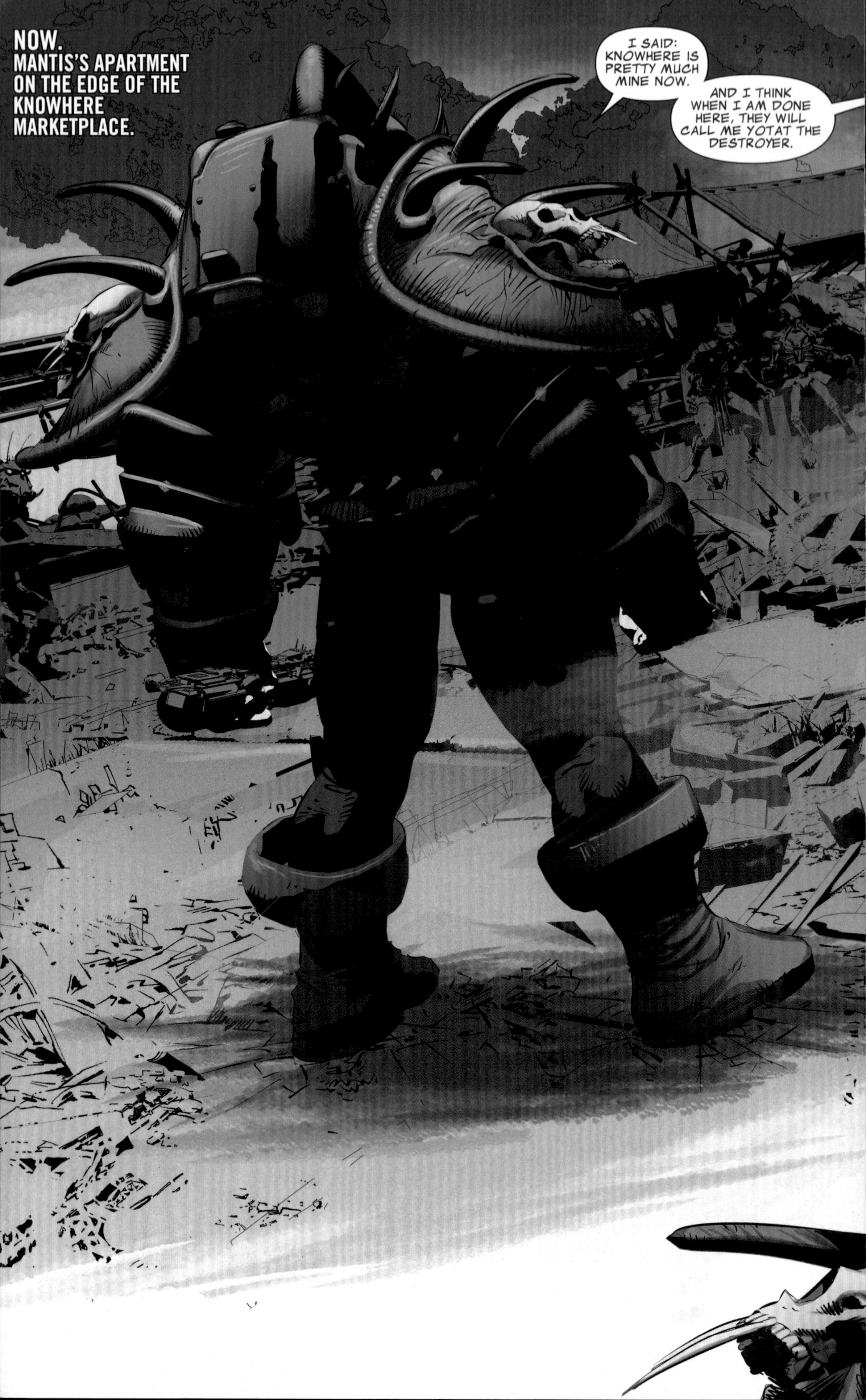
NOW.
MANTIS'S APARTMENT ON THE EDGE OF THE KNOWHERE MARKETPLACE.
I SAID: KNOWHERE IS PRETTY MUCH MINE NOW.
AND I THINK WHEN I AM DONE HERE, THEY WILL CALL ME YOTAT THE DESTROYER.

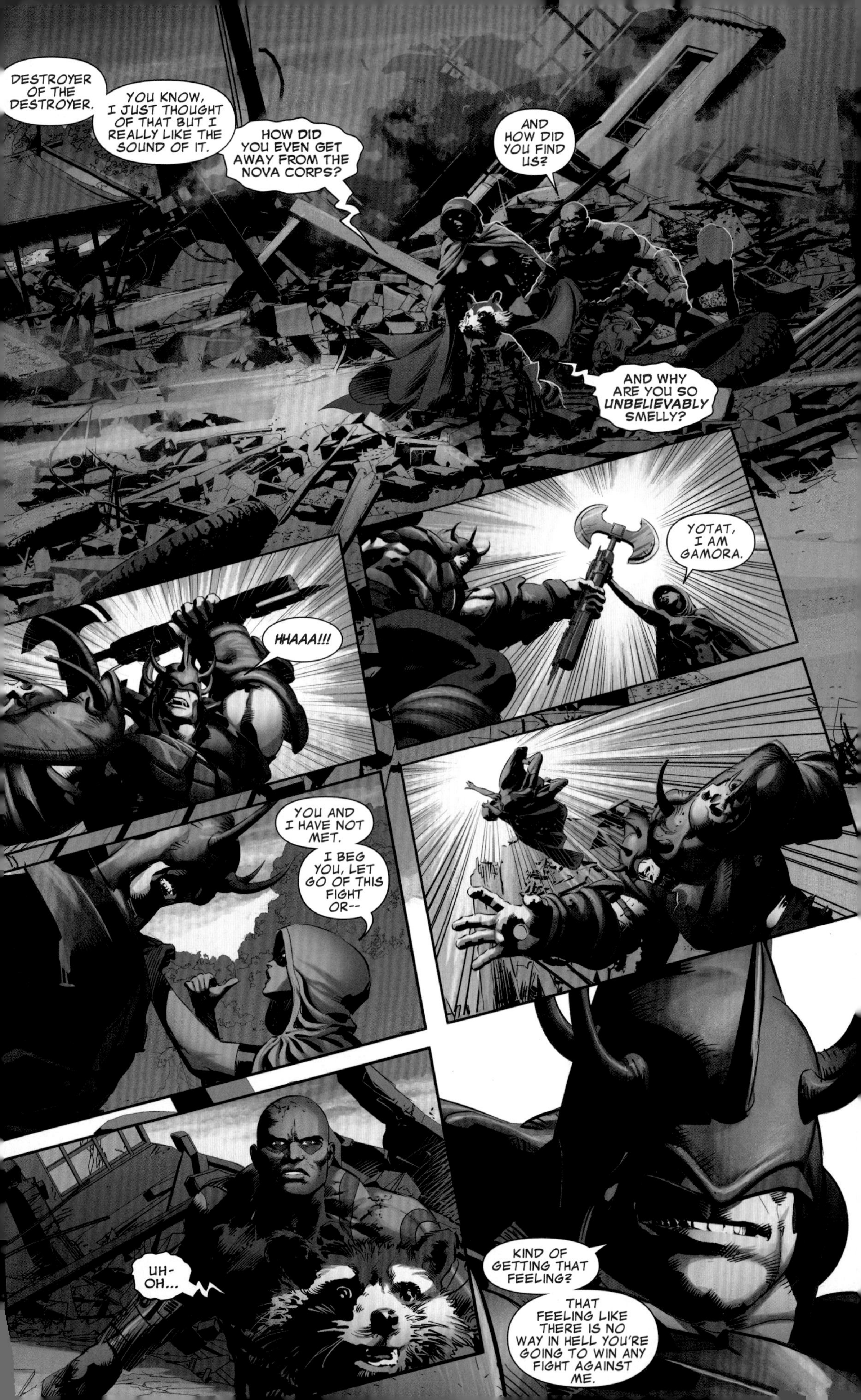
DESTROYER OF THE DESTROYER.
YOU KNOW, I JUST THOUGHT OF THAT BUT I REALLY LIKE THE SOUND OF IT.
HOW DID YOU EVEN GET AWAY FROM THE NOVA CORPS?
AND HOW DID YOU FIND US?
AND WHY ARE YOU SO UNBELIEVABLY SMELLY?
HHAAA!!!
YOTAT, I AM GAMORA.
YOU AND I HAVE NOT MET.
I BEG YOU, LET GO OF THIS FIGHT OR--
UH-OH...
KIND OF GETTING THAT FEELING?
THAT FEELING LIKE THERE IS NO WAY IN HELL YOU'RE GOING TO WIN ANY FIGHT AGAINST ME.

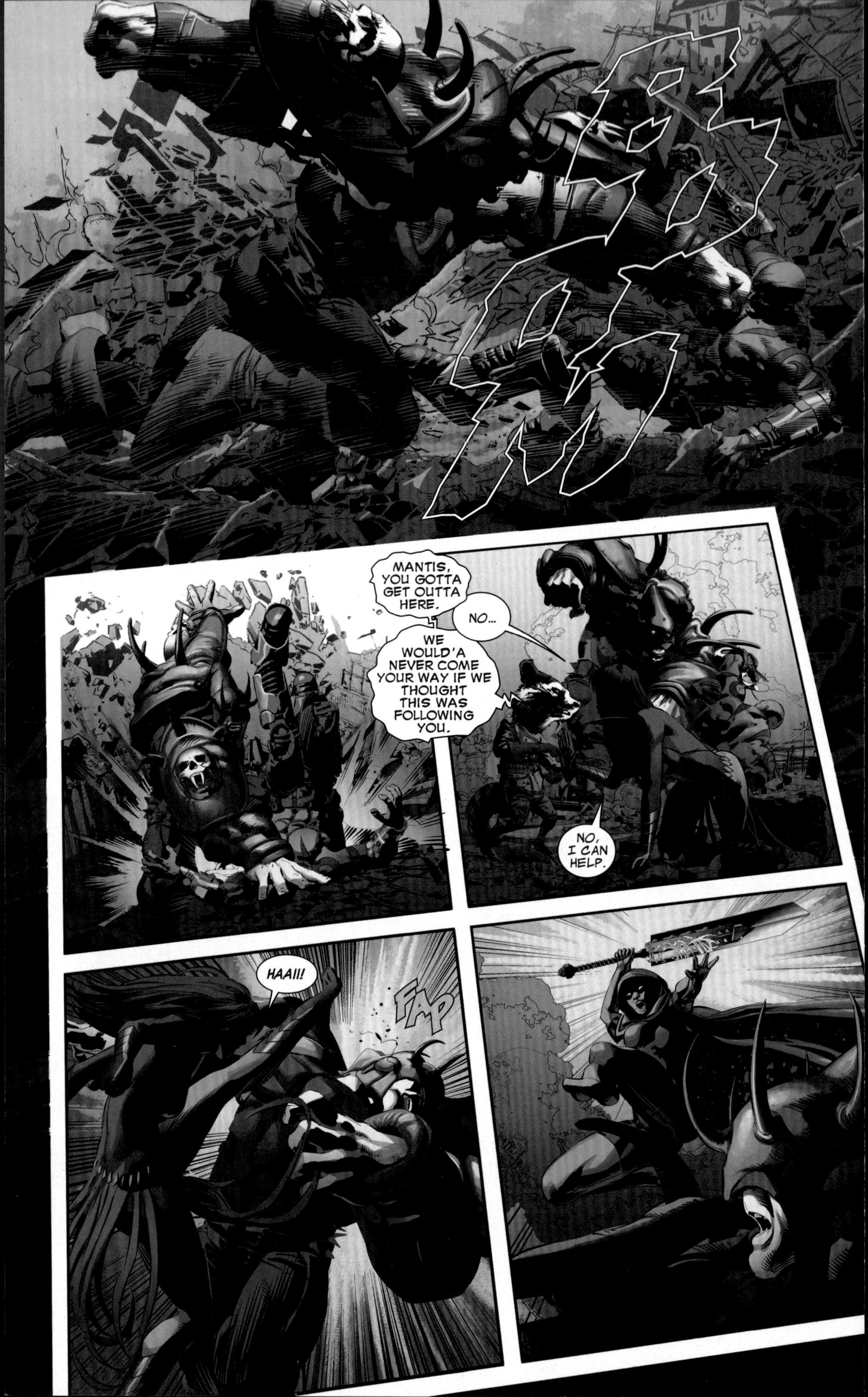
MANTIS, YOU GOTTA GET OUTTA HERE.
NO...
WE WOULD'A NEVER COME YOUR WAY IF WE THOUGHT THIS WAS FOLLOWING YOU.
NO, I CAN HELP.
HAAII!
FAP

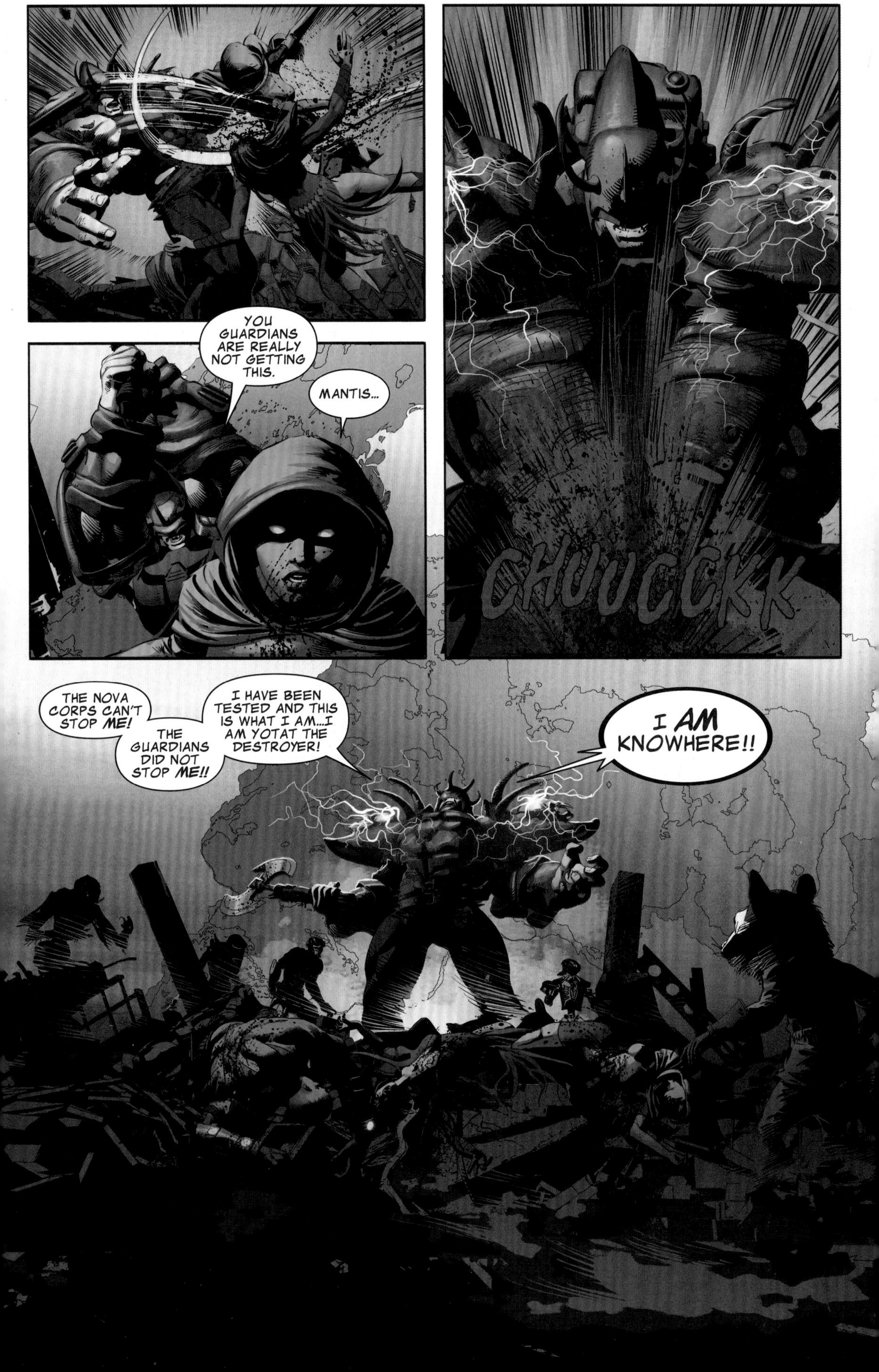
YOU GUARDIANS ARE REALLY NOT GETTING THIS.
MANTIS...
CHUUCCKK
THE NOVA CORPS CAN'T STOP ME!
THE GUARDIANS DID NOT STOP ME!!
I HAVE BEEN TESTED AND THIS IS WHAT I AM...I AM YOTAT THE DESTROYER!
I AM KNOWHERE!!

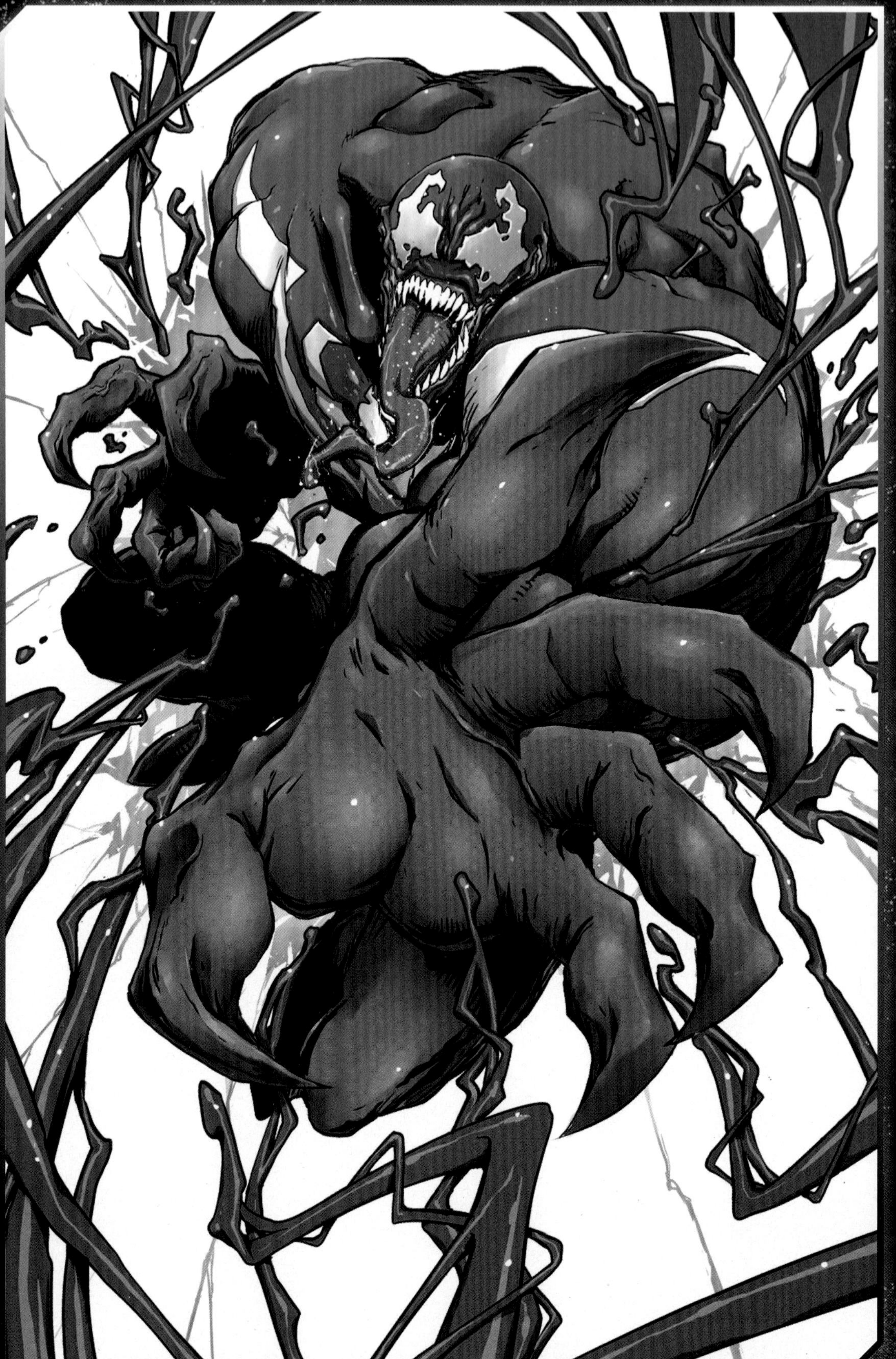

GUARDIANS OF KNOWHERE #3
MANGA VARIANT BY YASUHIRO NIGHTOW

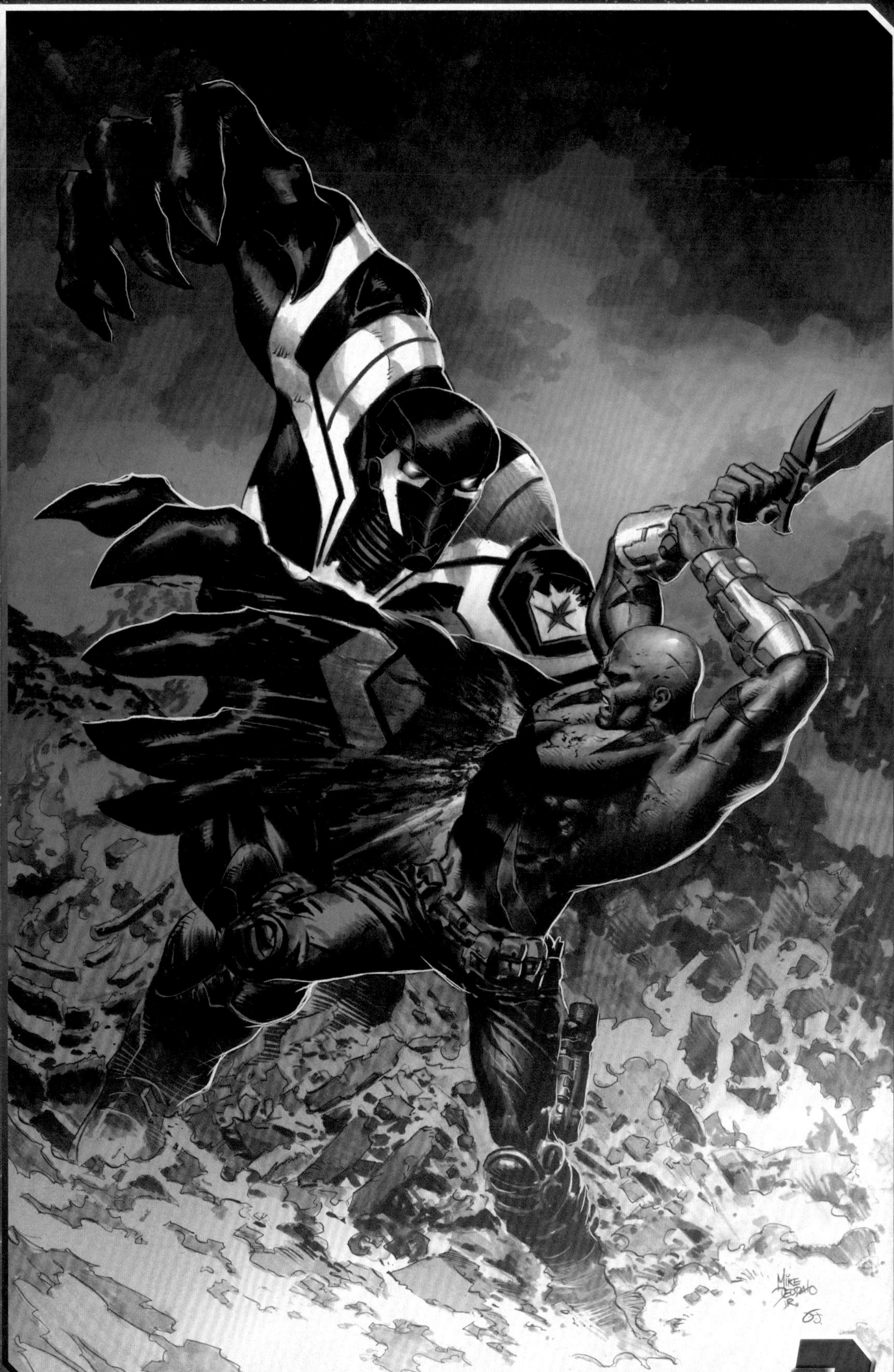
MIKE DEODATO JR.

3

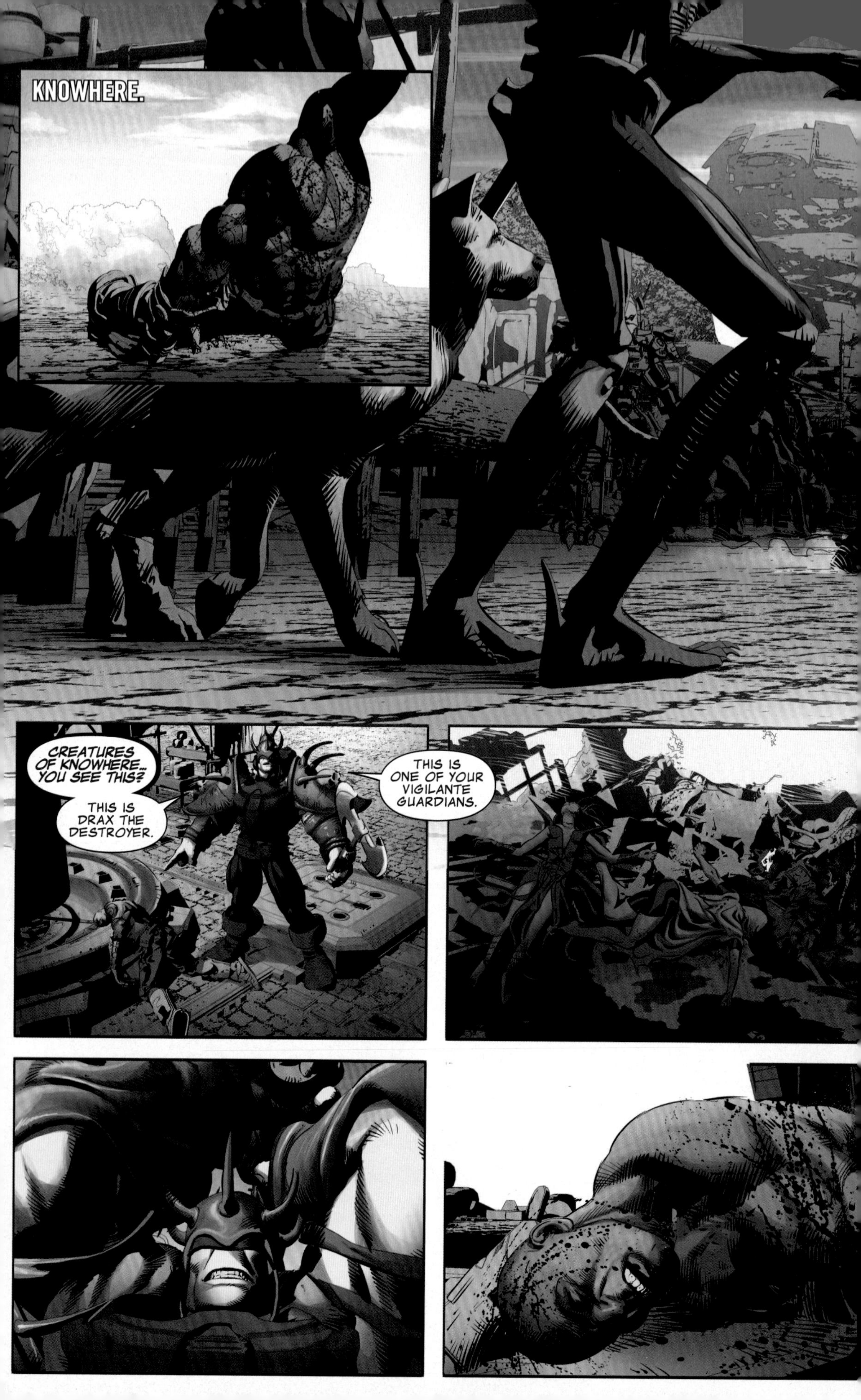
KNOWHERE.
CREATURES OF KNOWHERE... YOU SEE THIS?
THIS IS DRAX THE DESTROYER.
THIS IS ONE OF YOUR VIGILANTE GUARDIANS.

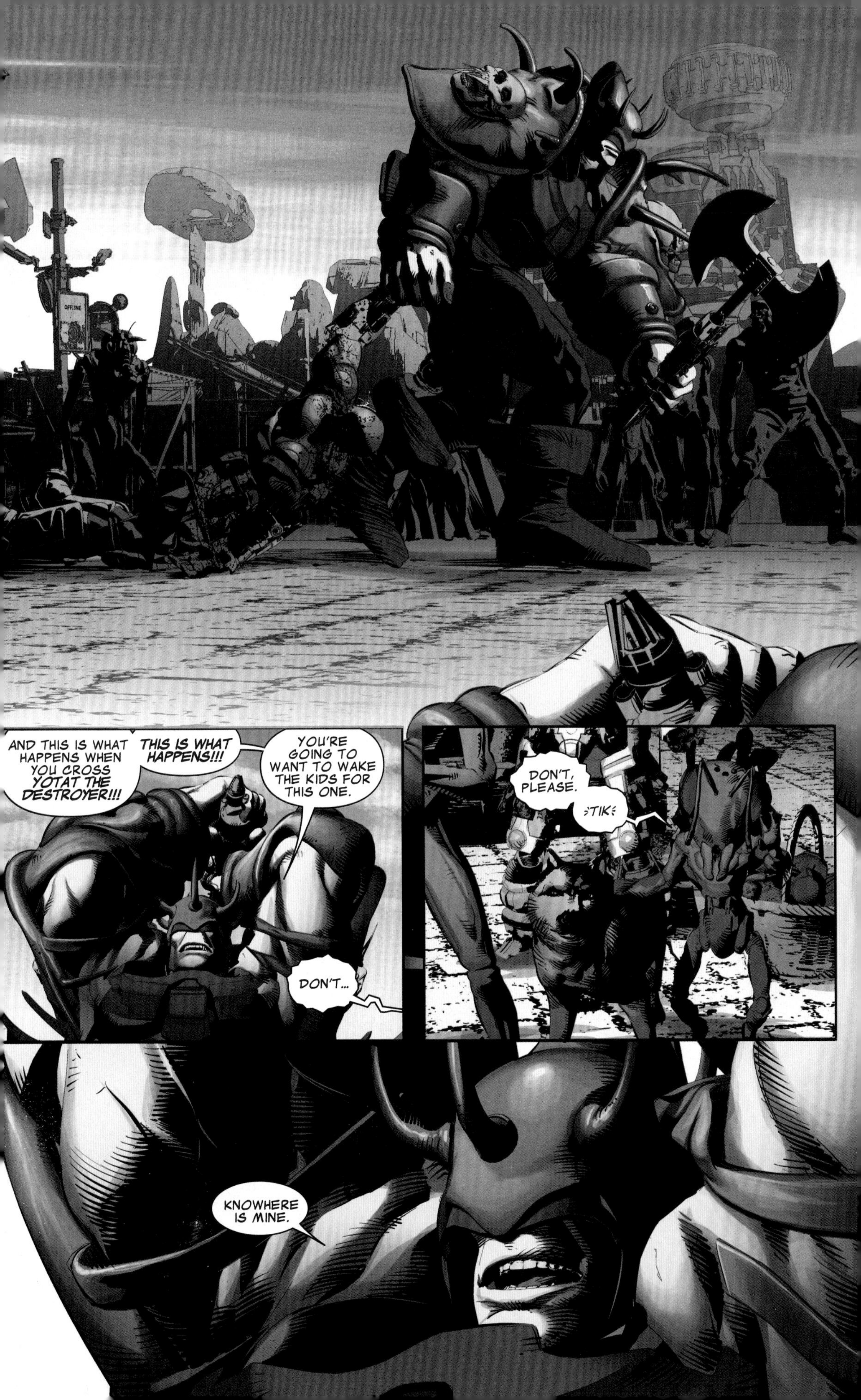
AND THIS IS WHAT HAPPENS WHEN YOU CROSS YOTAT THE DESTROYER!!!
THIS IS WHAT HAPPENS!!!
YOU'RE GOING TO WANT TO WAKE THE KIDS FOR THIS ONE.
DON'T...
DON'T, PLEASE.
TIK
KNOWHERE IS MINE.

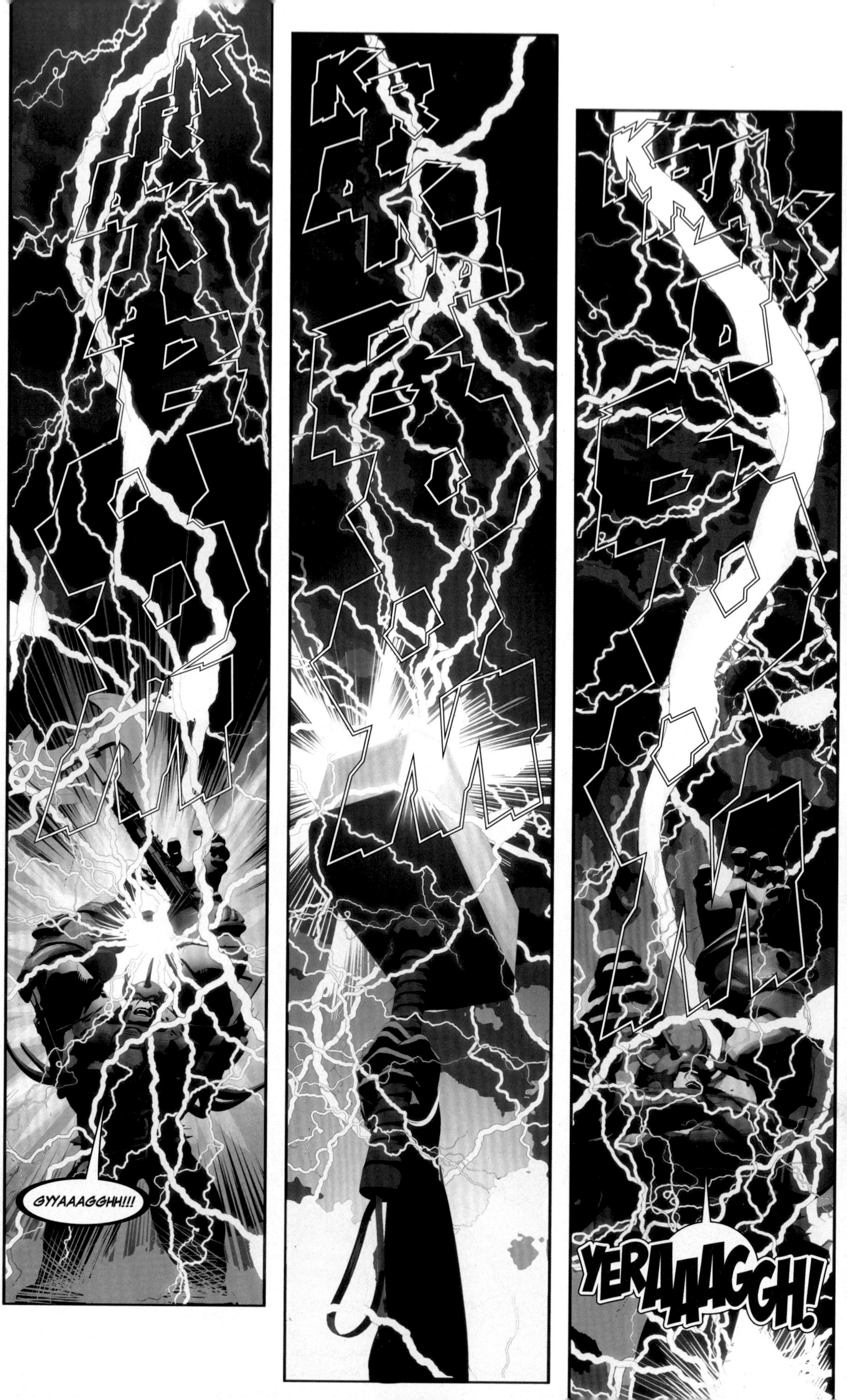
GYYAAAGGHH!!!
YERAAAGGH!

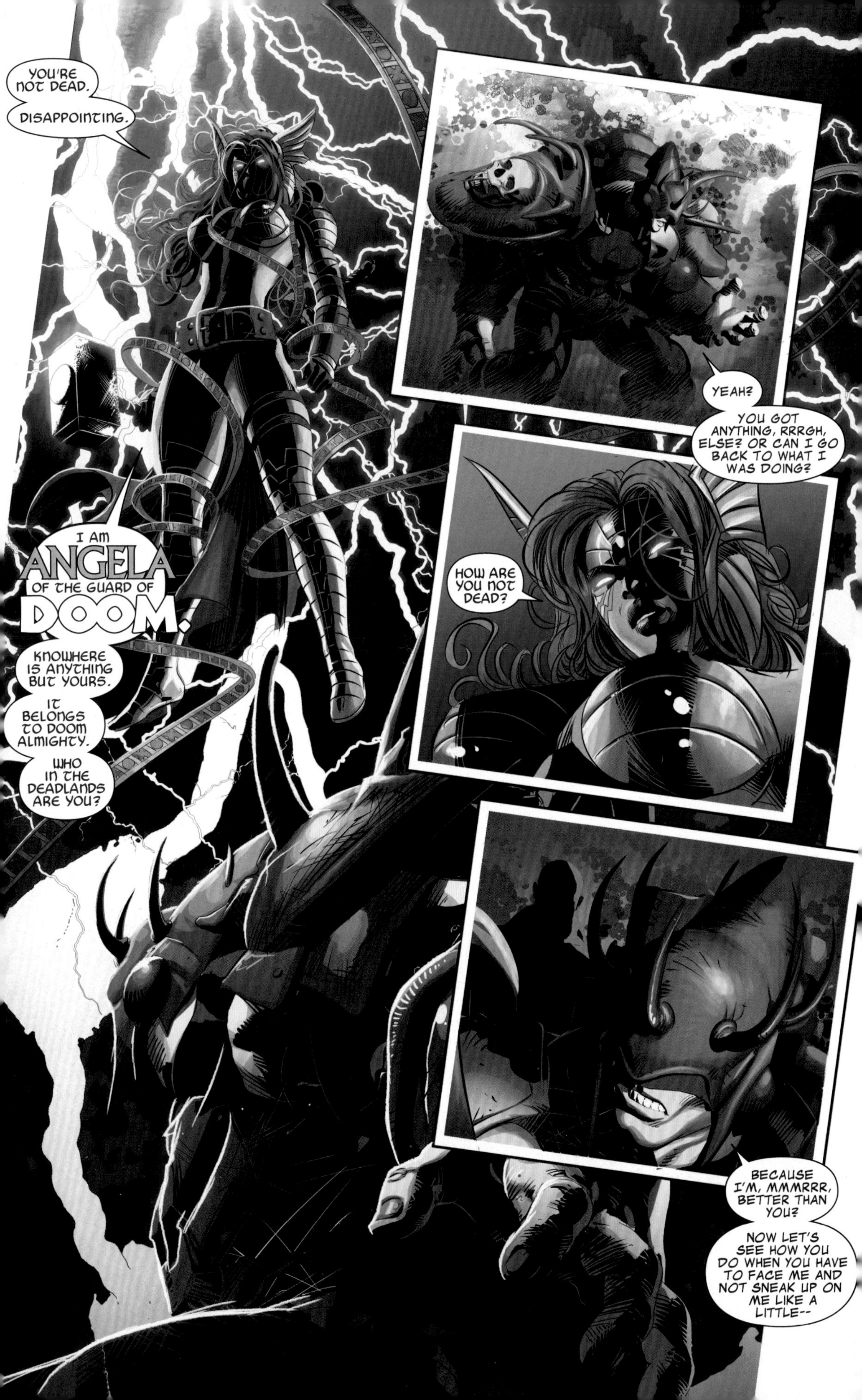
YOU'RE NOT DEAD.
DISAPPOINTING.
YEAH?
YOU GOT ANYTHING, RRRGH, ELSE? OR CAN I GO BACK TO WHAT I WAS DOING?
I AM ANGELA OF THE GUARD OF DOOM.
KNOWHERE IS ANYTHING BUT YOURS.
IT BELONGS TO DOOM ALMIGHTY.
WHO IN THE DEADLANDS ARE YOU?
HOW ARE YOU NOT DEAD?
BECAUSE I'M, MMMRRR, BETTER THAN YOU?
NOW LET'S SEE HOW YOU DO WHEN YOU HAVE TO FACE ME AND NOT SNEAK UP ON ME LIKE A LITTLE--

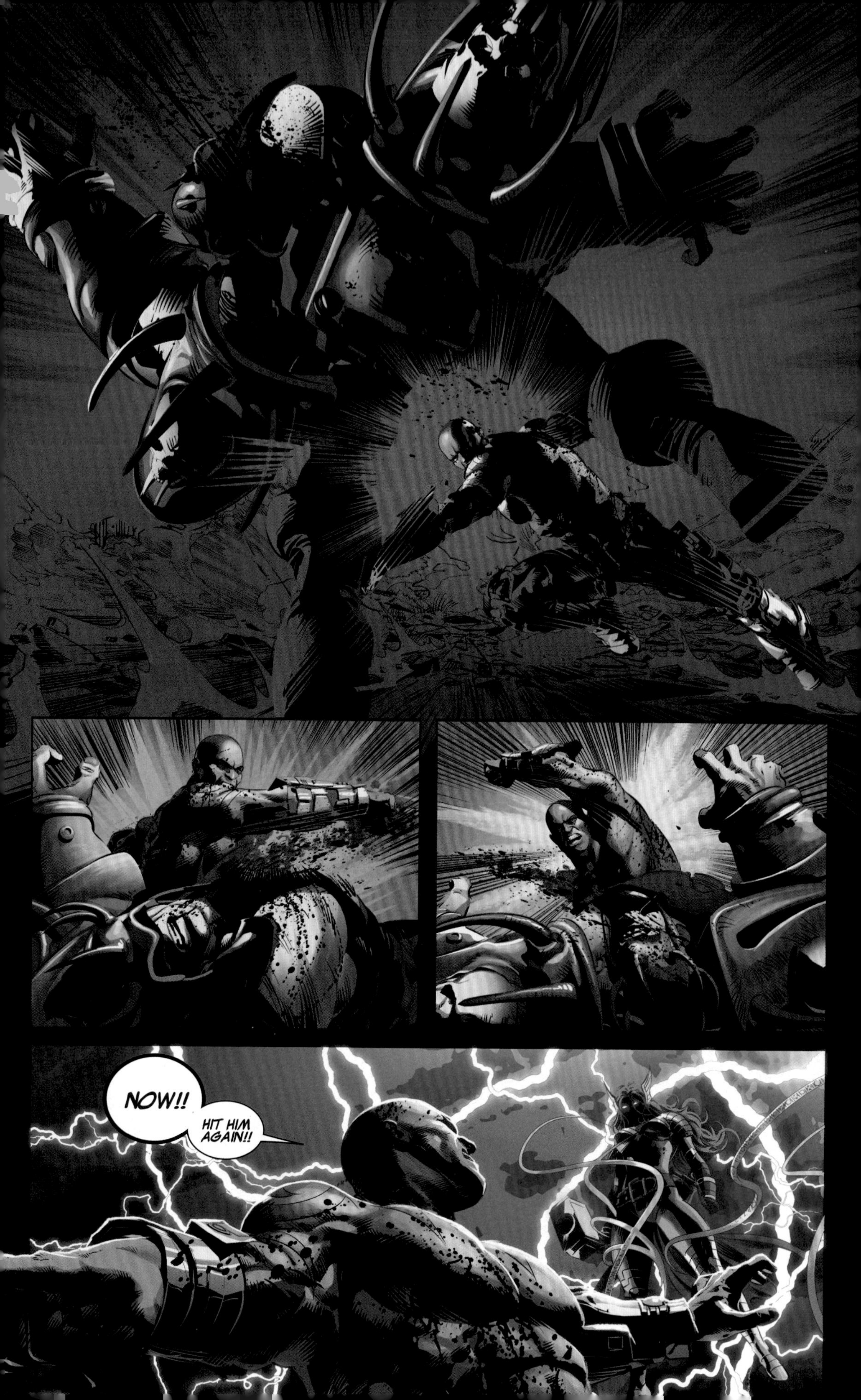
NOW!!
HIT HIM AGAIN!!

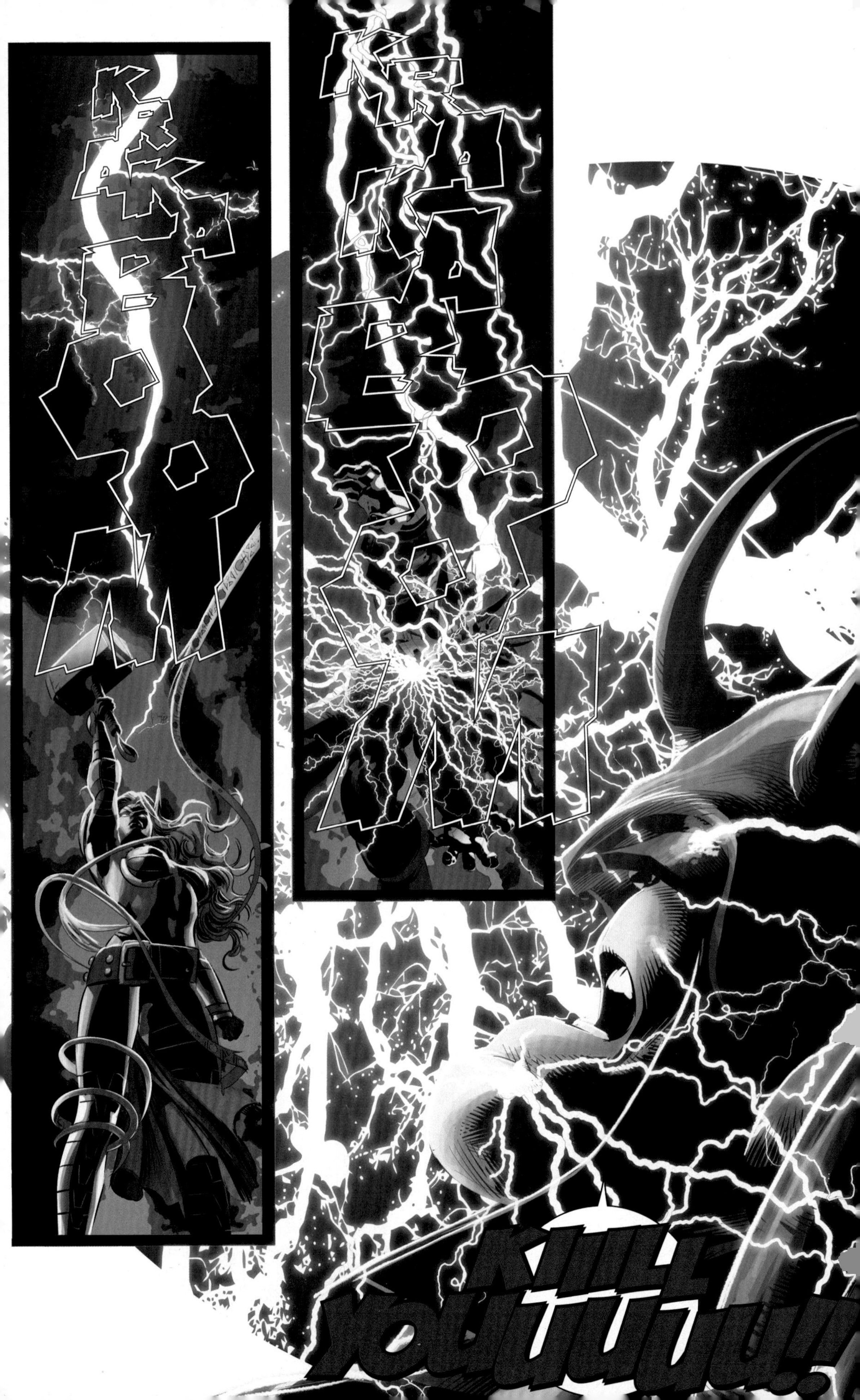
KILL YOUUUUU!!

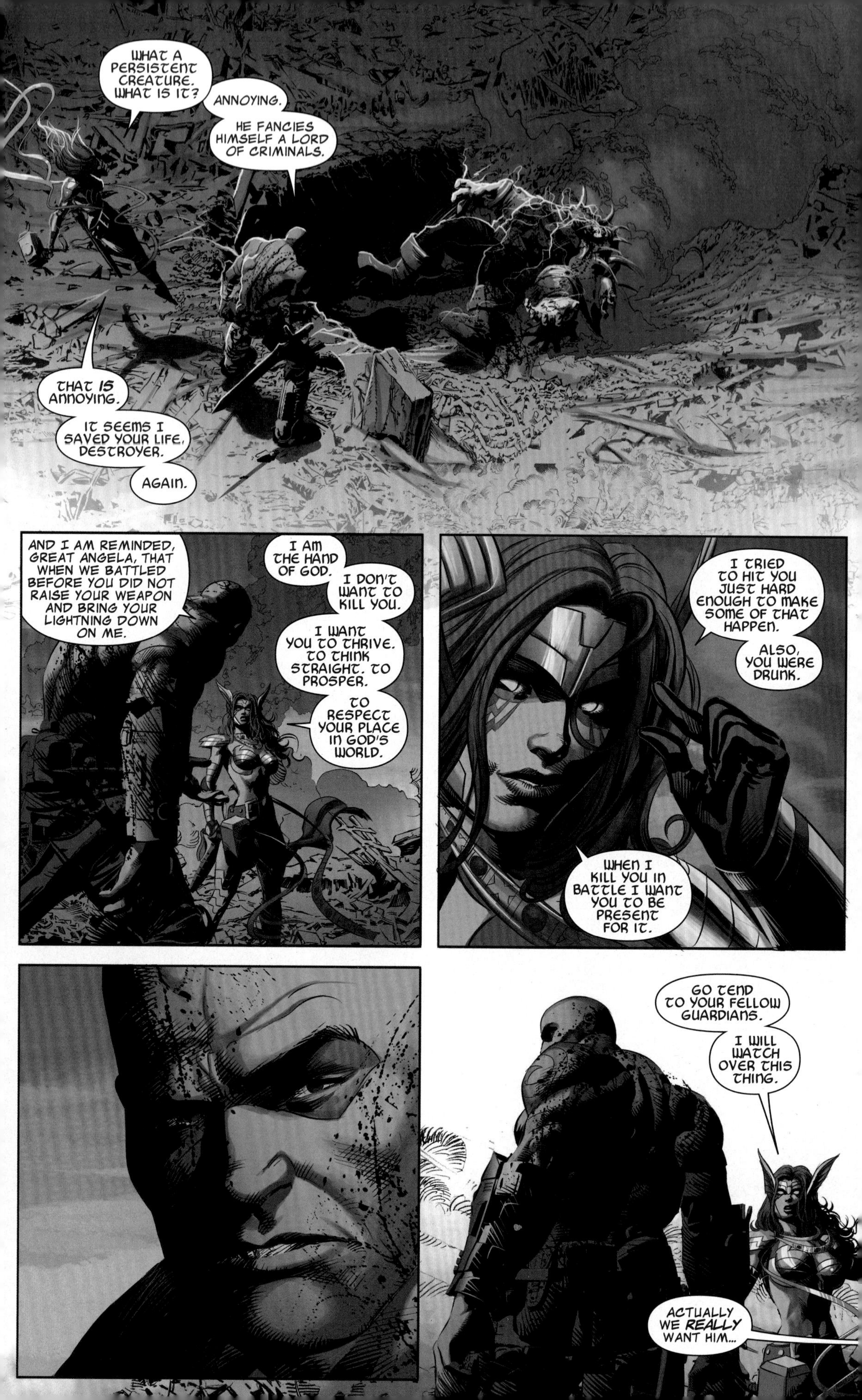
WHAT A PERSISTENT CREATURE. WHAT IS IT?
ANNOYING.
HE FANCIES HIMSELF A LORD OF CRIMINALS.
THAT IS ANNOYING.
IT SEEMS I SAVED YOUR LIFE, DESTROYER.
AGAIN.
AND I AM REMINDED, GREAT ANGELA, THAT WHEN WE BATTLED BEFORE YOU DID NOT RAISE YOUR WEAPON AND BRING YOUR LIGHTNING DOWN ON ME.
I AM THE HAND OF GOD.
I DON'T WANT TO KILL YOU.
I WANT YOU TO THRIVE. TO THINK STRAIGHT. TO PROSPER.
TO RESPECT YOUR PLACE IN GOD'S WORLD.
I TRIED TO HIT YOU JUST HARD ENOUGH TO MAKE SOME OF THAT HAPPEN.
ALSO, YOU WERE DRUNK.
WHEN I KILL YOU IN BATTLE I WANT YOU TO BE PRESENT FOR IT.
GO TEND TO YOUR FELLOW GUARDIANS.
I WILL WATCH OVER THIS THING.
ACTUALLY WE REALLY WANT HIM...

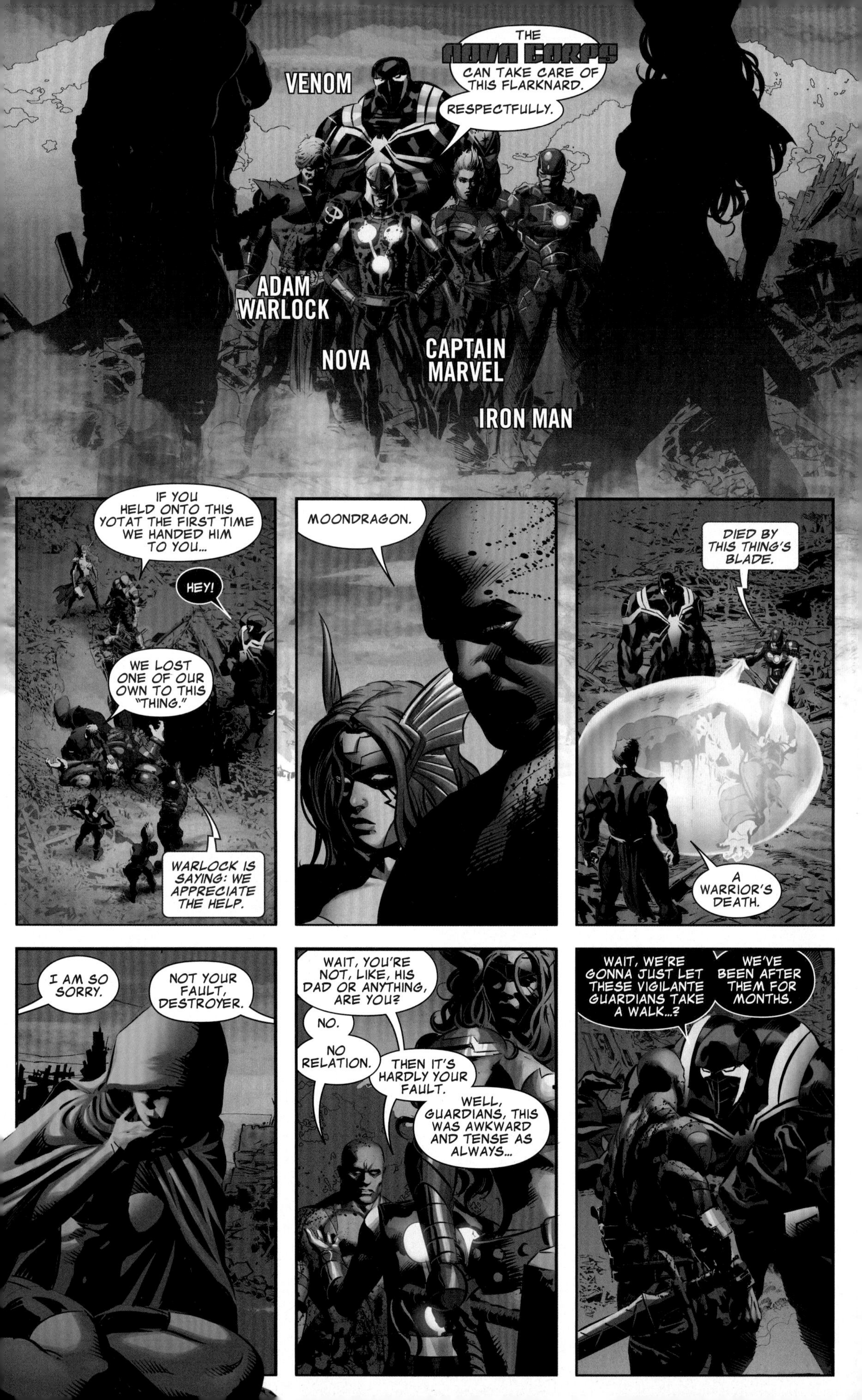
VENOM
THE NOVA CORPS CAN TAKE CARE OF THIS FLARKNARD.
RESPECTFULLY.
ADAM WARLOCK
NOVA
CAPTAIN MARVEL
IRON MAN
IF YOU HELD ONTO THIS YOTAT THE FIRST TIME WE HANDED HIM TO YOU...
HEY!
WE LOST ONE OF OUR OWN TO THIS "THING."
WARLOCK IS SAYING: WE APPRECIATE THE HELP.
MOONDRAGON.
DIED BY THIS THING'S BLADE.
A WARRIOR'S DEATH.
I AM SO SORRY.
NOT YOUR FAULT, DESTROYER.
WAIT, YOU'RE NOT, LIKE, HIS DAD OR ANYTHING, ARE YOU?
NO.
NO RELATION.
THEN IT'S HARDLY YOUR FAULT.
WELL, GUARDIANS, THIS WAS AWKWARD AND TENSE AS ALWAYS...
WAIT, WE'RE GONNA JUST LET THESE VIGILANTE GUARDIANS TAKE A WALK...?
WE'VE BEEN AFTER THEM FOR MONTHS.

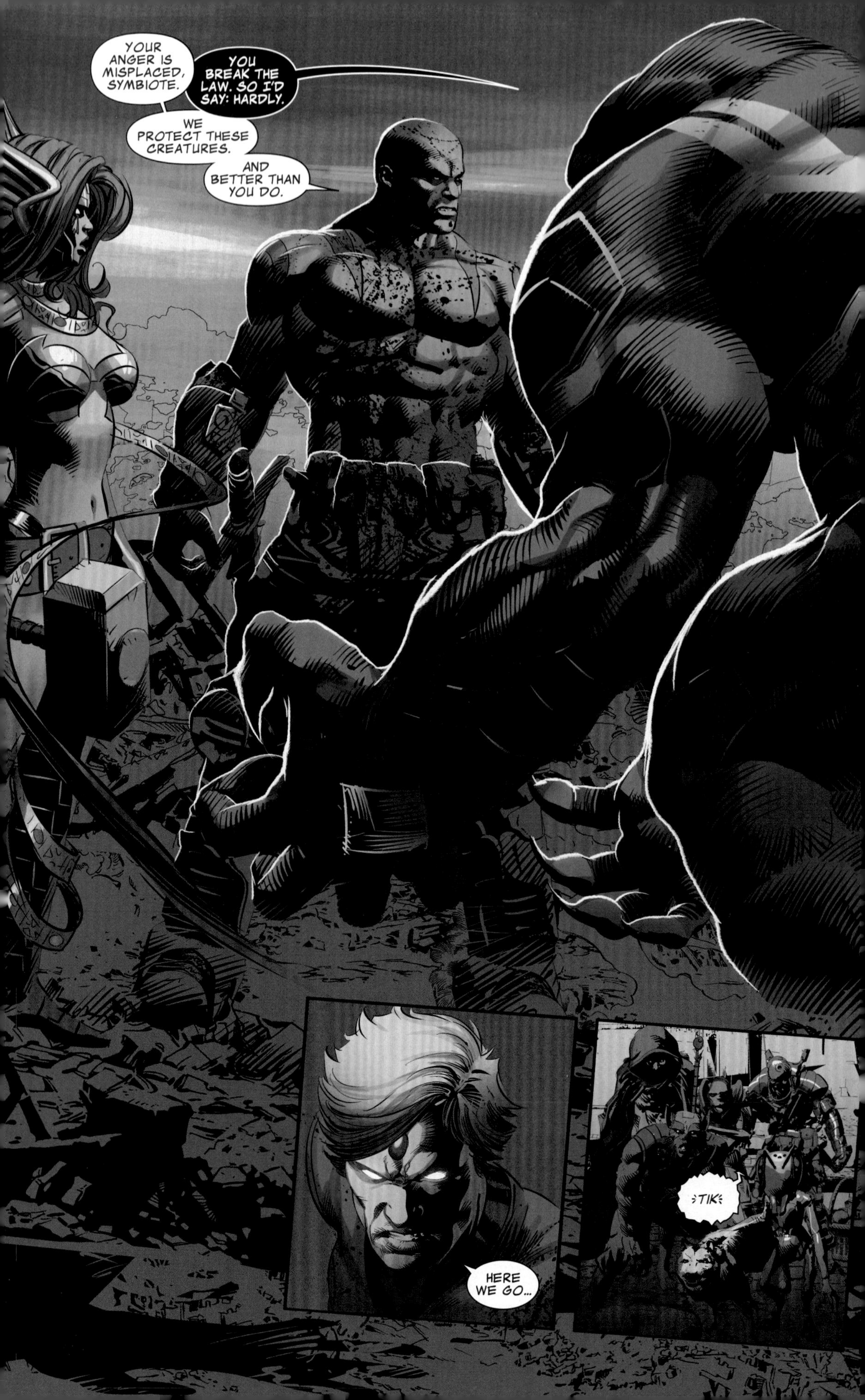
YOUR ANGER IS MISPLACED, SYMBIOTE.
YOU BREAK THE LAW. SO I'D SAY: HARDLY.
WE PROTECT THESE CREATURES.
AND BETTER THAN YOU DO.
HERE WE GO...
TIK

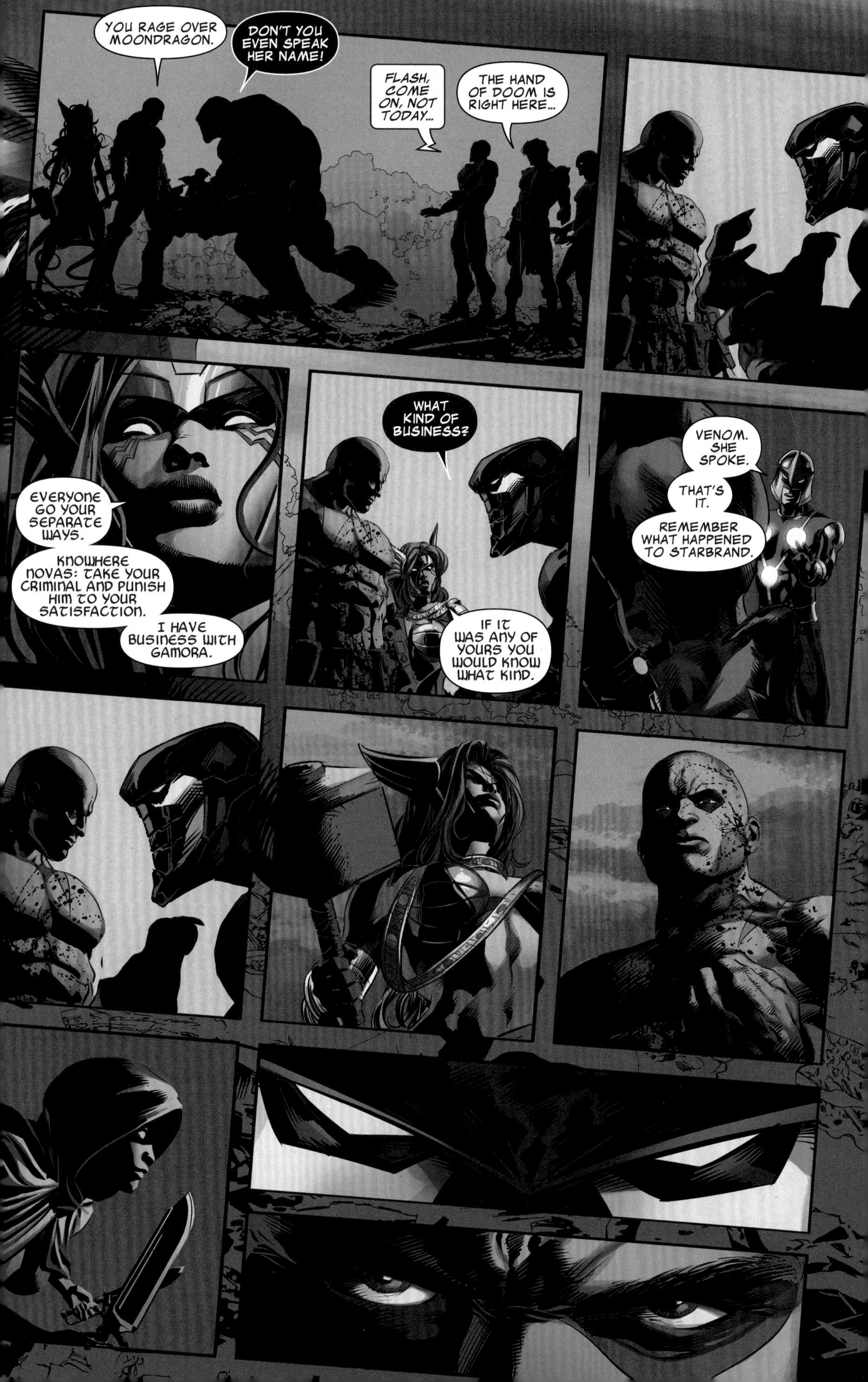
YOU RAGE OVER MOONDRAGON.
DON'T YOU EVEN SPEAK HER NAME!
FLASH, COME ON, NOT TODAY...
THE HAND OF DOOM IS RIGHT HERE...
EVERYONE GO YOUR SEPARATE WAYS.
KNOWHERE NOVAS: TAKE YOUR CRIMINAL AND PUNISH HIM TO YOUR SATISFACTION.
I HAVE BUSINESS WITH GAMORA.
WHAT KIND OF BUSINESS?
IF IT WAS ANY OF YOURS YOU WOULD KNOW WHAT KIND.
VENOM. SHE SPOKE.
THAT'S IT.
REMEMBER WHAT HAPPENED TO STARBRAND.

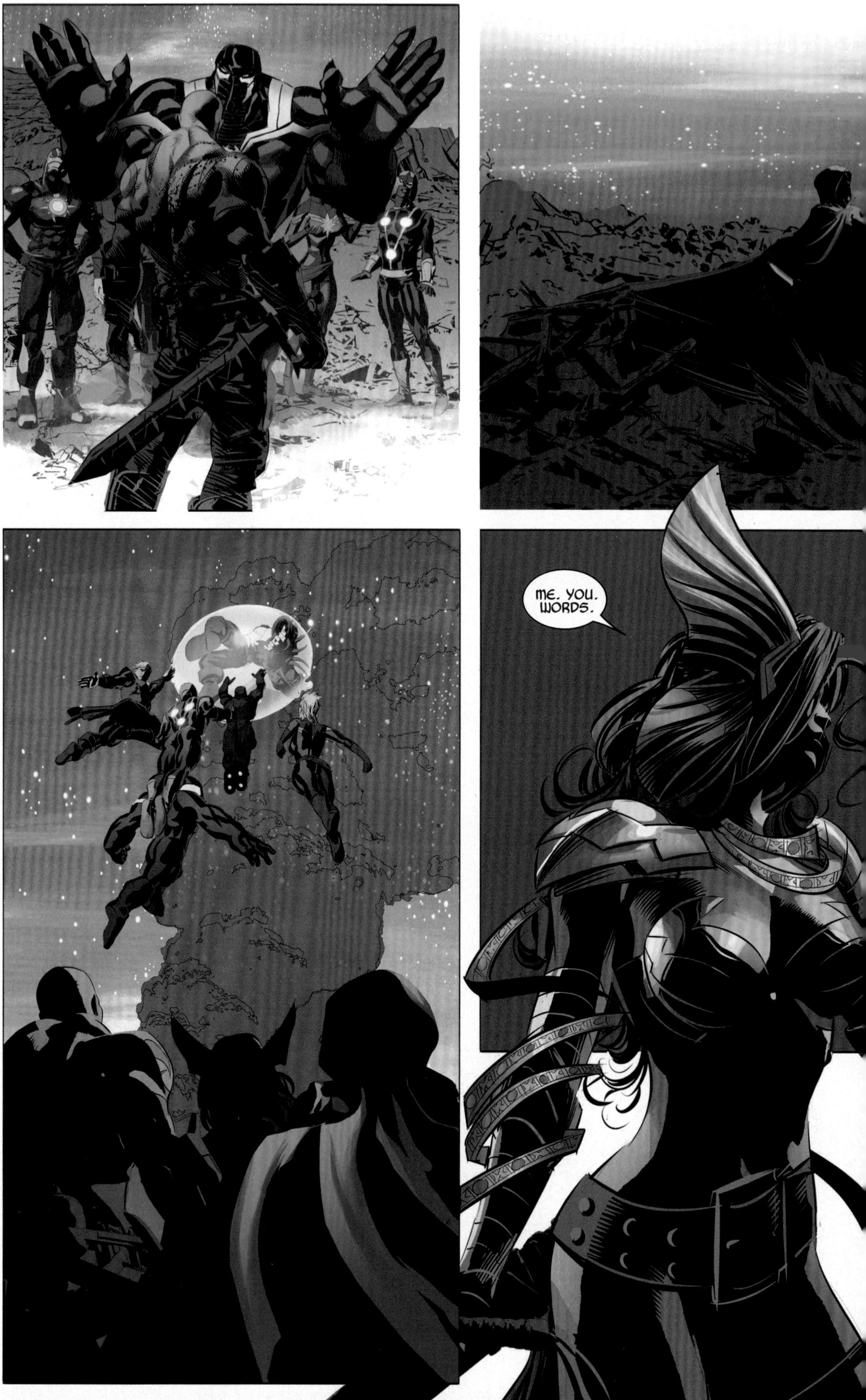
ME. YOU. WORDS.

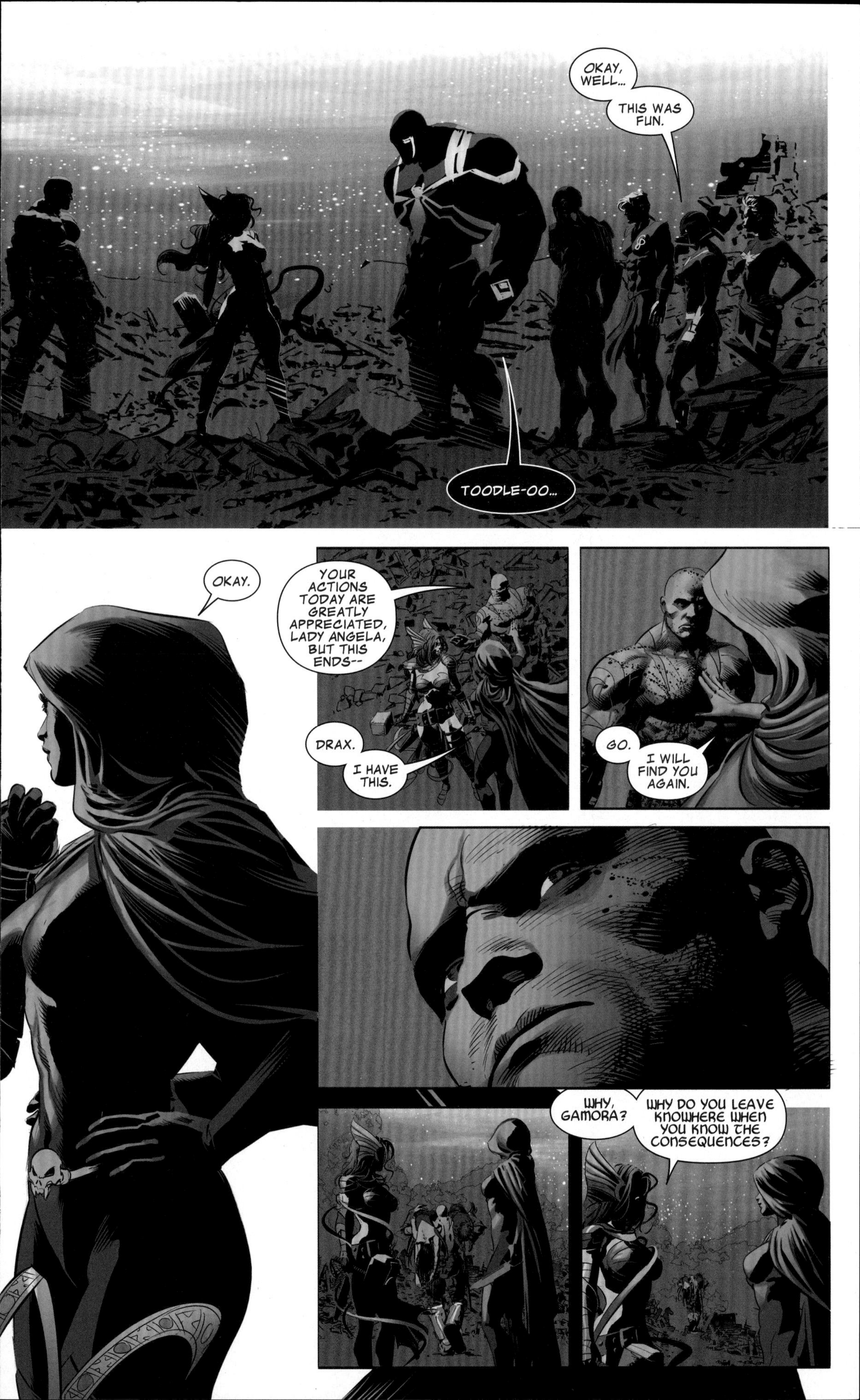
OKAY, WELL...
THIS WAS FUN.
TOODLE-OO...
OKAY.
YOUR ACTIONS TODAY ARE GREATLY APPRECIATED, LADY ANGELA, BUT THIS ENDS--
DRAX.
I HAVE THIS.
GO.
I WILL FIND YOU AGAIN.
WHY, GAMORA?
WHY DO YOU LEAVE KNOWHERE WHEN YOU KNOW THE CONSEQUENCES?

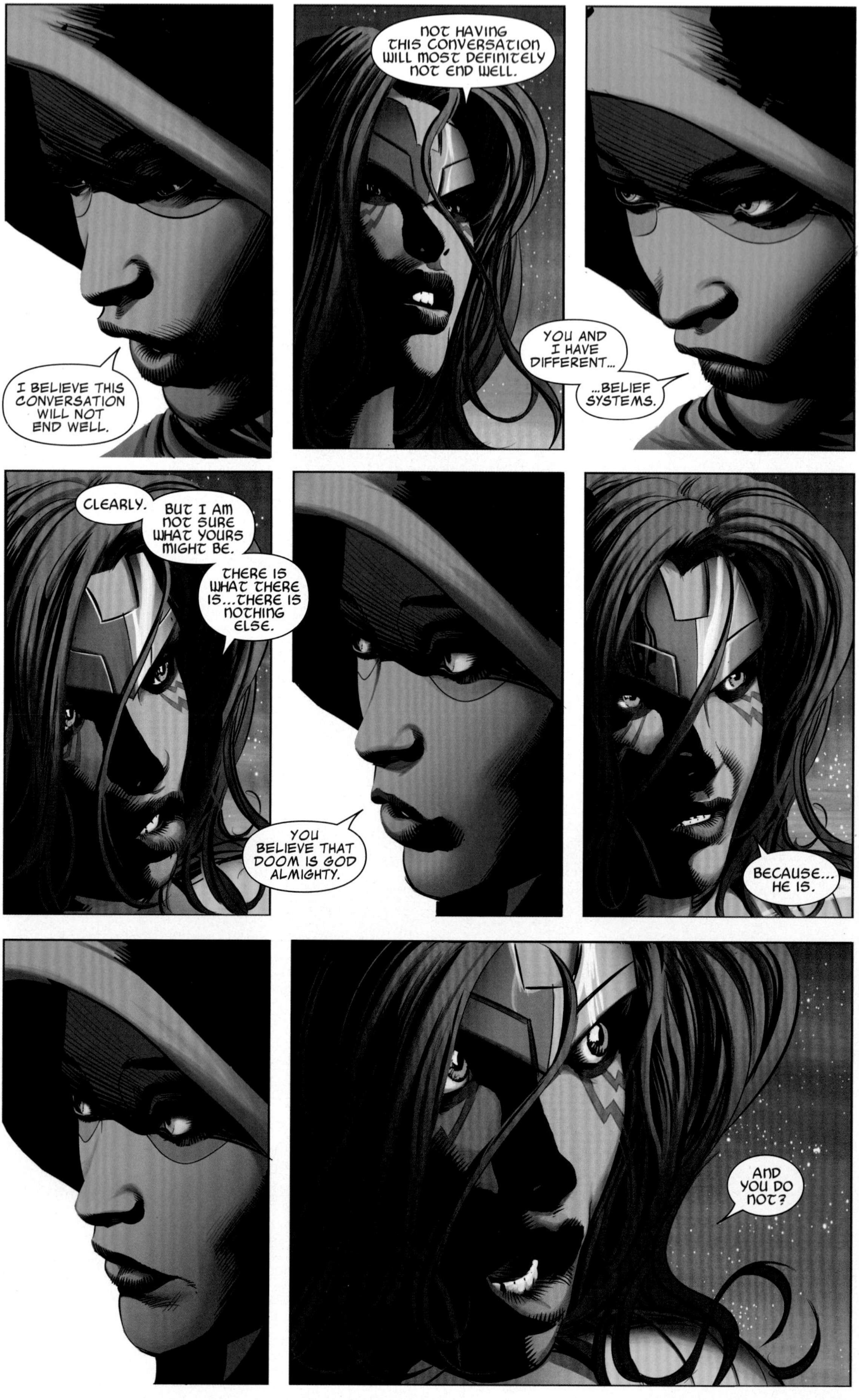
I BELIEVE THIS CONVERSATION WILL NOT END WELL.
NOT HAVING THIS CONVERSATION WILL MOST DEFINITELY NOT END WELL.
YOU AND I HAVE DIFFERENT...
...BELIEF SYSTEMS.
CLEARLY.
BUT I AM NOT SURE WHAT YOURS MIGHT BE.
THERE IS WHAT THERE IS...THERE IS NOTHING ELSE.
YOU BELIEVE THAT DOOM IS GOD ALMIGHTY.
BECAUSE... HE IS.
AND YOU DO NOT?

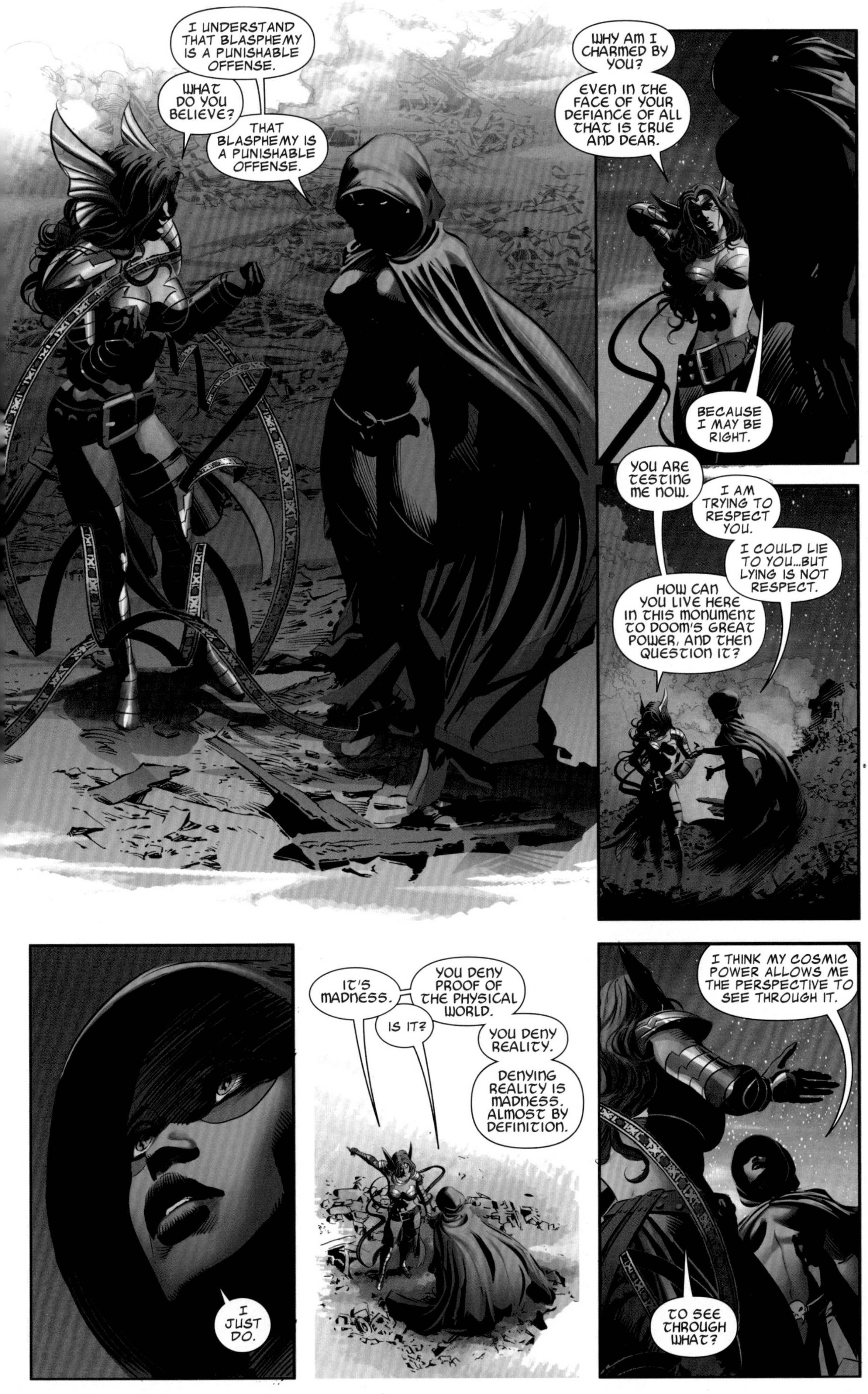
WHAT DO YOU BELIEVE?
I UNDERSTAND THAT BLASPHEMY IS A PUNISHABLE OFFENSE.
THAT BLASPHEMY IS A PUNISHABLE OFFENSE.
WHY AM I CHARMED BY YOU?
EVEN IN THE FACE OF YOUR DEFIANCE OF ALL THAT IS TRUE AND DEAR.
BECAUSE I MAY BE RIGHT.
YOU ARE TESTING ME NOW.
I AM TRYING TO RESPECT YOU.
I COULD LIE TO YOU...BUT LYING IS NOT RESPECT.
HOW CAN YOU LIVE HERE IN THIS MONUMENT TO DOOM'S GREAT POWER, AND THEN QUESTION IT?
I JUST DO.
IT'S MADNESS.
YOU DENY PROOF OF THE PHYSICAL WORLD.
IS IT?
YOU DENY REALITY.
DENYING REALITY IS MADNESS. ALMOST BY DEFINITION.
I THINK MY COSMIC POWER ALLOWS ME THE PERSPECTIVE TO SEE THROUGH IT.
TO SEE THROUGH WHAT?

THIS ILLUSION.

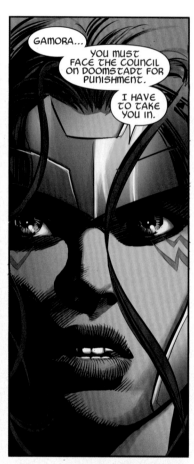

GAMORA... YOU MUST FACE THE COUNCIL ON DOOMSTADT FOR PUNISHMENT.

I HAVE TO TAKE YOU IN.

I KNOW YOU THINK YOU DO.

I CAN WALK AWAY FROM THIS IF YOU GIVE ME EVEN A SMALL REASON TO.

CONSIDER YOUR WORDS.

SPEAK WISELY OF OUR LORD AND SAVIOR...

I'M SORRY.

I CAN'T DO THAT.

IF DOOM IS NOT OUR LORD AND YOU ARE NOT LIVING OFF OF HIS GENEROSITY AND POWER, THEN WHAT IS THERE...

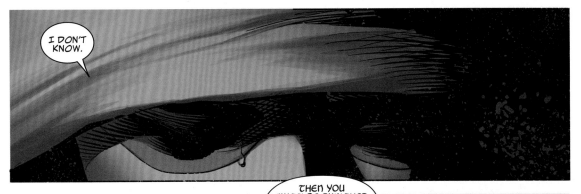

I DON'T KNOW.

THEN YOU MUST BE PUNISHED FOR YOUR BLASPHEMY AND MAY DOOM HAVE MERCY ON YOUR SOUL!

KRAK

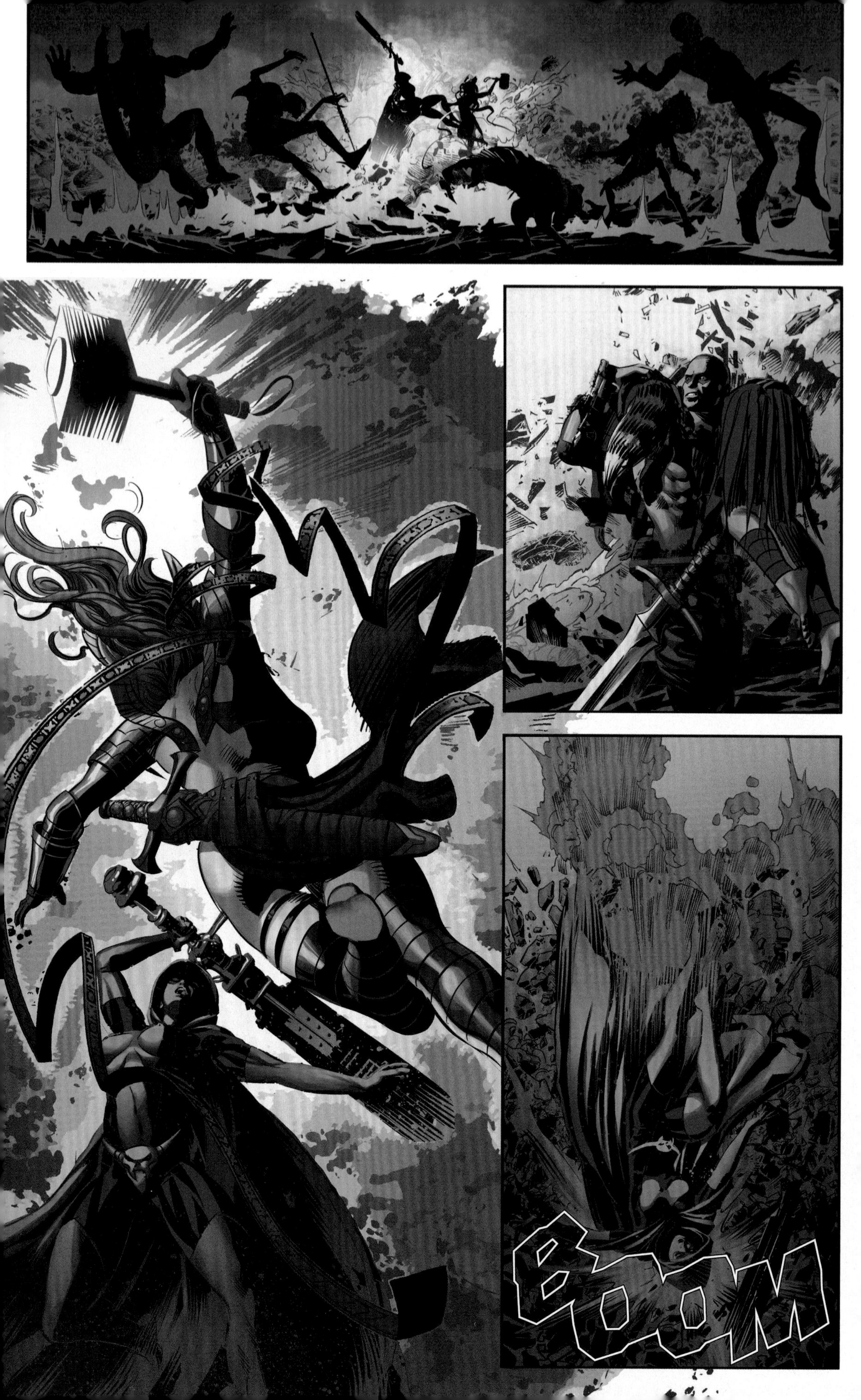
BOOOM

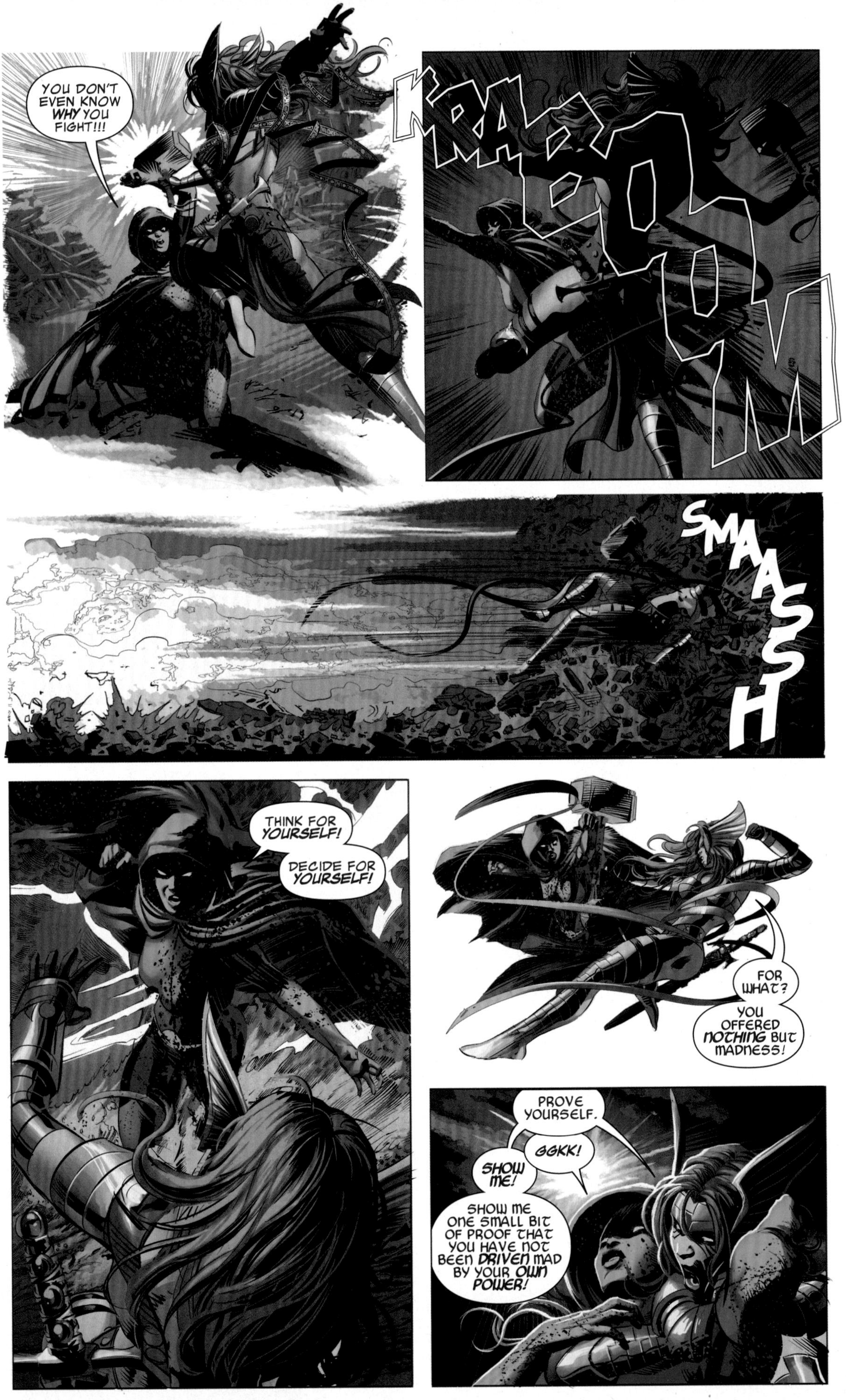

YOU DON'T EVEN KNOW **WHY** YOU FIGHT!!!
KRAKOOM
SMAASH
THINK FOR *YOURSELF!*
DECIDE FOR *YOURSELF!*
FOR WHAT?
YOU OFFERED **NOTHING** BUT MADNESS!
PROVE YOURSELF.
GGKK!
SHOW ME!
SHOW ME ONE SMALL BIT OF PROOF THAT YOU HAVE NOT BEEN **DRIVEN** MAD BY YOUR **OWN POWER!**

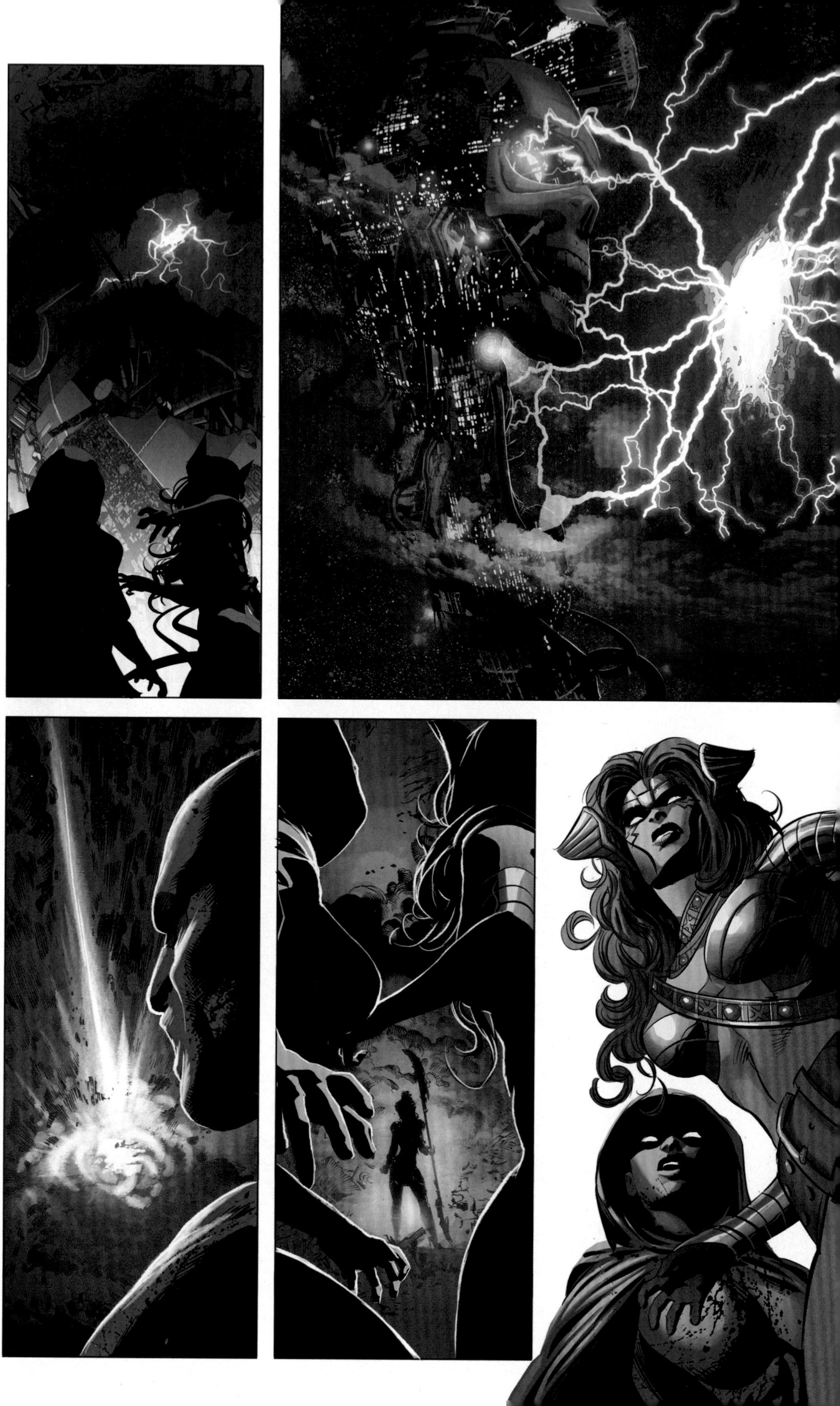

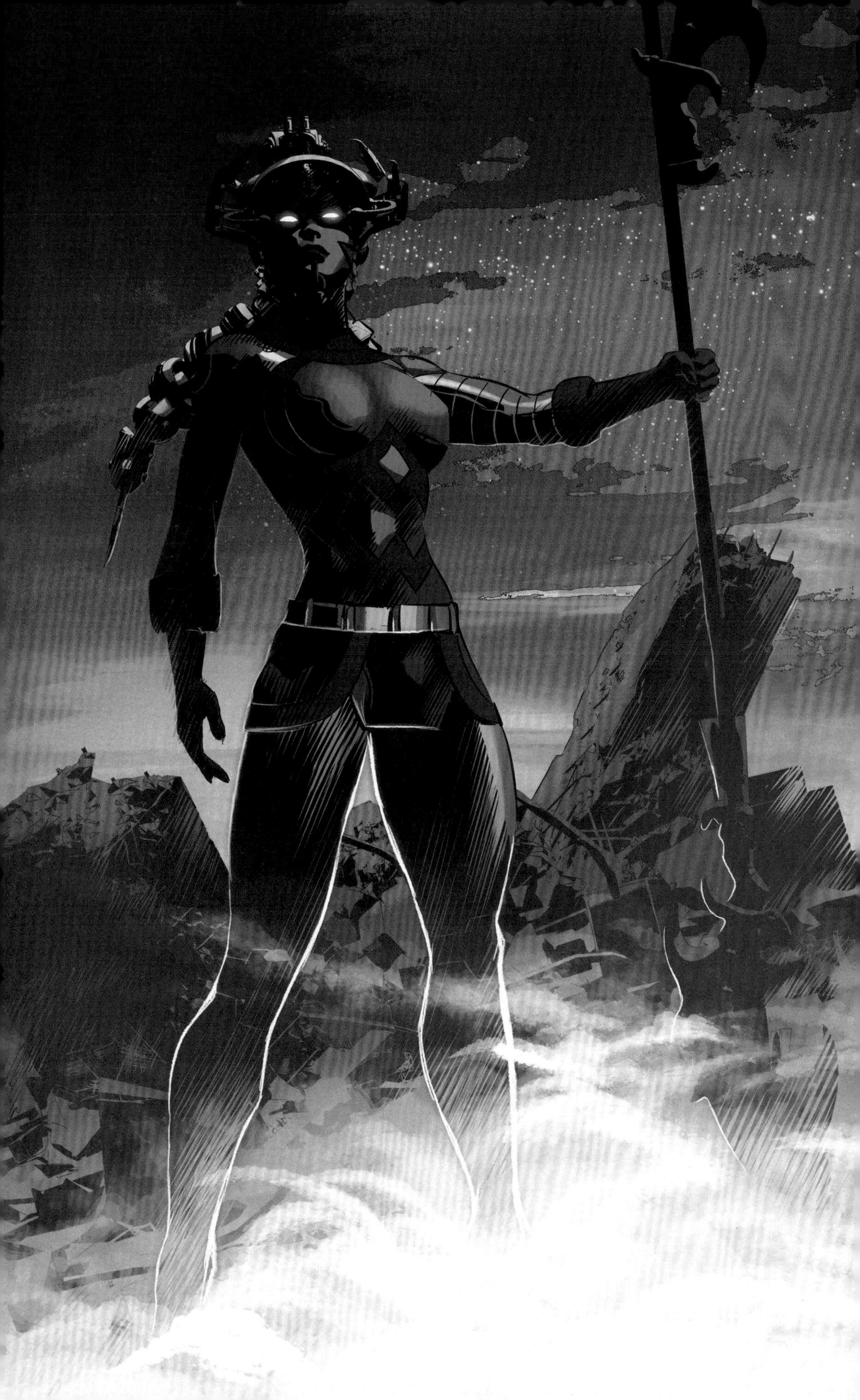

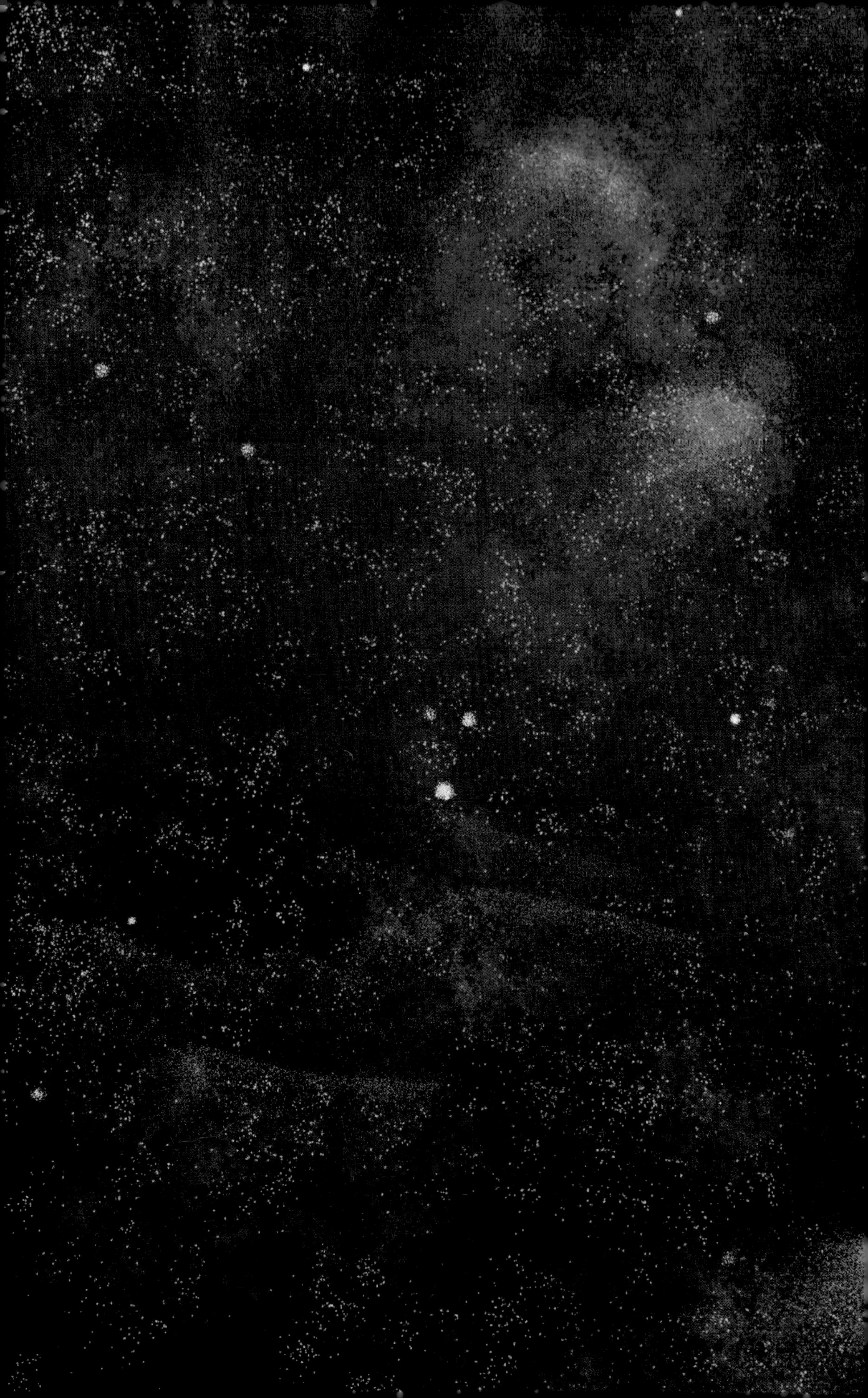

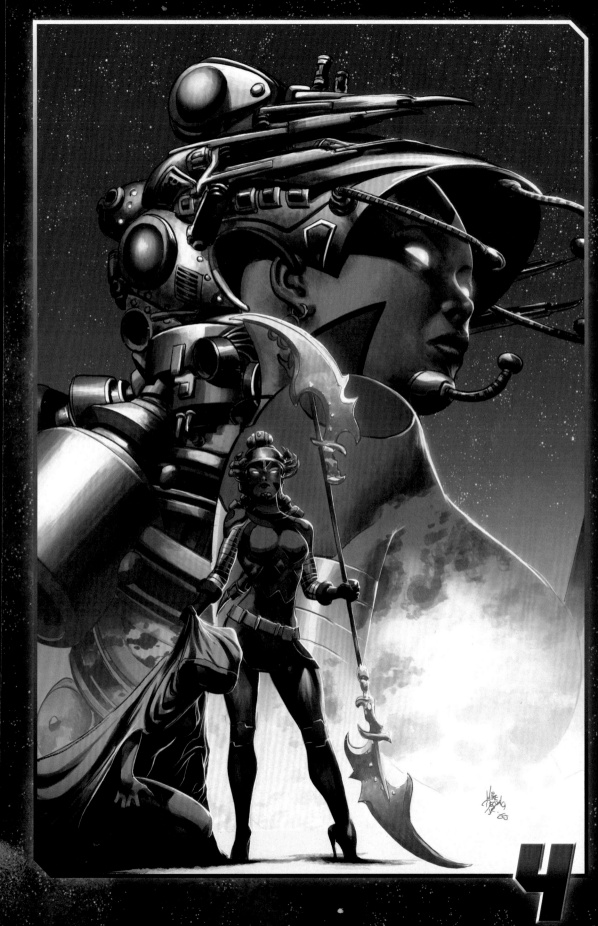

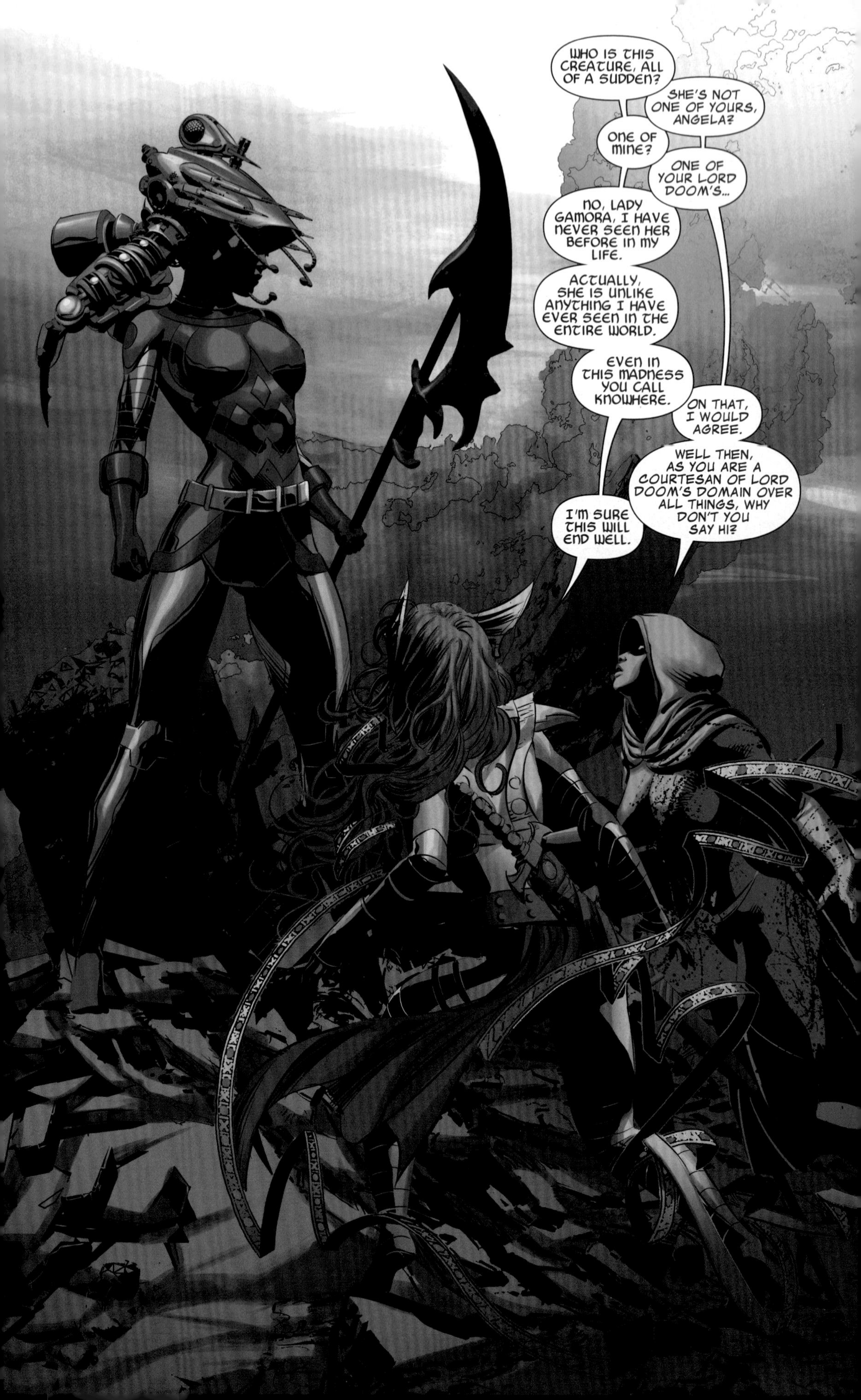
WHO IS THIS CREATURE, ALL OF A SUDDEN?
SHE'S NOT ONE OF YOURS, ANGELA?
ONE OF MINE?
ONE OF YOUR LORD DOOM'S...
NO, LADY GAMORA, I HAVE NEVER SEEN HER BEFORE IN MY LIFE.
ACTUALLY, SHE IS UNLIKE ANYTHING I HAVE EVER SEEN IN THE ENTIRE WORLD.
EVEN IN THIS MADNESS YOU CALL KNOWHERE.
ON THAT, I WOULD AGREE.
WELL THEN, AS YOU ARE A COURTESAN OF LORD DOOM'S DOMAIN OVER ALL THINGS, WHY DON'T YOU SAY HI?
I'M SURE THIS WILL END WELL.

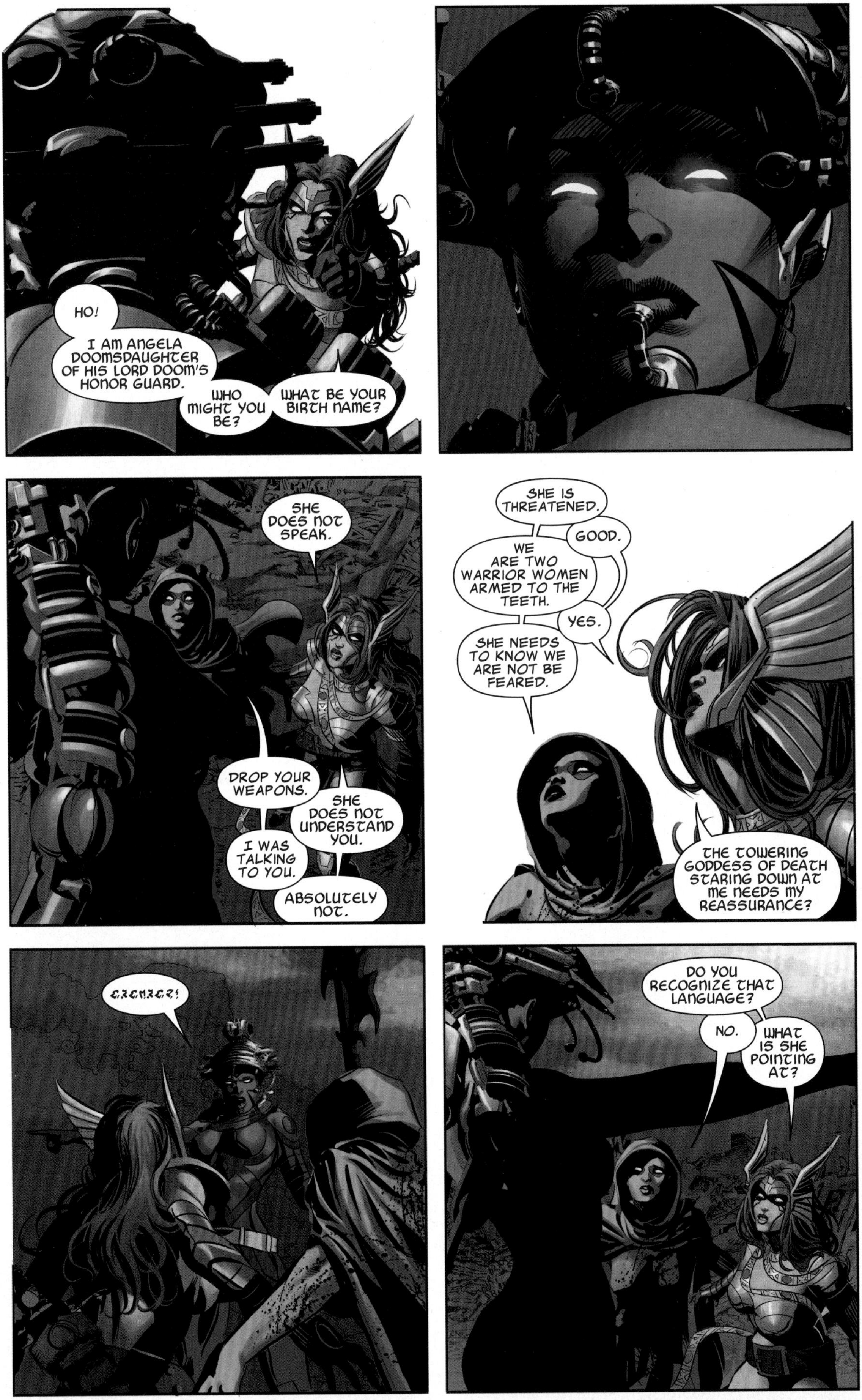
HO!
I AM ANGELA DOOMSDAUGHTER OF HIS LORD DOOM'S HONOR GUARD.
WHO MIGHT YOU BE?
WHAT BE YOUR BIRTH NAME?
SHE DOES NOT SPEAK.
DROP YOUR WEAPONS.
SHE DOES NOT UNDERSTAND YOU.
I WAS TALKING TO YOU.
ABSOLUTELY NOT.
SHE IS THREATENED.
GOOD.
WE ARE TWO WARRIOR WOMEN ARMED TO THE TEETH.
YES.
SHE NEEDS TO KNOW WE ARE NOT BE FEARED.
THE TOWERING GODDESS OF DEATH STARING DOWN AT ME NEEDS MY REASSURANCE?
DO YOU RECOGNIZE THAT LANGUAGE?
NO.
WHAT IS SHE POINTING AT?

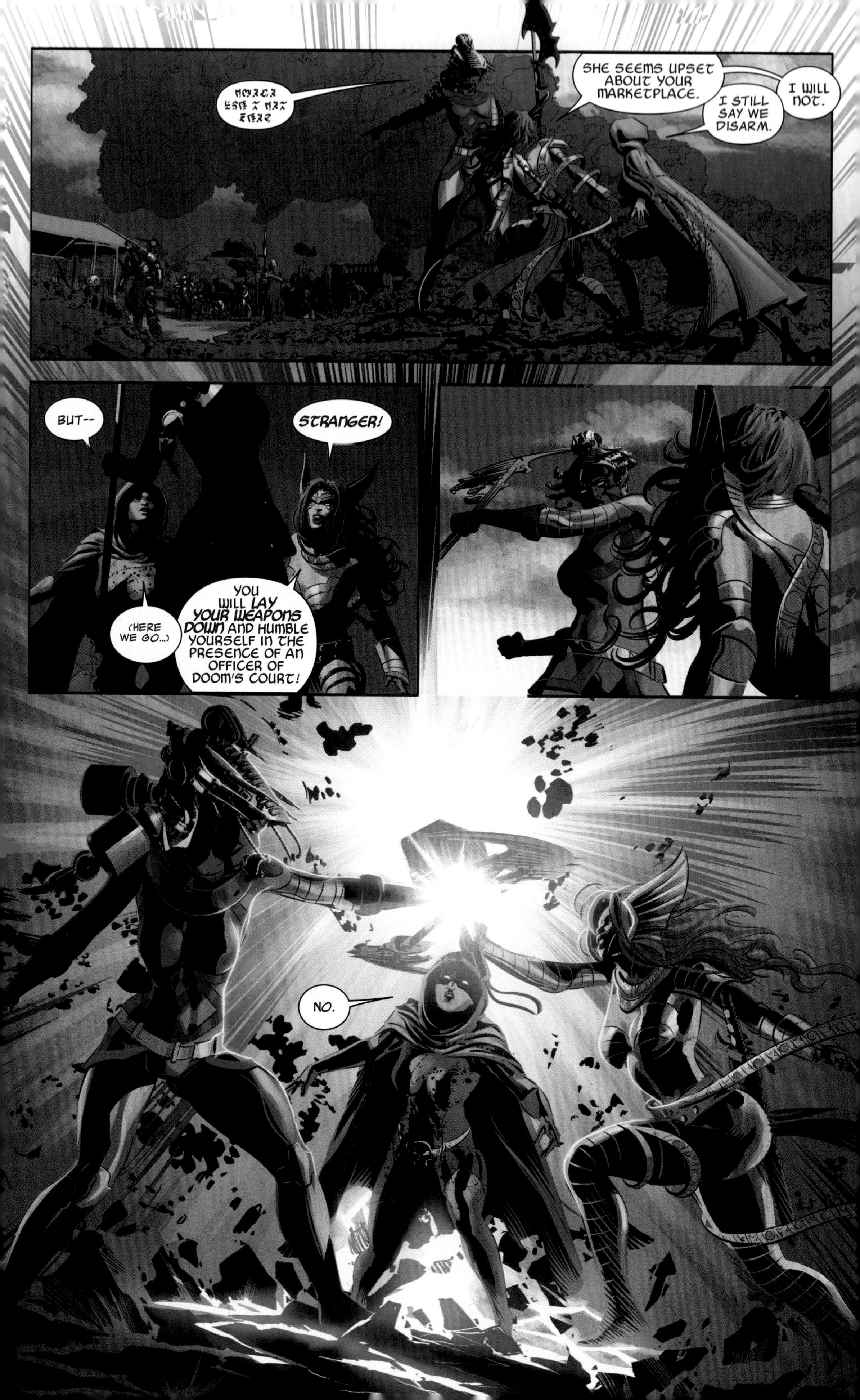

SHE SEEMS UPSET ABOUT YOUR MARKETPLACE.
I WILL NOT.
I STILL SAY WE DISARM.
BUT--
STRANGER!
YOU WILL LAY YOUR WEAPONS DOWN AND HUMBLE YOURSELF IN THE PRESENCE OF AN OFFICER OF DOOM'S COURT!
(HERE WE GO...)
NO.

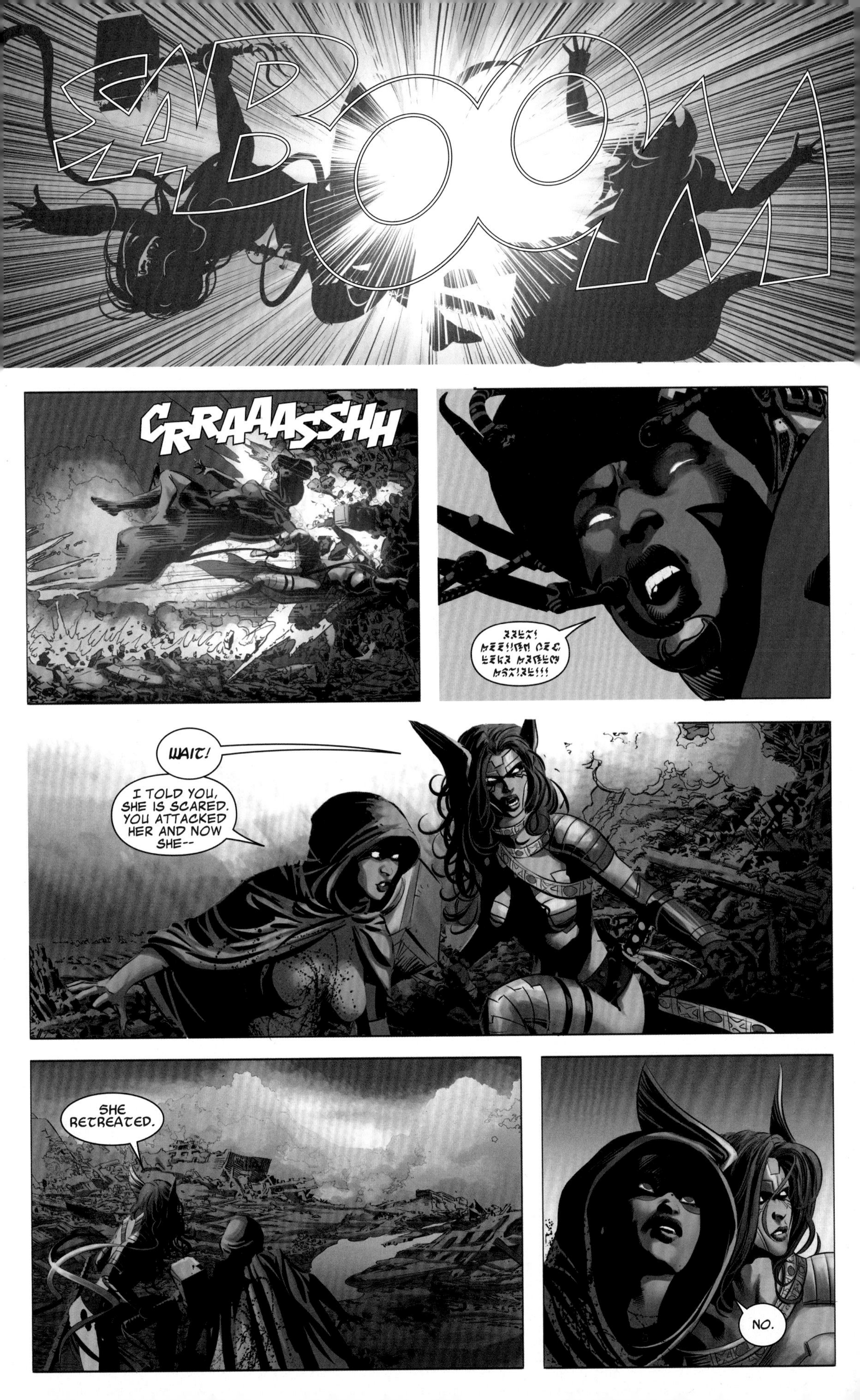
CRRAAASSHH
WAIT!
I TOLD YOU, SHE IS SCARED. YOU ATTACKED HER AND NOW SHE--
SHE RETREATED.
NO.

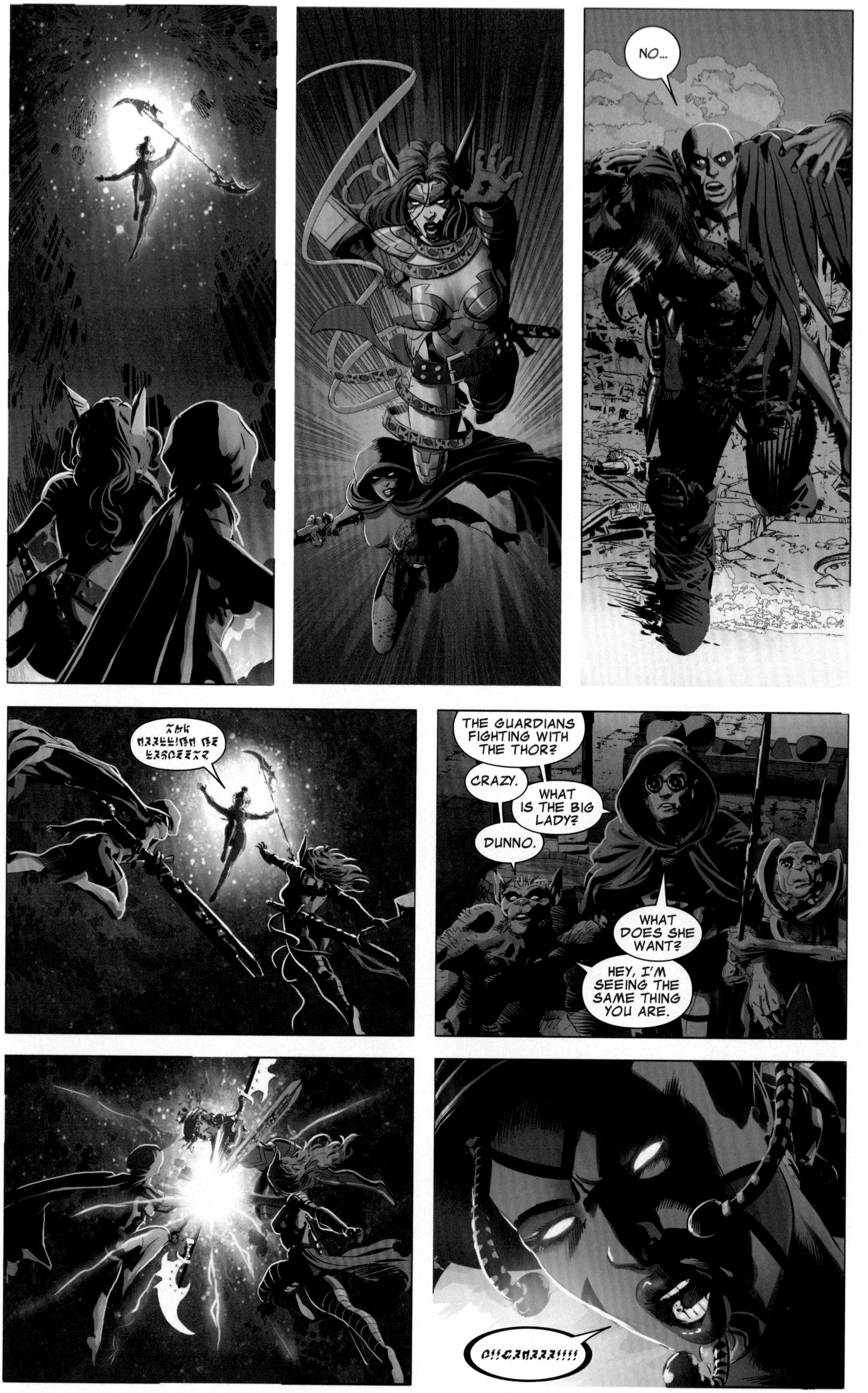
NO...
THE GUARDIANS FIGHTING WITH THE THOR?
CRAZY.
WHAT IS THE BIG LADY?
DUNNO.
WHAT DOES SHE WANT?
HEY, I'M SEEING THE SAME THING YOU ARE.

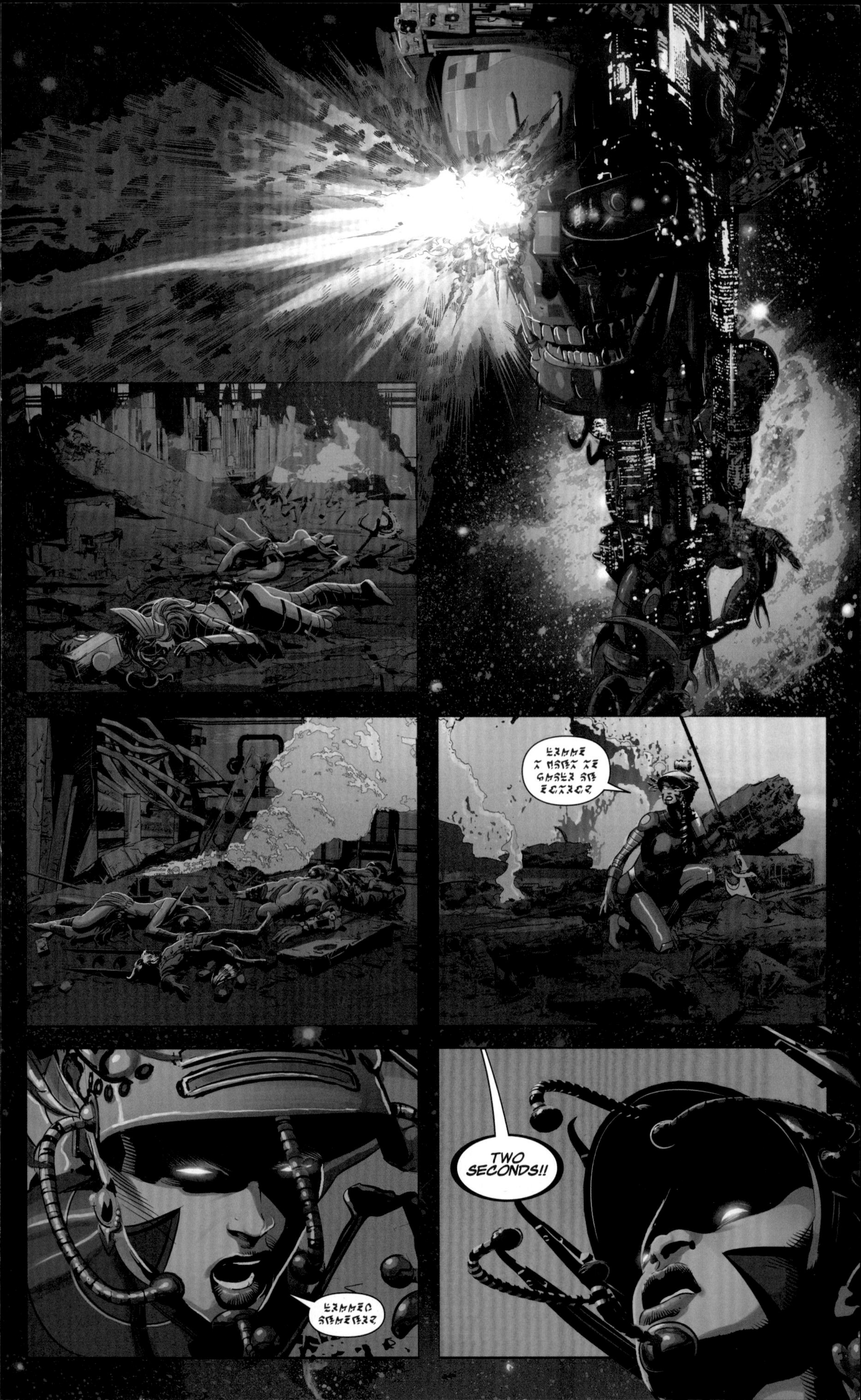
TWO SECONDS!!

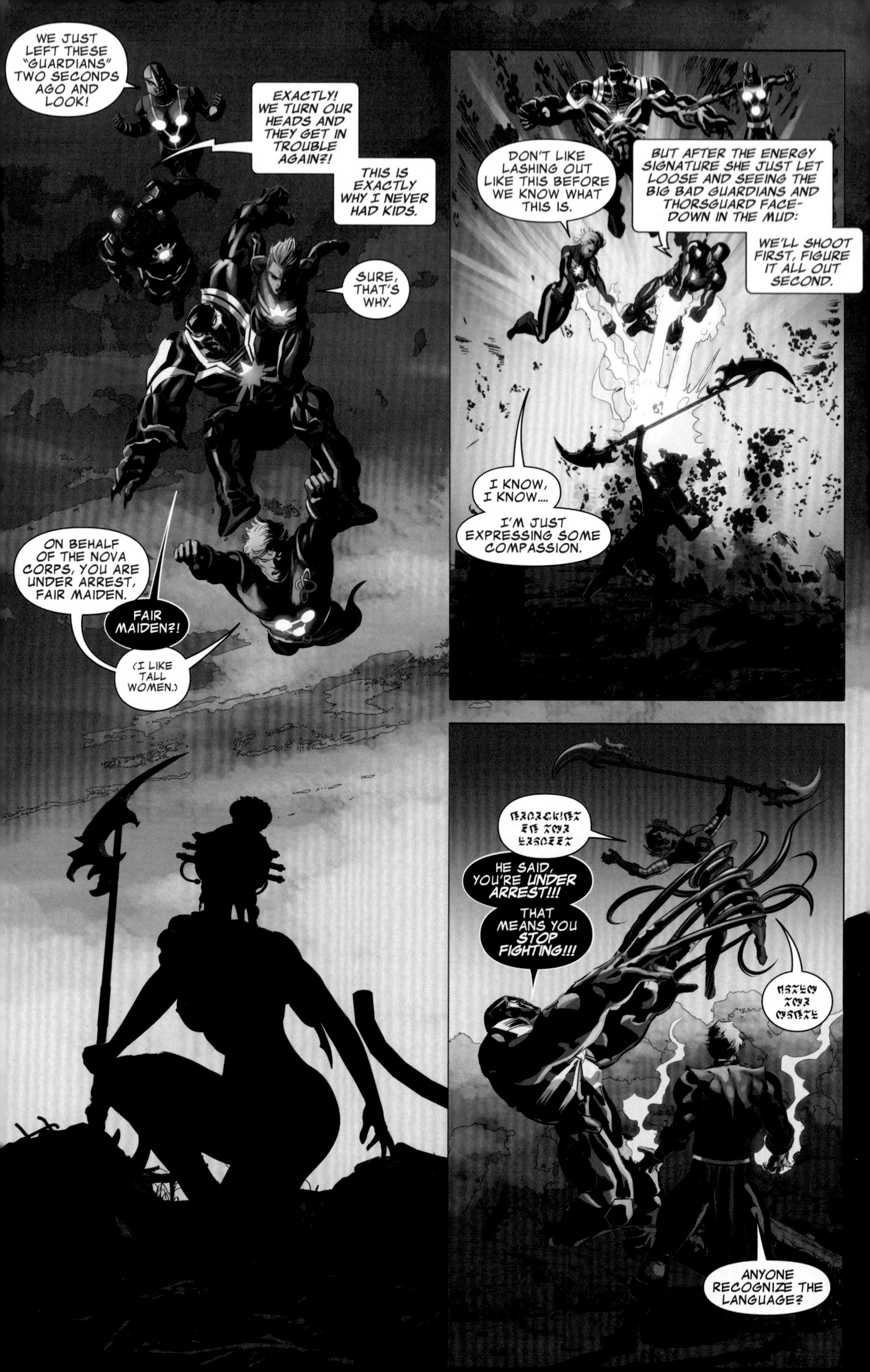
WE JUST LEFT THESE "GUARDIANS" TWO SECONDS AGO AND LOOK!
EXACTLY! WE TURN OUR HEADS AND THEY GET IN TROUBLE AGAIN?!
THIS IS EXACTLY WHY I NEVER HAD KIDS.
SURE, THAT'S WHY.
ON BEHALF OF THE NOVA CORPS, YOU ARE UNDER ARREST, FAIR MAIDEN.
FAIR MAIDEN?!
(I LIKE TALL WOMEN.)
DON'T LIKE LASHING OUT LIKE THIS BEFORE WE KNOW WHAT THIS IS.
BUT AFTER THE ENERGY SIGNATURE SHE JUST LET LOOSE AND SEEING THE BIG BAD GUARDIANS AND THORSGUARD FACE-DOWN IN THE MUD:
WE'LL SHOOT FIRST, FIGURE IT ALL OUT SECOND.
I KNOW, I KNOW....
I'M JUST EXPRESSING SOME COMPASSION.
HE SAID, YOU'RE UNDER ARREST!!!
THAT MEANS YOU STOP FIGHTING!!!
ANYONE RECOGNIZE THE LANGUAGE?

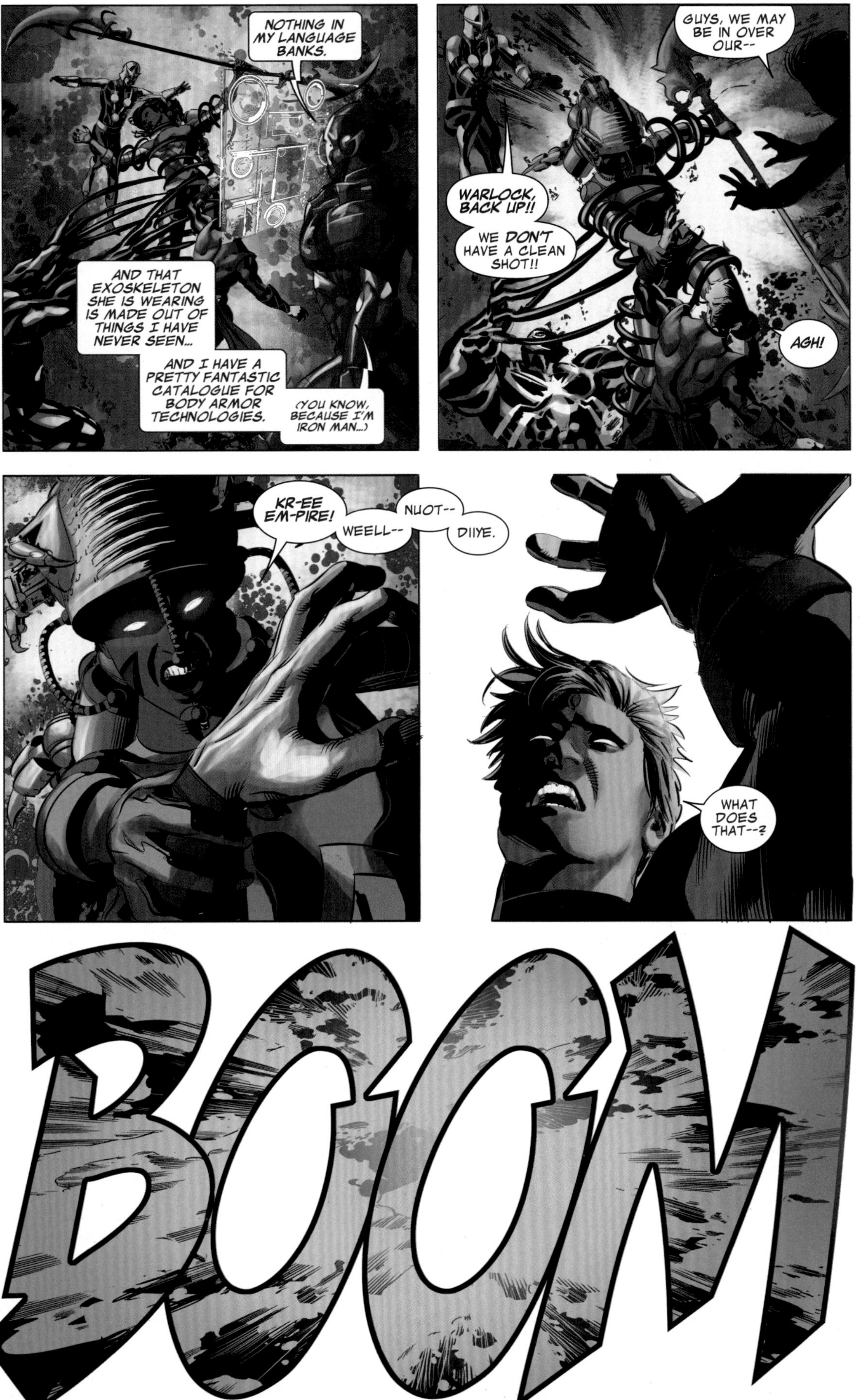
NOTHING IN MY LANGUAGE BANKS.
AND THAT EXOSKELETON SHE IS WEARING IS MADE OUT OF THINGS I HAVE NEVER SEEN...
AND I HAVE A PRETTY FANTASTIC CATALOGUE FOR BODY ARMOR TECHNOLOGIES.
(YOU KNOW, BECAUSE I'M IRON MAN...)
GUYS, WE MAY BE IN OVER OUR--
WARLOCK, BACK UP!!
WE DON'T HAVE A CLEAN SHOT!!
AGH!
KR-EE EM-PIRE!
WEELL--
NUOT--
DIIYE.
WHAT DOES THAT--?
BOOM

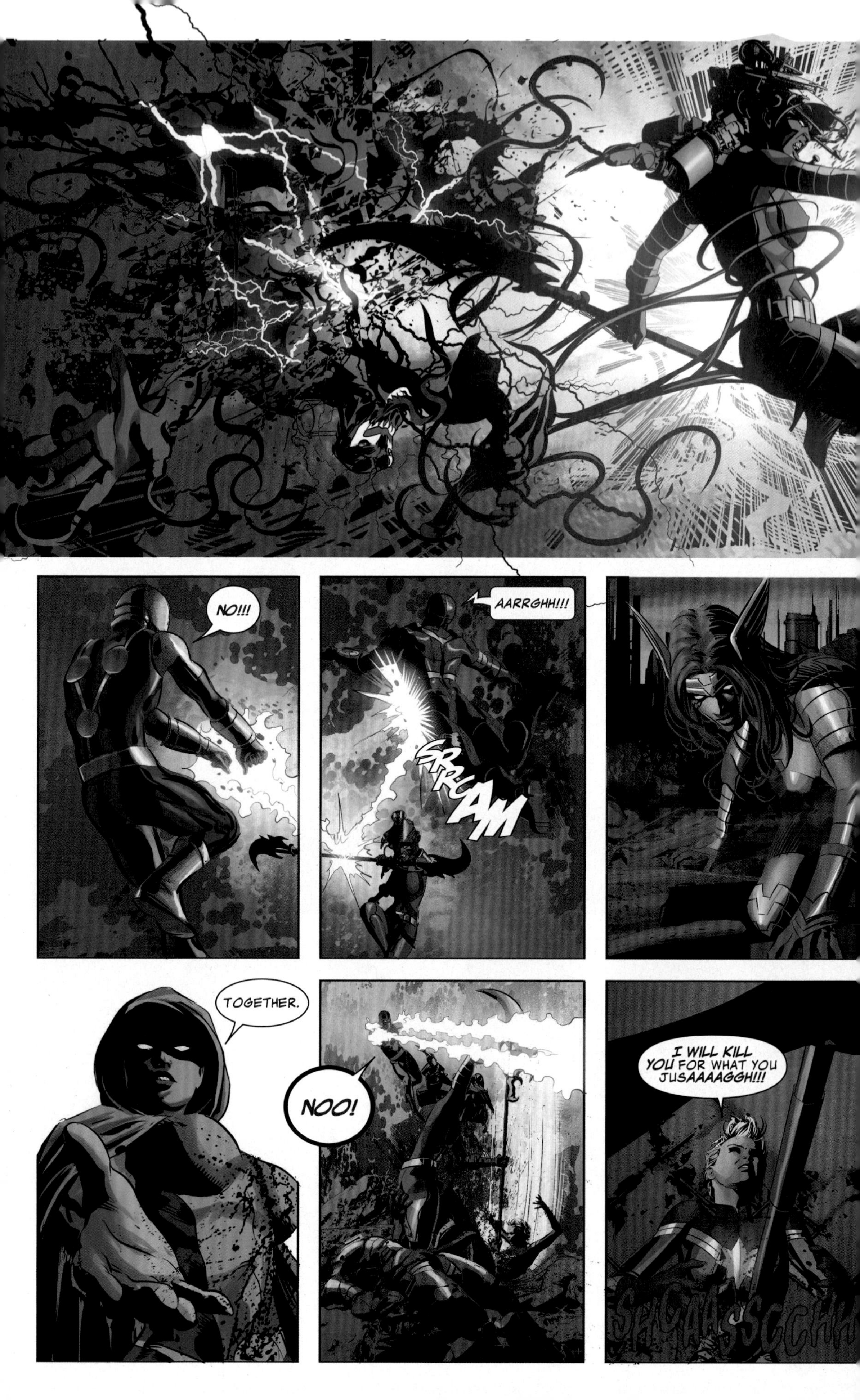
NO!!!
AARRGHH!!!
SRRCAM
TOGETHER.
NOO!
I WILL KILL YOU FOR WHAT YOU JUSAAAAGGH!!!

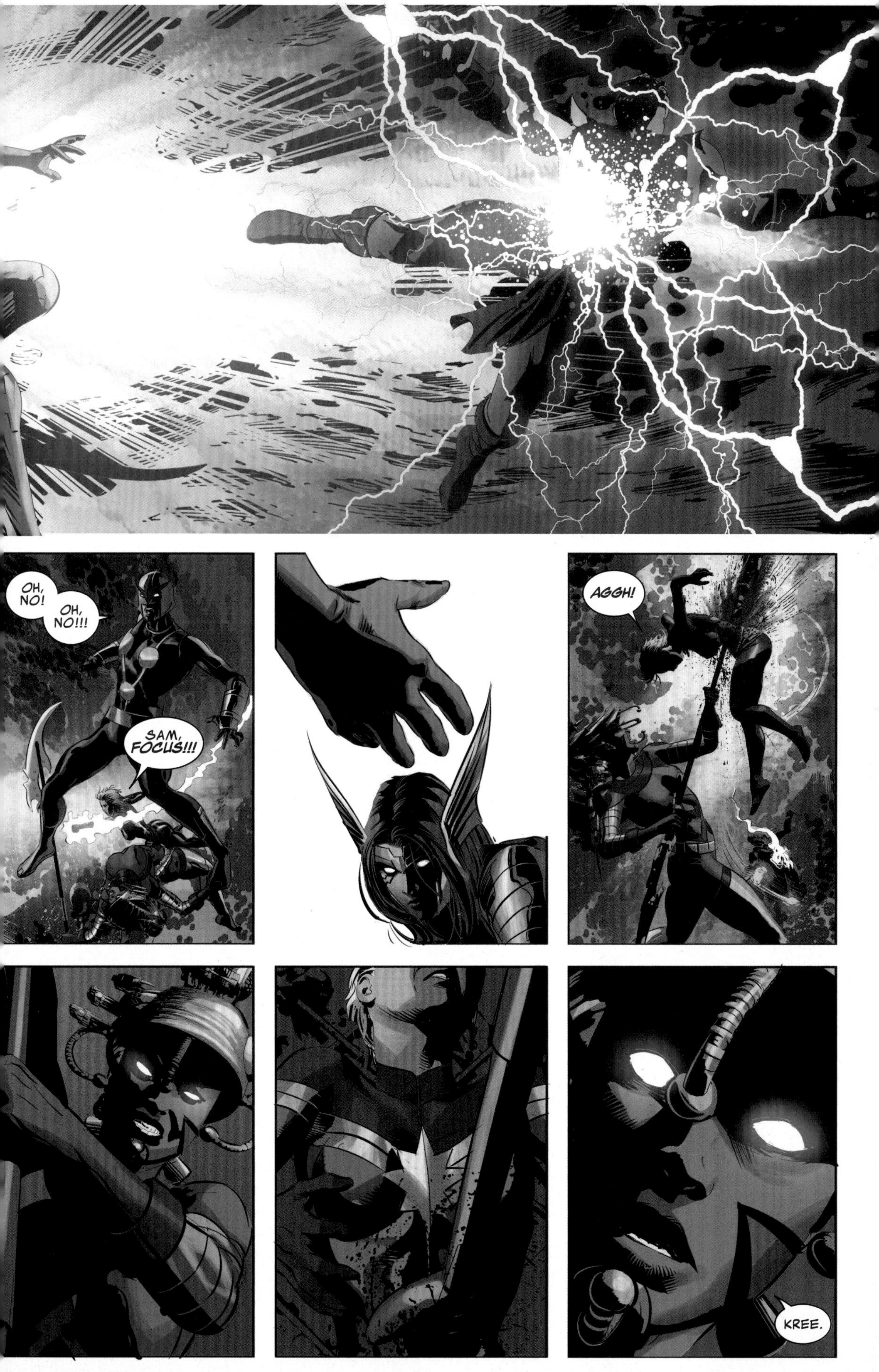
OH, NO!
OH, NO!!!
SAM, FOCUS!!!
AGGH!
KREE.

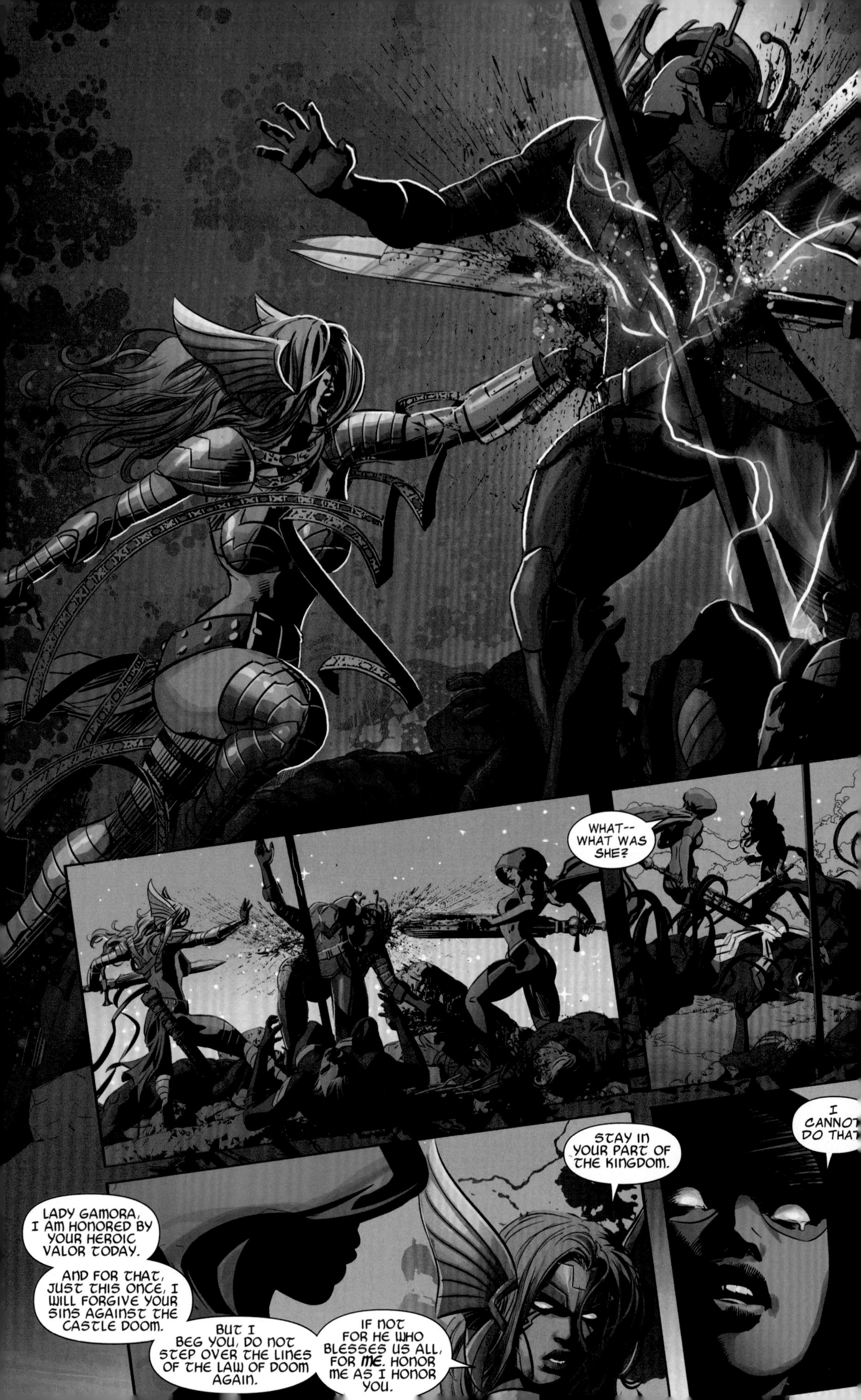
WHAT--
WHAT WAS
SHE?
STAY IN
YOUR PART OF
THE KINGDOM.
I
CANNOT
DO THAT
LADY GAMORA,
I AM HONORED BY
YOUR HEROIC
VALOR TODAY.
AND FOR THAT,
JUST THIS ONCE, I
WILL FORGIVE YOUR
SINS AGAINST THE
CASTLE DOOM.
BUT I
BEG YOU, DO NOT
STEP OVER THE LINES
OF THE LAW OF DOOM
AGAIN.
IF NOT
FOR HE WHO
BLESSES US ALL,
FOR ME. HONOR
ME AS I HONOR
YOU.

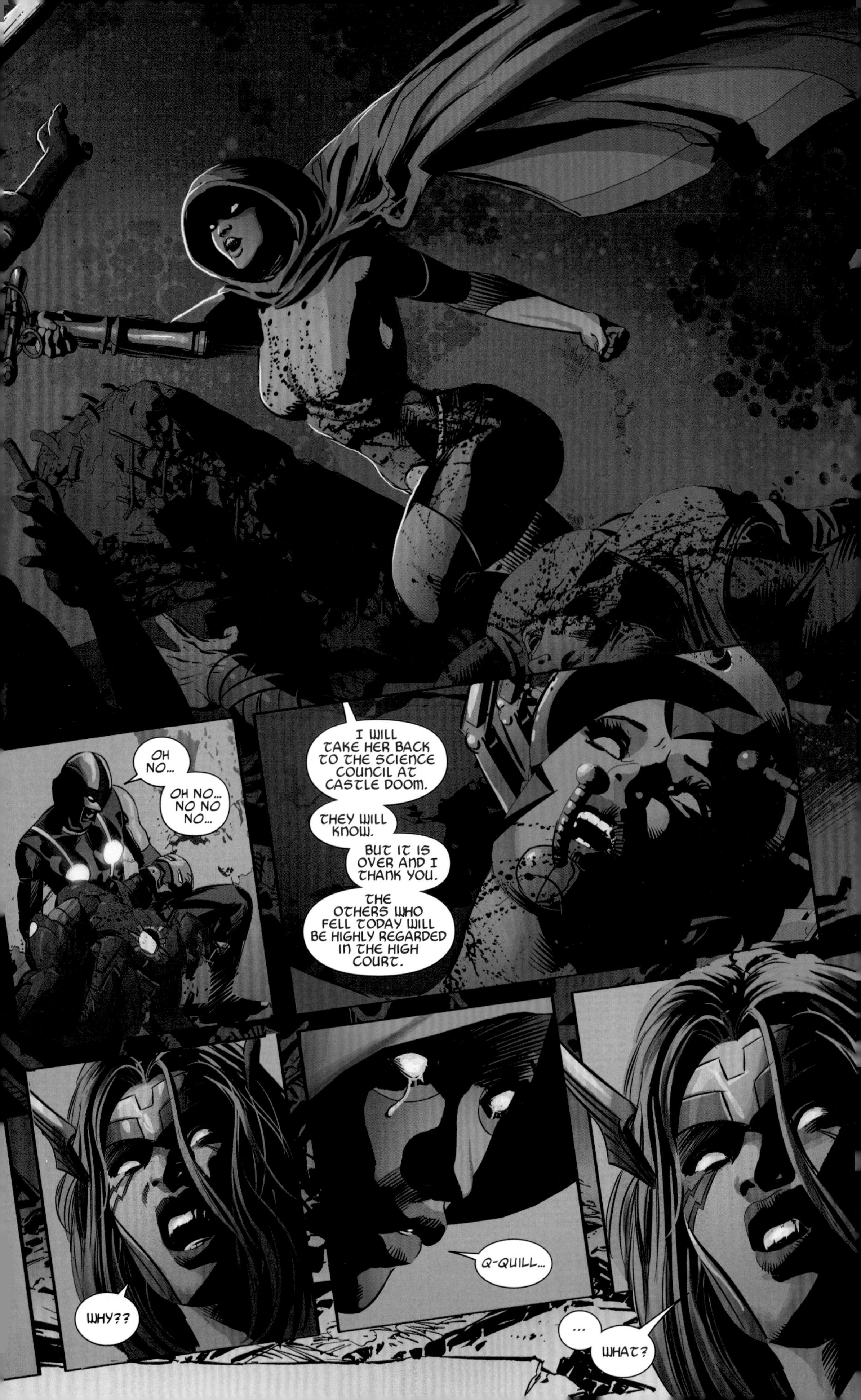
OH NO...
OH NO... NO NO NO...
I WILL TAKE HER BACK TO THE SCIENCE COUNCIL AT CASTLE DOOM.
THEY WILL KNOW.
BUT IT IS OVER AND I THANK YOU.
THE OTHERS WHO FELL TODAY WILL BE HIGHLY REGARDED IN THE HIGH COURT.
WHY??
Q-QUILL...
...
WHAT?

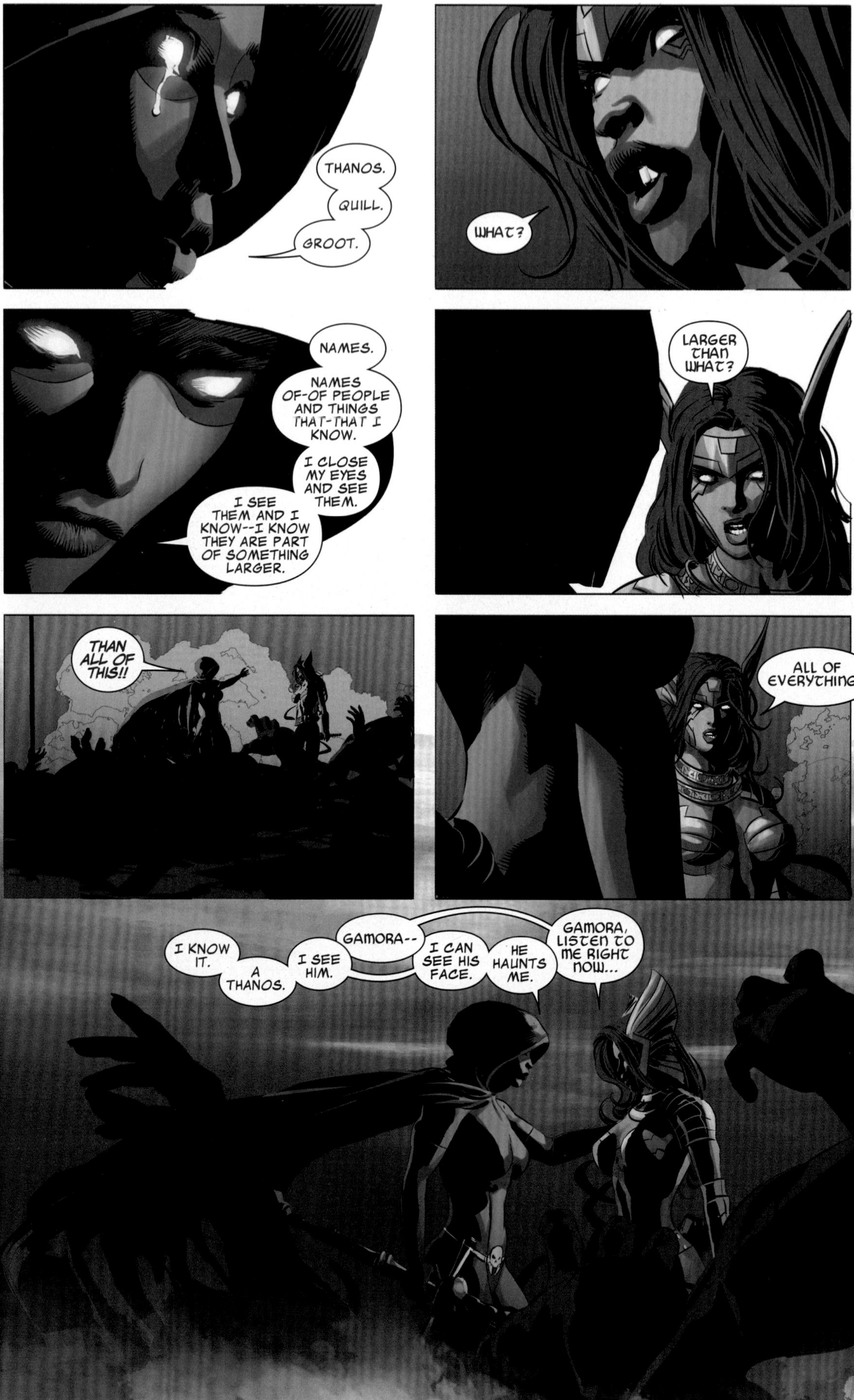
THANOS.
QUILL.
GROOT.
WHAT?
NAMES.
NAMES OF-OF PEOPLE AND THINGS THAT-THAT I KNOW.
I CLOSE MY EYES AND SEE THEM.
I SEE THEM AND I KNOW--I KNOW THEY ARE PART OF SOMETHING LARGER.
LARGER THAN WHAT?
THAN ALL OF THIS!!
ALL OF EVERYTHING?
I KNOW IT.
A THANOS.
I SEE HIM.
GAMORA--
I CAN SEE HIS FACE.
HE HAUNTS ME.
GAMORA, LISTEN TO ME RIGHT NOW...

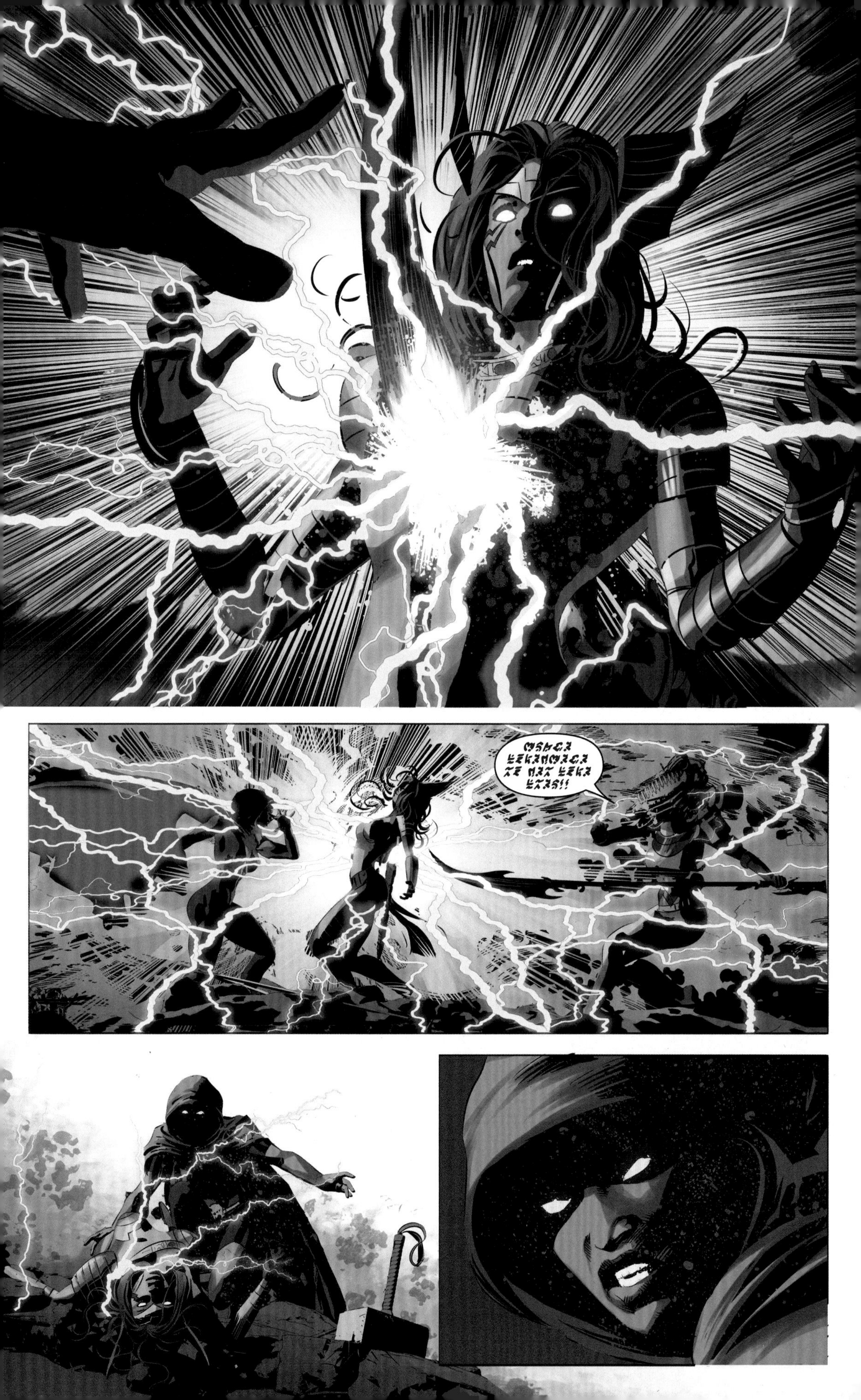

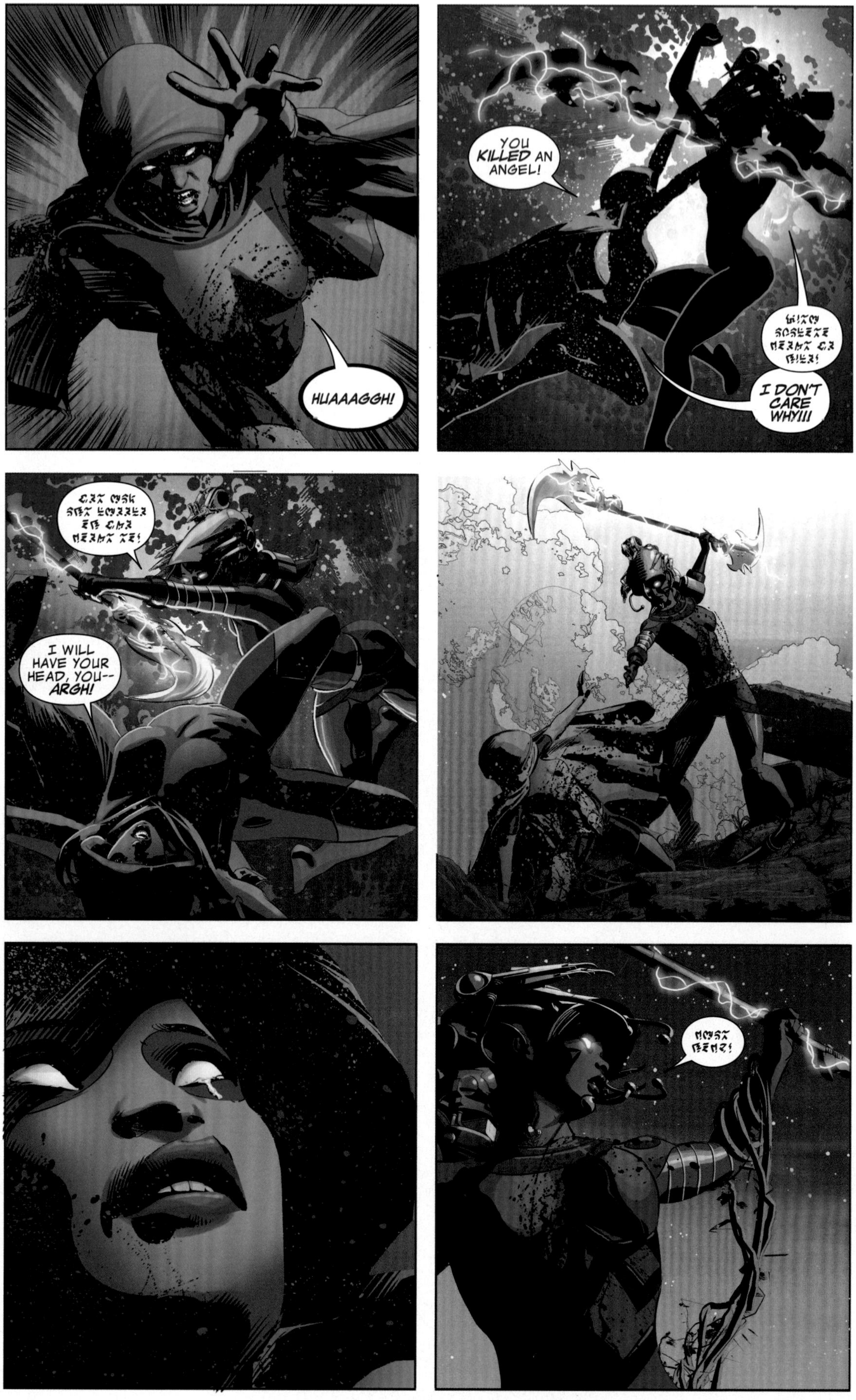
HUAAAGGH!
YOU KILLED AN ANGEL!
I DON'T CARE WHY!!!
I WILL HAVE YOUR HEAD, YOU-- ARGH!

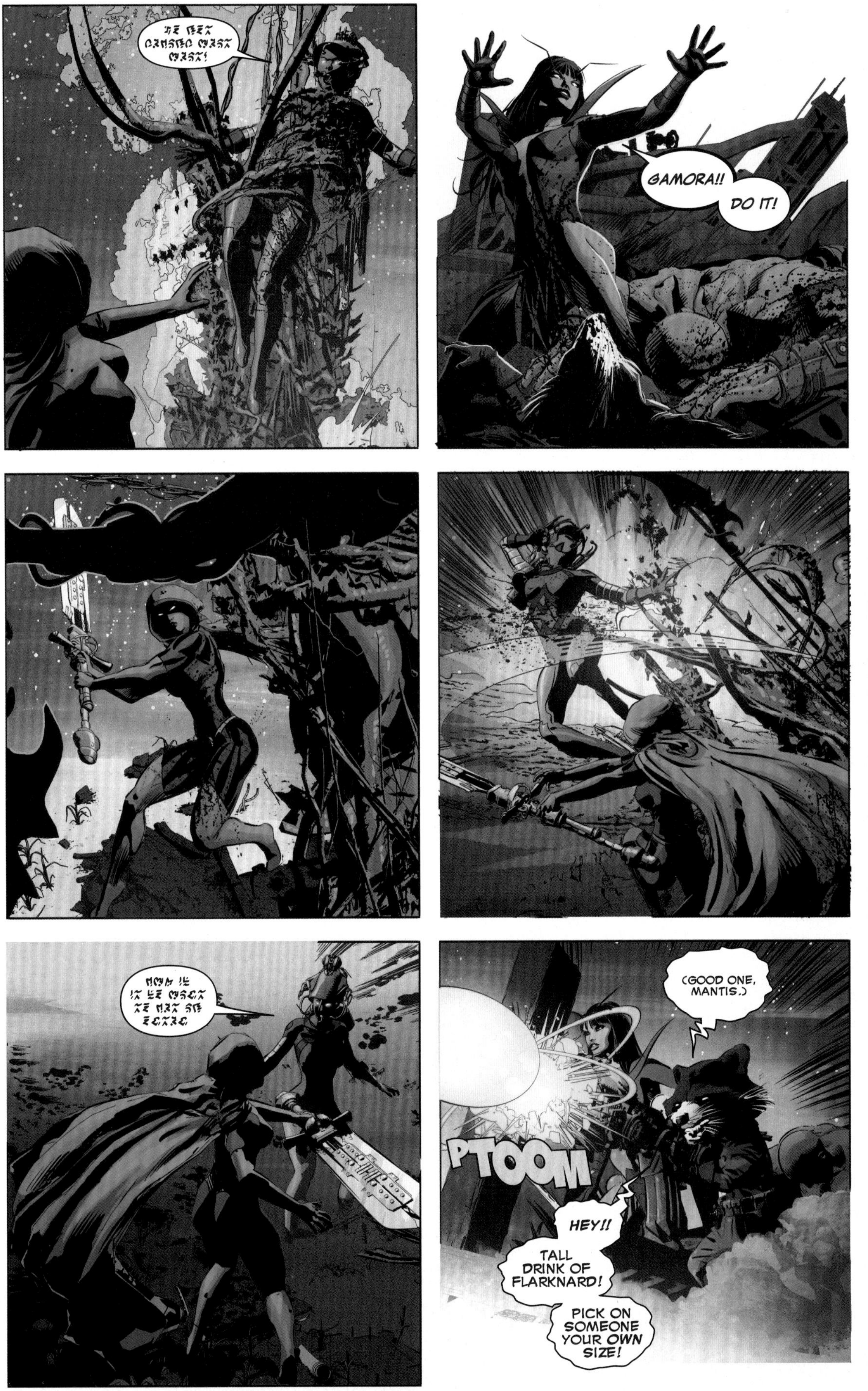
GAMORA!!
DO IT!
(GOOD ONE, MANTIS.)
PTOOM
HEY!!
TALL DRINK OF FLARKNARD!
PICK ON SOMEONE YOUR OWN SIZE!

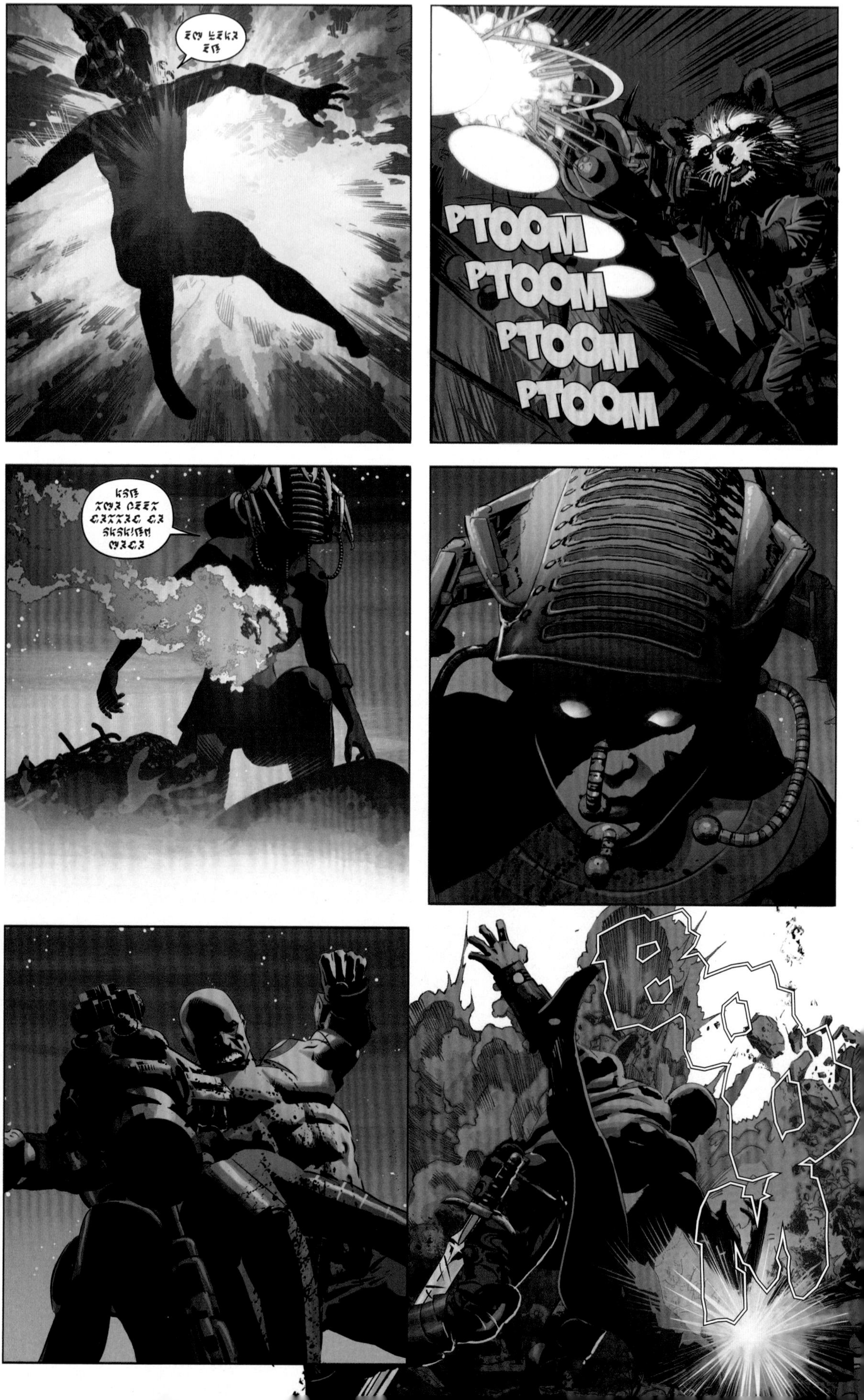
PTOOM
PTOOM
PTOOM
PTOOM

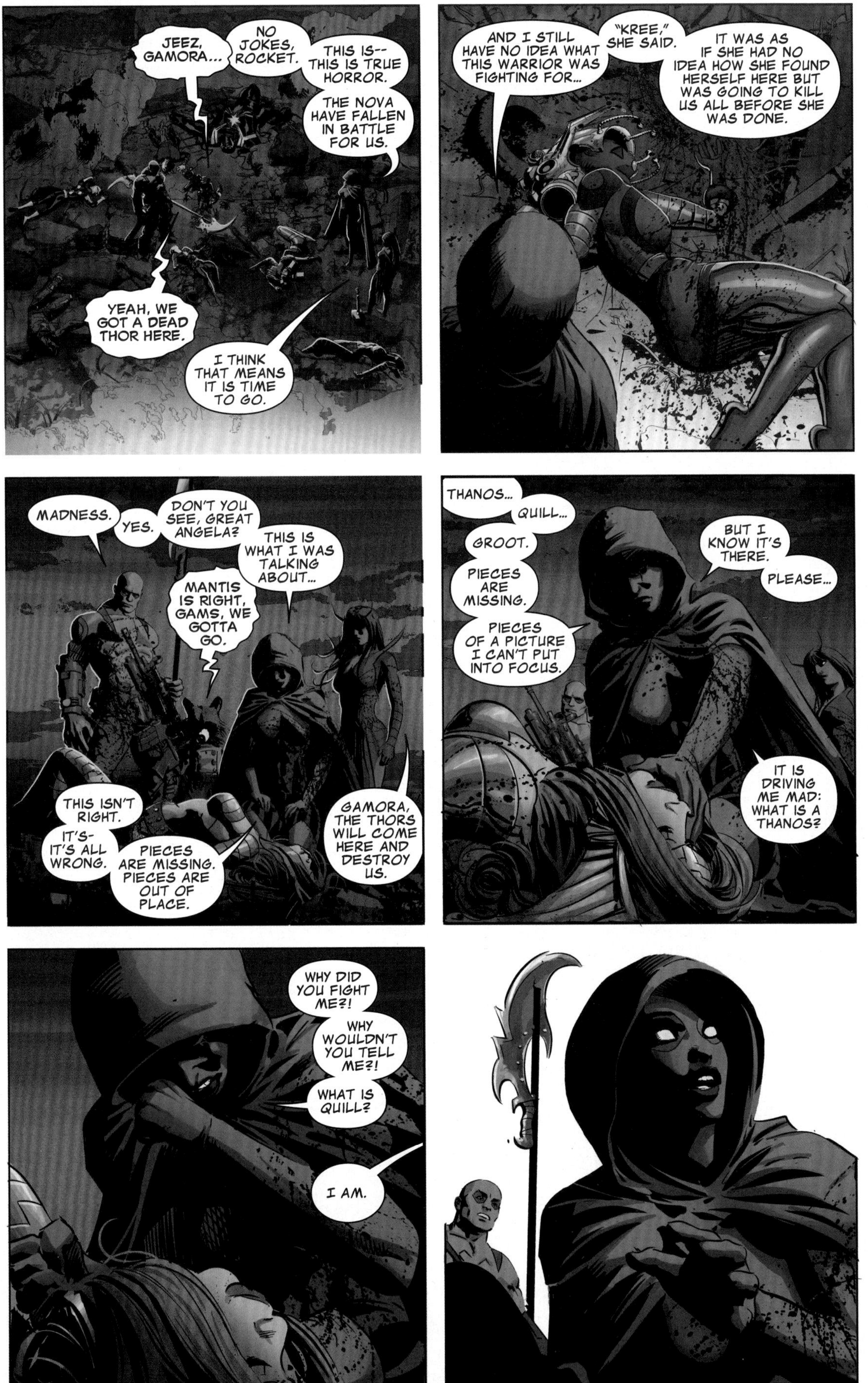
JEEZ, GAMORA...
NO JOKES, ROCKET.
THIS IS-- THIS IS TRUE HORROR.
THE NOVA HAVE FALLEN IN BATTLE FOR US.
YEAH, WE GOT A DEAD THOR HERE.
I THINK THAT MEANS IT IS TIME TO GO.
AND I STILL HAVE NO IDEA WHAT THIS WARRIOR WAS FIGHTING FOR...
"KREE," SHE SAID.
IT WAS AS IF SHE HAD NO IDEA HOW SHE FOUND HERSELF HERE BUT WAS GOING TO KILL US ALL BEFORE SHE WAS DONE.
MADNESS.
YES.
DON'T YOU SEE, GREAT ANGELA?
THIS IS WHAT I WAS TALKING ABOUT...
MANTIS IS RIGHT, GAMS, WE GOTTA GO.
THIS ISN'T RIGHT.
IT'S- IT'S ALL WRONG.
PIECES ARE MISSING. PIECES ARE OUT OF PLACE.
GAMORA, THE THORS WILL COME HERE AND DESTROY US.
THANOS...
QUILL...
GROOT.
PIECES ARE MISSING.
PIECES OF A PICTURE I CAN'T PUT INTO FOCUS.
BUT I KNOW IT'S THERE.
PLEASE...
IT IS DRIVING ME MAD: WHAT IS A THANOS?
WHY DID YOU FIGHT ME?!
WHY WOULDN'T YOU TELL ME?!
WHAT IS QUILL?
I AM.

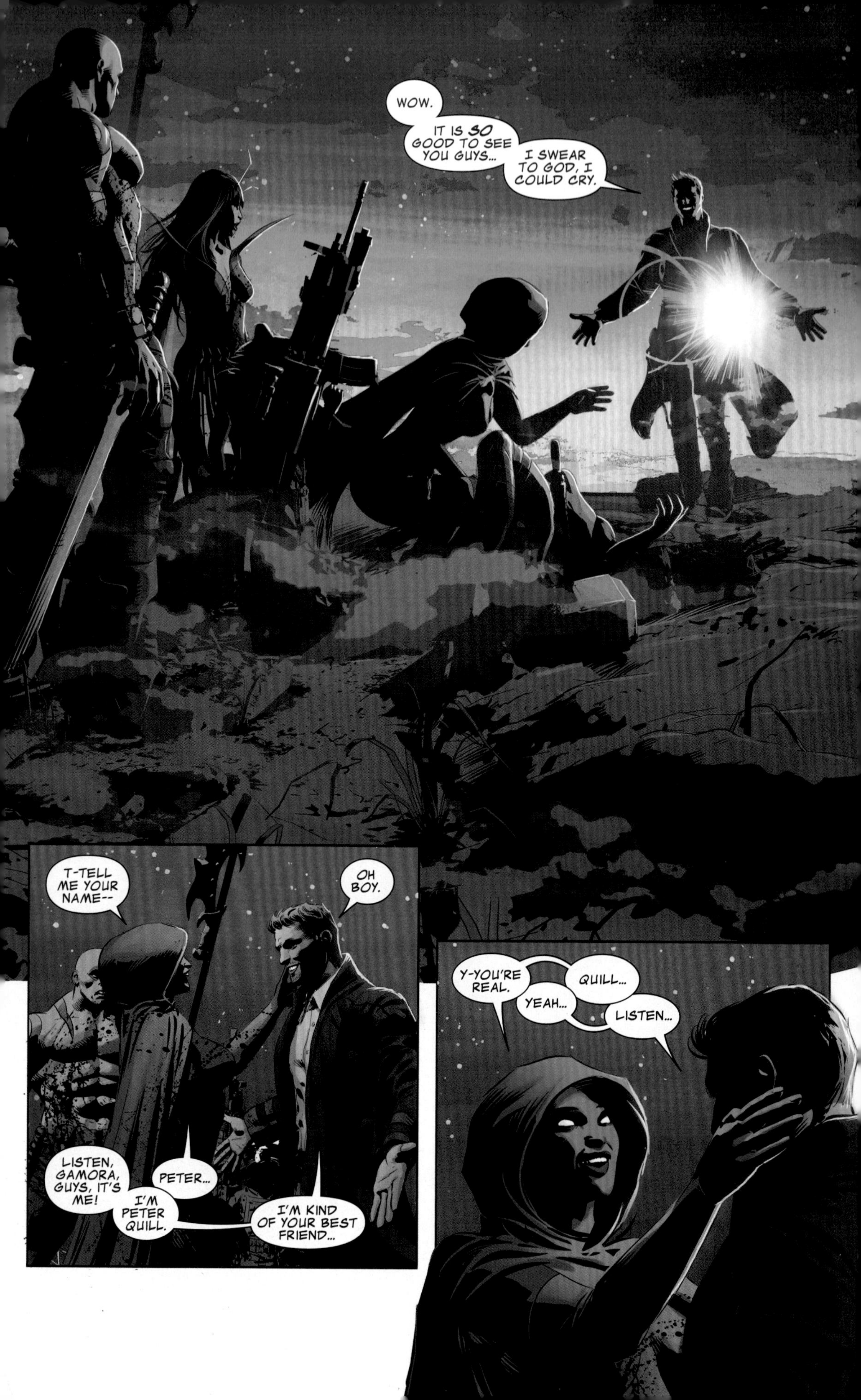
WOW.
IT IS SO GOOD TO SEE YOU GUYS...
I SWEAR TO GOD, I COULD CRY.
T-TELL ME YOUR NAME--
OH BOY.
LISTEN, GAMORA, GUYS, IT'S ME!
PETER...
I'M PETER QUILL.
I'M KIND OF YOUR BEST FRIEND...
Y-YOU'RE REAL.
QUILL...
YEAH...
LISTEN...

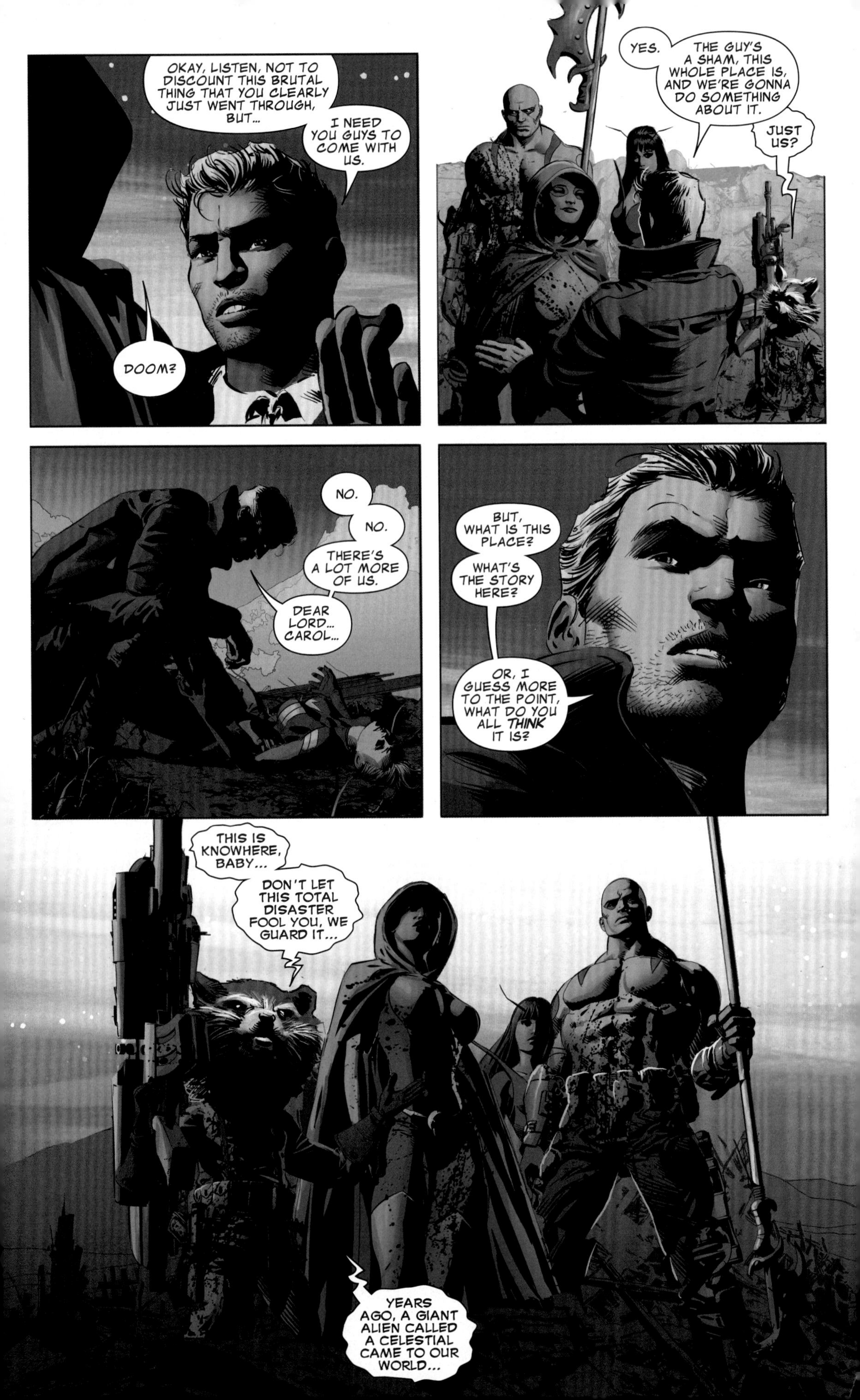
OKAY, LISTEN, NOT TO DISCOUNT THIS BRUTAL THING THAT YOU CLEARLY JUST WENT THROUGH, BUT...
I NEED YOU GUYS TO COME WITH US.
DOOM?
YES.
THE GUY'S A SHAM, THIS WHOLE PLACE IS, AND WE'RE GONNA DO SOMETHING ABOUT IT.
JUST US?
NO.
NO.
THERE'S A LOT MORE OF US.
DEAR LORD... CAROL...
BUT, WHAT IS THIS PLACE?
WHAT'S THE STORY HERE?
OR, I GUESS MORE TO THE POINT, WHAT DO YOU ALL *THINK* IT IS?
THIS IS KNOWHERE, BABY...
DON'T LET THIS TOTAL DISASTER FOOL YOU, WE GUARD IT...
YEARS AGO, A GIANT ALIEN CALLED A CELESTIAL CAME TO OUR WORLD...

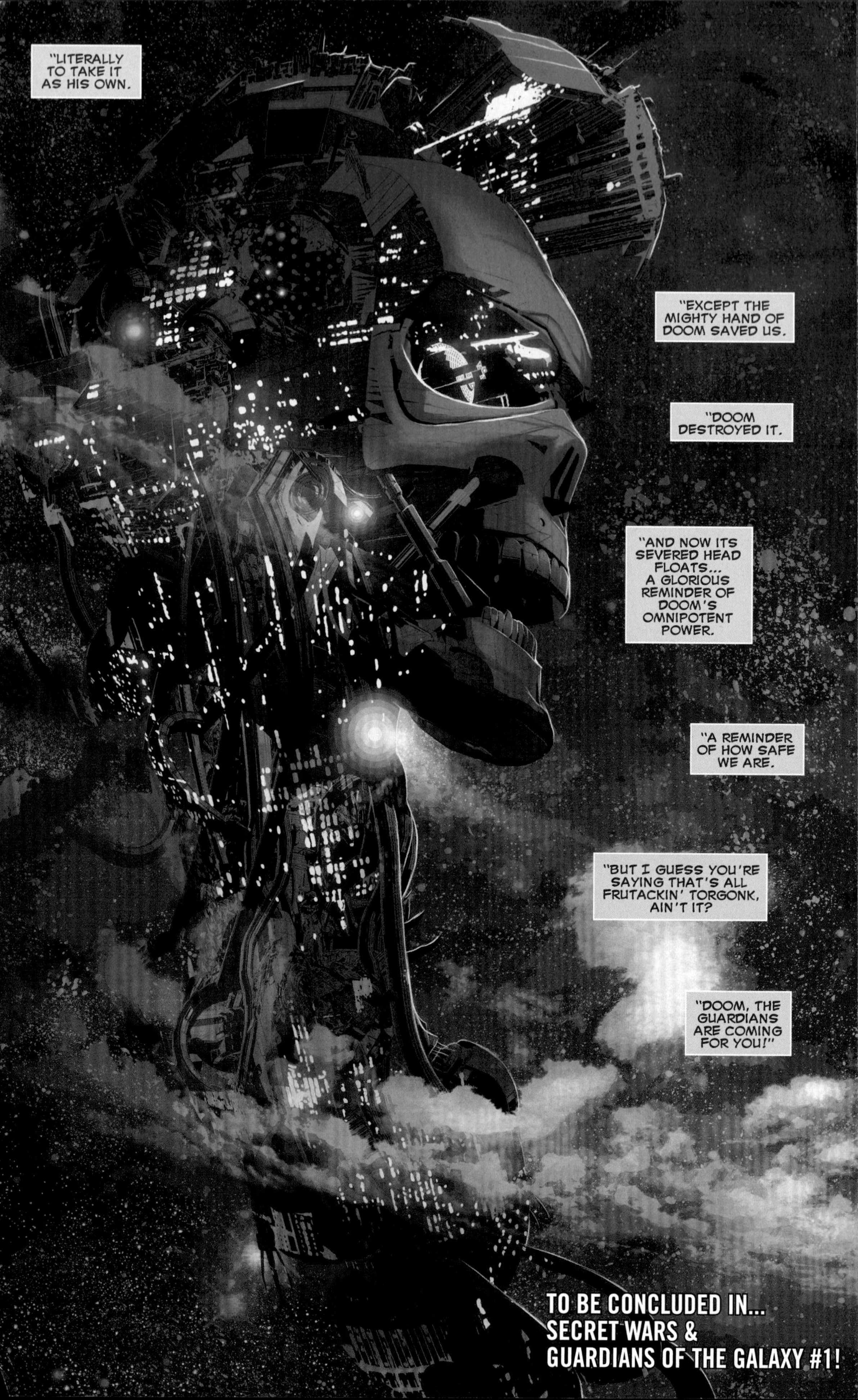
"LITERALLY TO TAKE IT AS HIS OWN.
"EXCEPT THE MIGHTY HAND OF DOOM SAVED US.
"DOOM DESTROYED IT.
"AND NOW ITS SEVERED HEAD FLOATS... A GLORIOUS REMINDER OF DOOM'S OMNIPOTENT POWER.
"A REMINDER OF HOW SAFE WE ARE.
"BUT I GUESS YOU'RE SAYING THAT'S ALL FRUTACKIN' TORGONK, AIN'T IT?
"DOOM, THE GUARDIANS ARE COMING FOR YOU!"
TO BE CONCLUDED IN... SECRET WARS & GUARDIANS OF THE GALAXY #1!

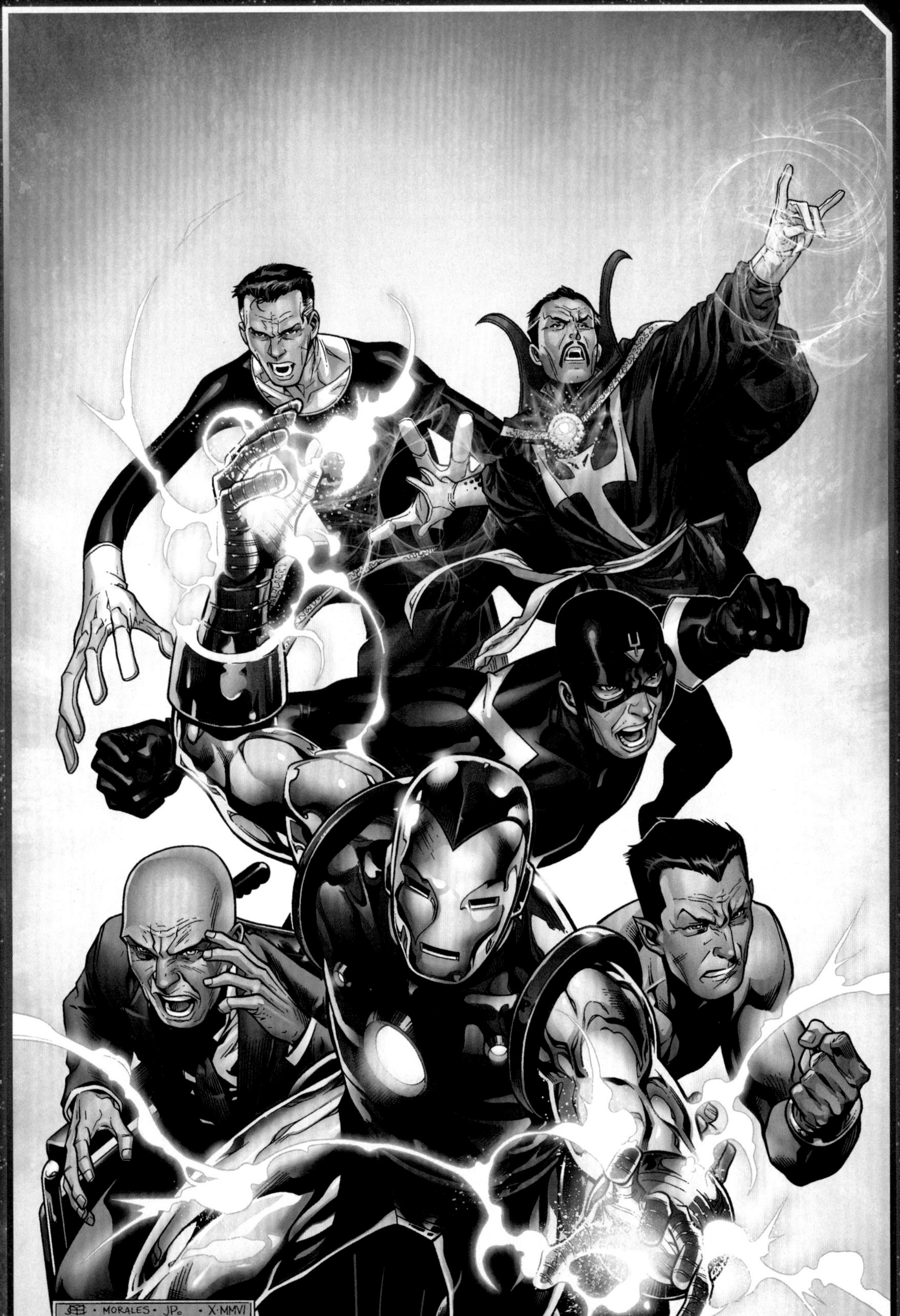
· MORALES · JPo · X·MMVI

NEW AVENGERS: ILLUMINATI (2007) #3

THE NEW AVENGERS
ILLUMINATI

The Illuminati is a secret organization comprised of several of the world's most powerful heroes: Sorcerer Supreme Doctor Strange; Black Bolt, King of the Inhumans; Charles Xavier, founder of the X-Men and mutant rights activist; Reed Richards, founding member of the Fantastic Four; Namor, the Sub-Mariner, Ruler of Atlantis; and Iron Man, founding member of the Avengers.

These six men have worked together to shape the superhuman world. To keep the trust between the group members, the Illuminati's existence has been kept secret from everyone, including the members' teammates and families.

What they've done together has remained a mystery…until now…

Years ago, a mysterious entity known as the Beyonder picked up heroes and villains from Earth and pitted them against each other on the faraway Battleworld in order to better understand human emotion. Those who were taken banded together and escaped the Battleworld, leaving the Beyonder alone...

Writers	Penciler	Inker	Colorist	Letterer
Brian Michael Bendis & Brian Reed	Jim Cheung	Mark Morales	Justin Ponsor	VC's Cory Petit

Production	Assistant Editor	Editor	Editor in Chief	Publisher
Kate Levin	Molly Lazer	Tom Brevoort	Joe Quesada	Dan Buckley

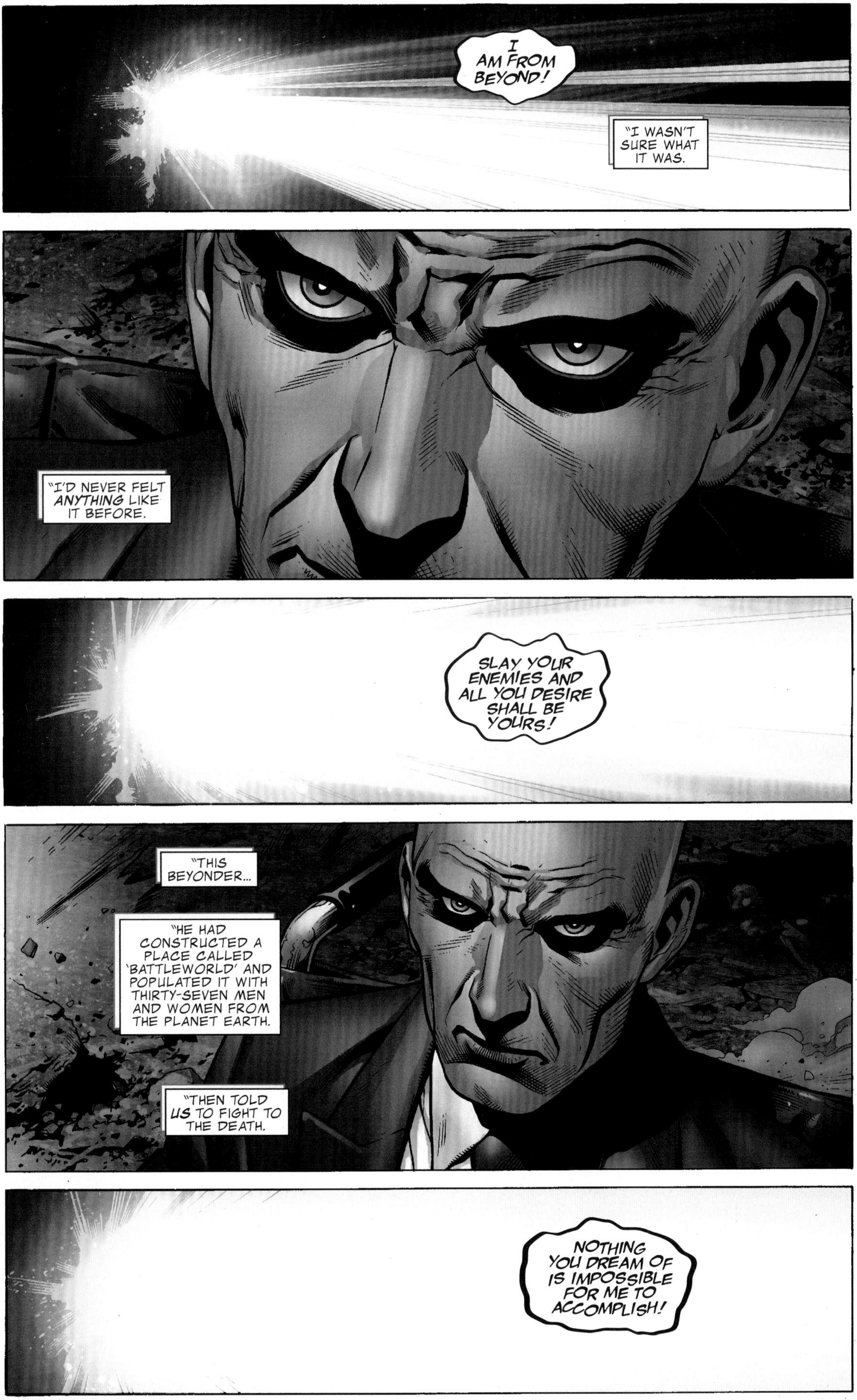
I AM FROM BEYOND!
"I WASN'T SURE WHAT IT WAS.
"I'D NEVER FELT ANYTHING LIKE IT BEFORE.
SLAY YOUR ENEMIES AND ALL YOU DESIRE SHALL BE YOURS!
"THIS BEYONDER...
"HE HAD CONSTRUCTED A PLACE CALLED 'BATTLEWORLD' AND POPULATED IT WITH THIRTY-SEVEN MEN AND WOMEN FROM THE PLANET EARTH.
"THEN TOLD US TO FIGHT TO THE DEATH.
NOTHING YOU DREAM OF IS IMPOSSIBLE FOR ME TO ACCOMPLISH!

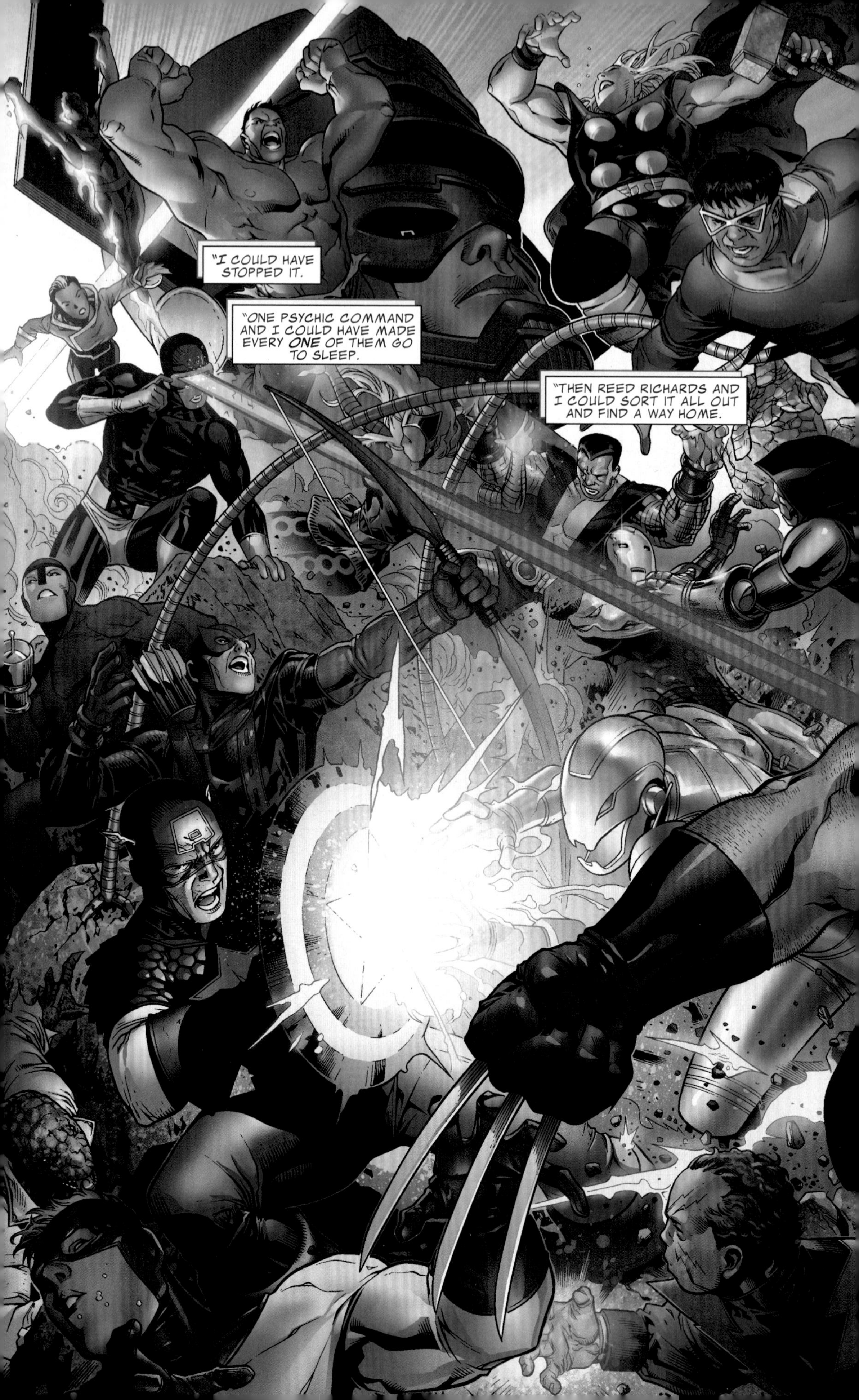
"I COULD HAVE STOPPED IT.
"ONE PSYCHIC COMMAND AND I COULD HAVE MADE EVERY ONE OF THEM GO TO SLEEP.
"THEN REED RICHARDS AND I COULD SORT IT ALL OUT AND FIND A WAY HOME.

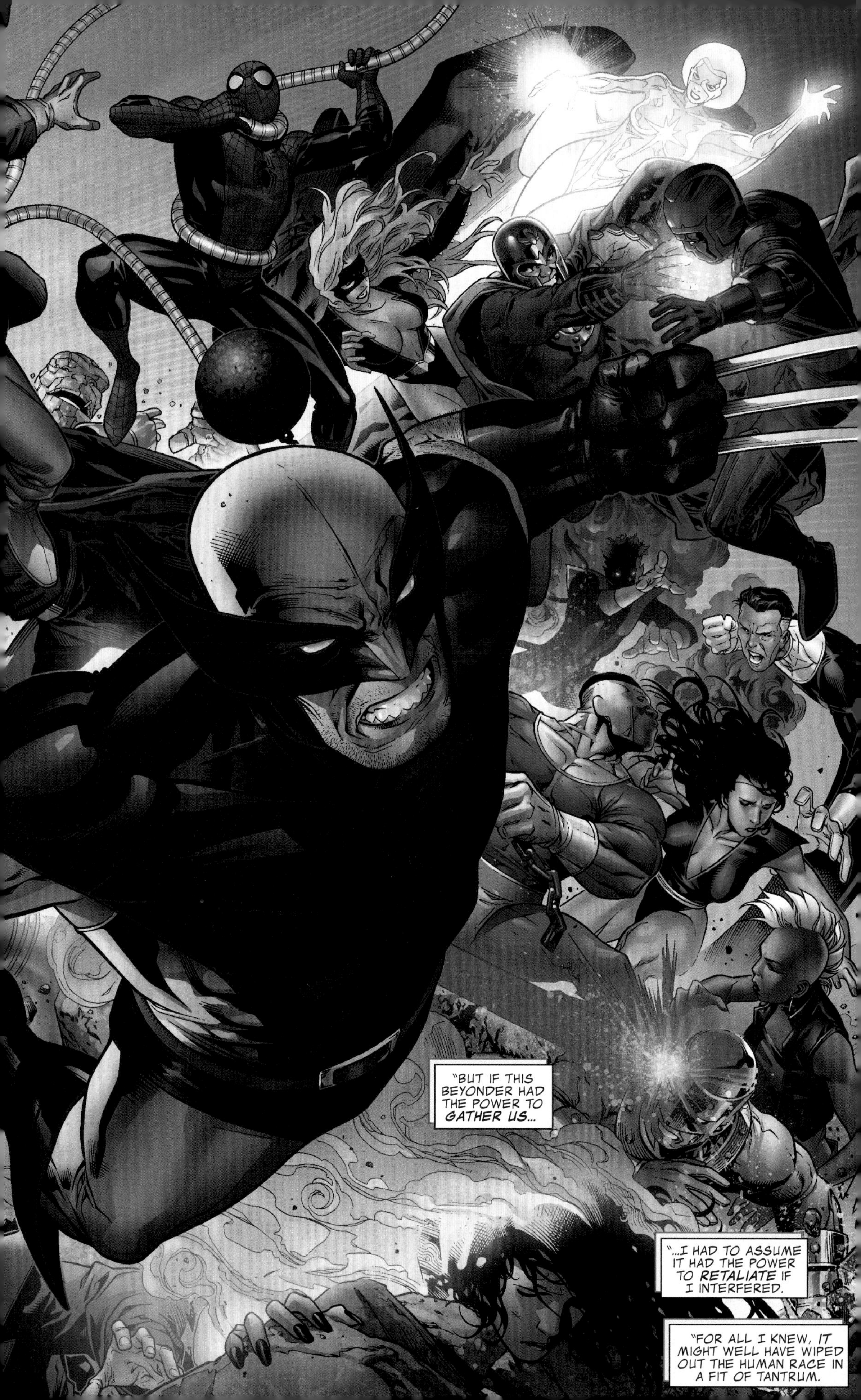
"BUT IF THIS BEYONDER HAD THE POWER TO *GATHER US*...
"...I HAD TO ASSUME IT HAD THE POWER TO *RETALIATE* IF I INTERFERED.
"FOR ALL I KNEW, *IT* MIGHT WELL HAVE WIPED OUT THE HUMAN RACE IN A FIT OF TANTRUM.

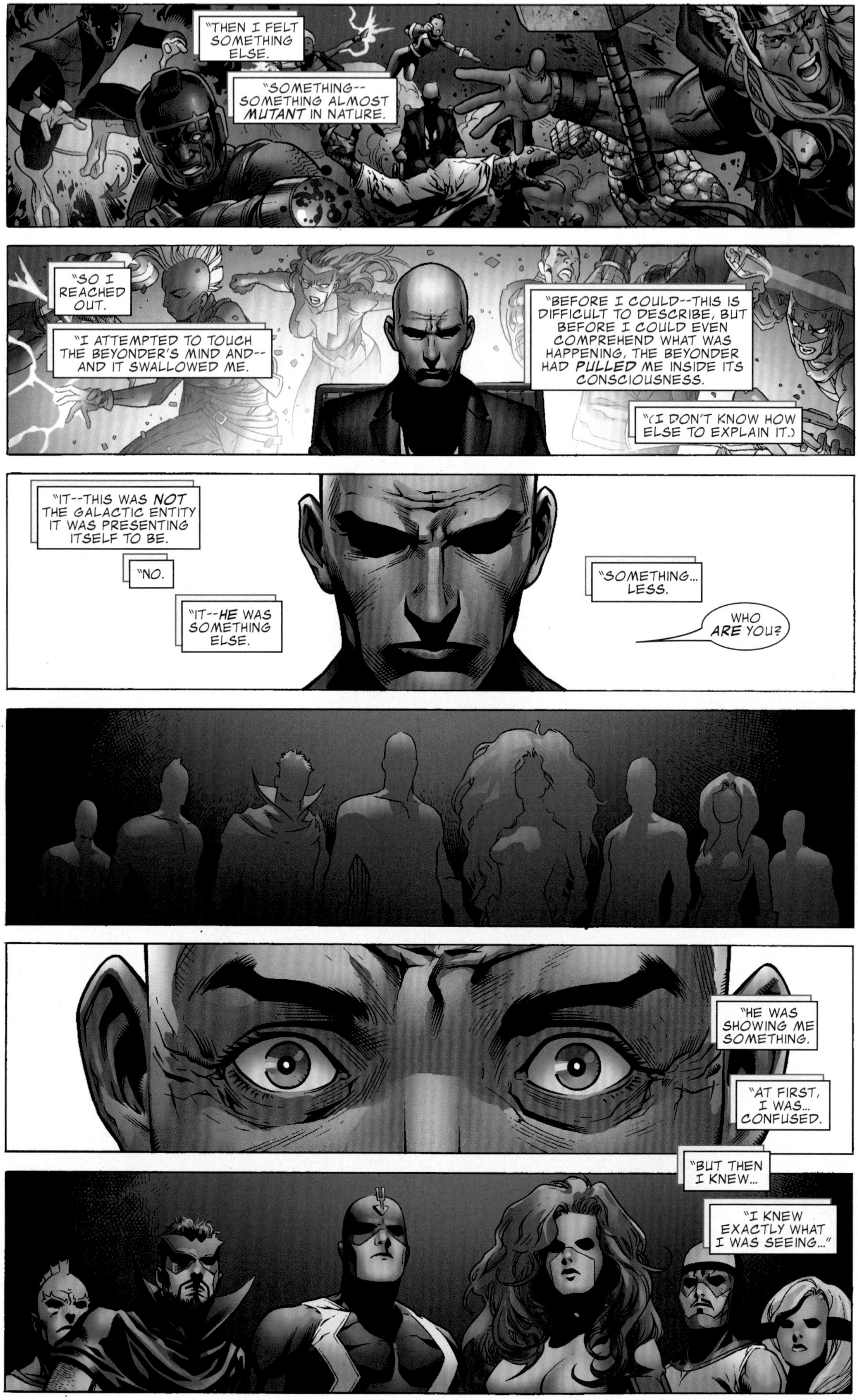
"THEN I FELT SOMETHING ELSE.
"SOMETHING--SOMETHING ALMOST *MUTANT* IN NATURE.
"SO I REACHED OUT.
"I ATTEMPTED TO TOUCH THE BEYONDER'S MIND AND--AND IT SWALLOWED ME.
"BEFORE I COULD--THIS IS DIFFICULT TO DESCRIBE, BUT BEFORE I COULD EVEN COMPREHEND WHAT WAS HAPPENING, THE BEYONDER HAD *PULLED* ME INSIDE ITS CONSCIOUSNESS.
"(I DON'T KNOW HOW ELSE TO EXPLAIN IT.)
"IT--THIS WAS **NOT** THE GALACTIC ENTITY IT WAS PRESENTING ITSELF TO BE.
"NO.
"IT--**HE** WAS SOMETHING ELSE.
"SOMETHING... LESS.
WHO **ARE** YOU?
"HE WAS SHOWING ME SOMETHING.
"AT FIRST, I WAS... CONFUSED.
"BUT THEN I KNEW...
"I KNEW EXACTLY WHAT I WAS SEEING..."

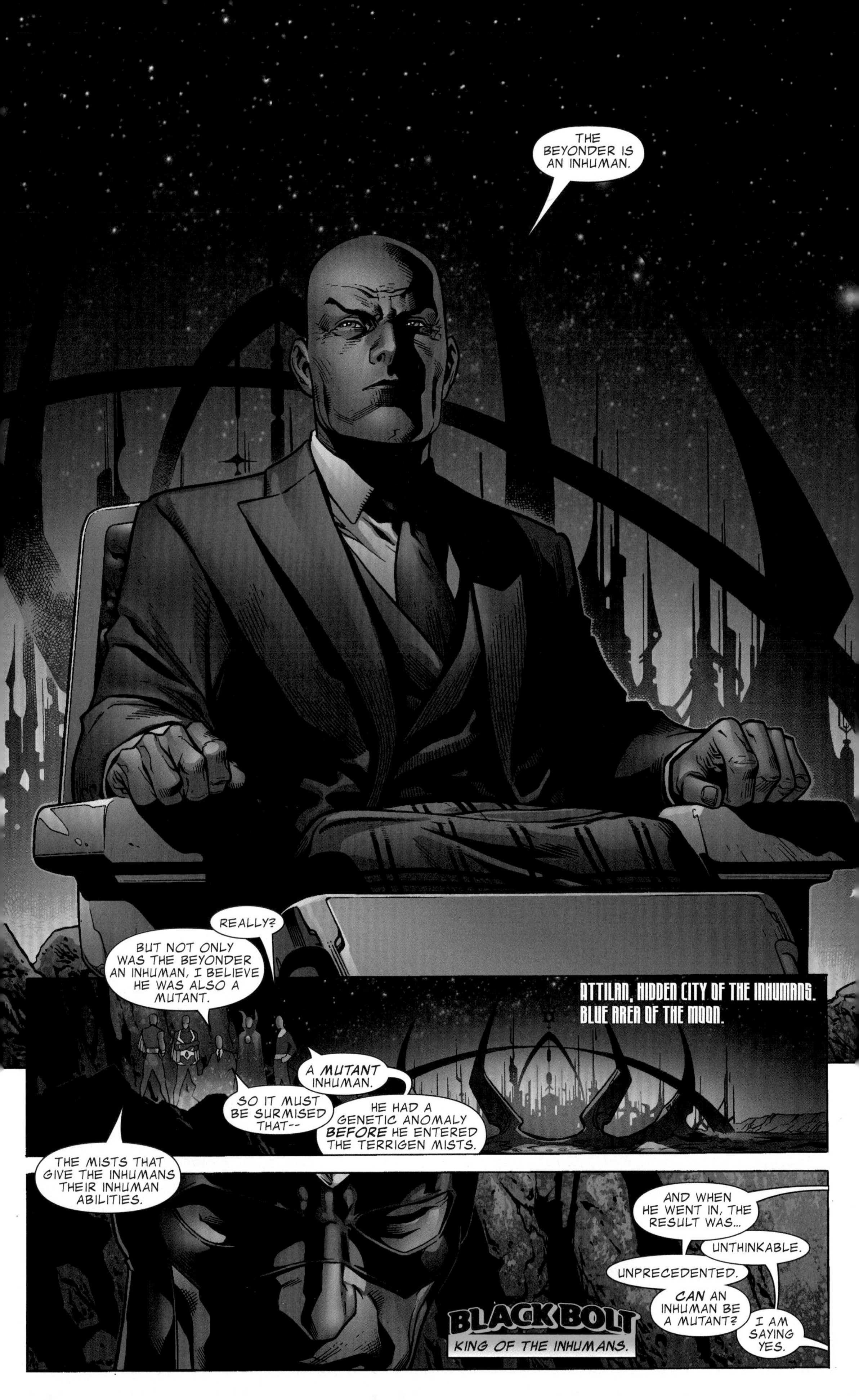
THE BEYONDER IS AN INHUMAN.
REALLY?
BUT NOT ONLY WAS THE BEYONDER AN INHUMAN, I BELIEVE HE WAS ALSO A MUTANT.
ATTILAN, HIDDEN CITY OF THE INHUMANS. BLUE AREA OF THE MOON.
A MUTANT INHUMAN.
SO IT MUST BE SURMISED THAT--
HE HAD A GENETIC ANOMALY BEFORE HE ENTERED THE TERRIGEN MISTS.
THE MISTS THAT GIVE THE INHUMANS THEIR INHUMAN ABILITIES.
AND WHEN HE WENT IN, THE RESULT WAS...
UNTHINKABLE.
UNPRECEDENTED.
CAN AN INHUMAN BE A MUTANT?
I AM SAYING YES.
BLACK BOLT
KING OF THE INHUMANS.

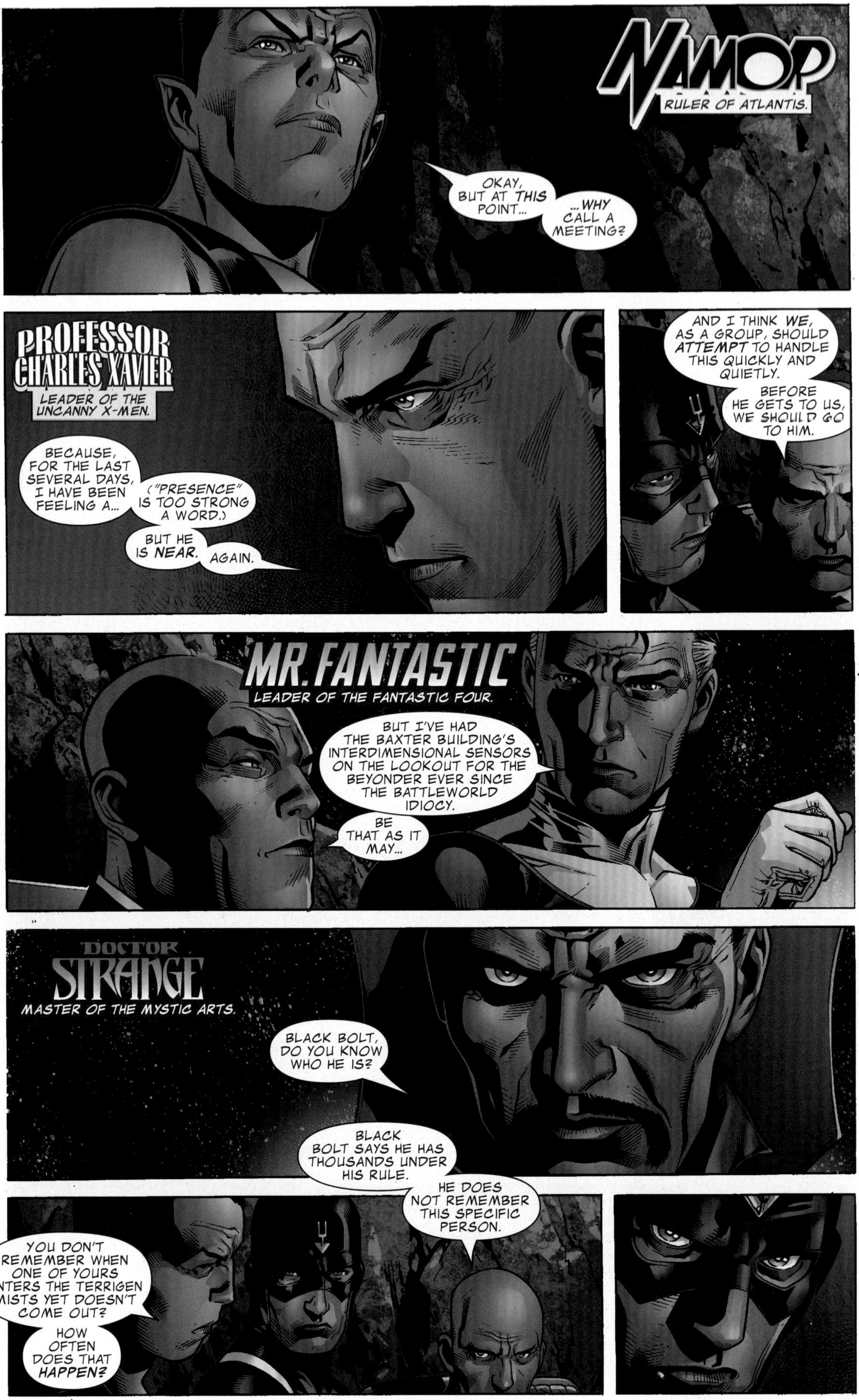
NAMOR
RULER OF ATLANTIS.
OKAY, BUT AT THIS POINT...
...WHY CALL A MEETING?
PROFESSOR CHARLES XAVIER
LEADER OF THE UNCANNY X-MEN.
BECAUSE, FOR THE LAST SEVERAL DAYS, I HAVE BEEN FEELING A...
("PRESENCE" IS TOO STRONG A WORD.)
BUT HE IS NEAR.
AGAIN.
AND I THINK WE, AS A GROUP, SHOULD ATTEMPT TO HANDLE THIS QUICKLY AND QUIETLY.
BEFORE HE GETS TO US, WE SHOULD GO TO HIM.
MR. FANTASTIC
LEADER OF THE FANTASTIC FOUR.
BUT I'VE HAD THE BAXTER BUILDING'S INTERDIMENSIONAL SENSORS ON THE LOOKOUT FOR THE BEYONDER EVER SINCE THE BATTLEWORLD IDIOCY.
BE THAT AS IT MAY...
DOCTOR STRANGE
MASTER OF THE MYSTIC ARTS.
BLACK BOLT, DO YOU KNOW WHO HE IS?
BLACK BOLT SAYS HE HAS THOUSANDS UNDER HIS RULE.
HE DOES NOT REMEMBER THIS SPECIFIC PERSON.
YOU DON'T REMEMBER WHEN ONE OF YOURS ENTERS THE TERRIGEN MISTS YET DOESN'T COME OUT?
HOW OFTEN DOES THAT HAPPEN?

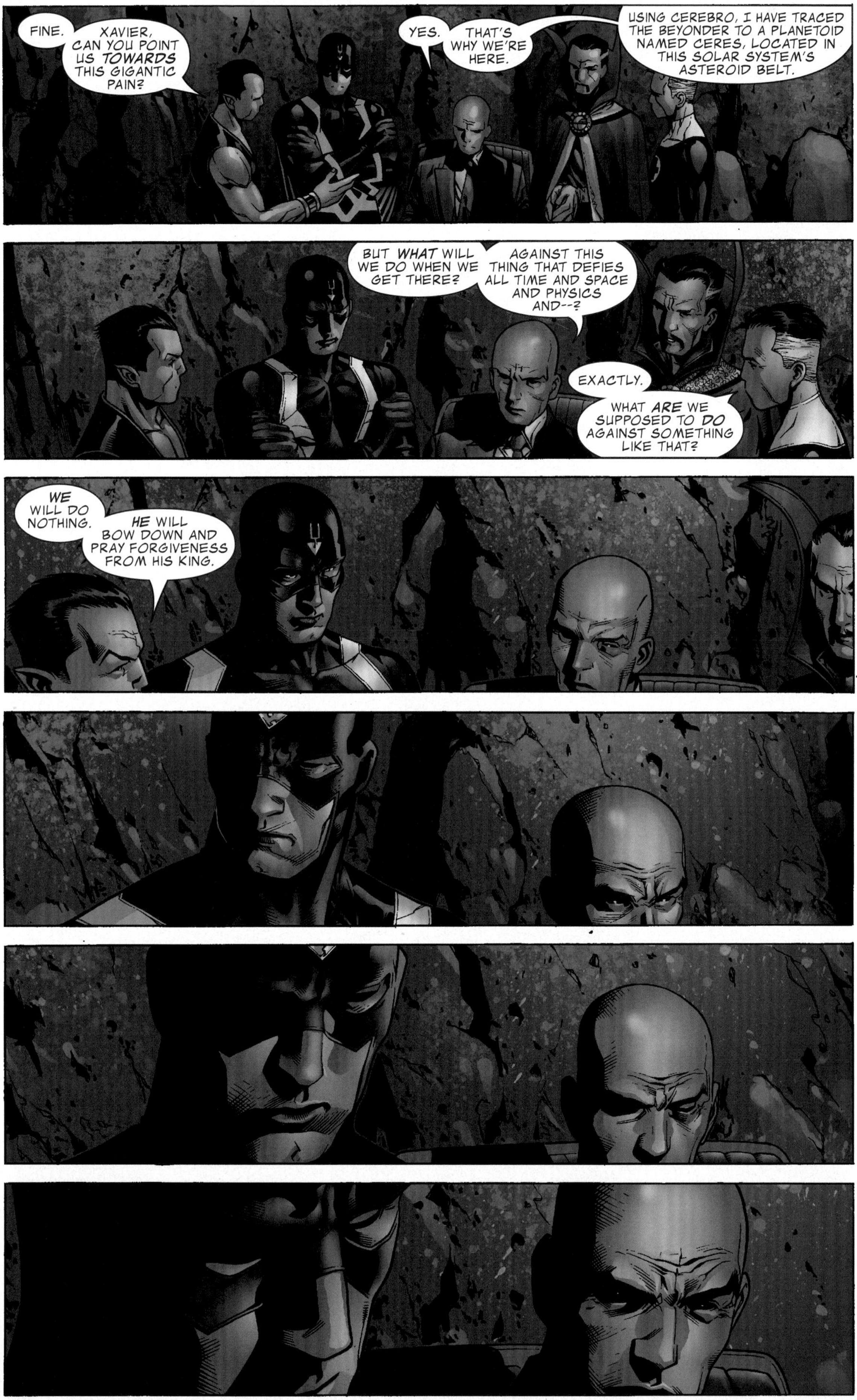
FINE.
XAVIER, CAN YOU POINT US TOWARDS THIS GIGANTIC PAIN?
YES.
THAT'S WHY WE'RE HERE.
USING CEREBRO, I HAVE TRACED THE BEYONDER TO A PLANETOID NAMED CERES, LOCATED IN THIS SOLAR SYSTEM'S ASTEROID BELT.
BUT WHAT WILL WE DO WHEN WE GET THERE?
AGAINST THIS THING THAT DEFIES ALL TIME AND SPACE AND PHYSICS AND--?
EXACTLY.
WHAT ARE WE SUPPOSED TO DO AGAINST SOMETHING LIKE THAT?
WE WILL DO NOTHING.
HE WILL BOW DOWN AND PRAY FORGIVENESS FROM HIS KING.

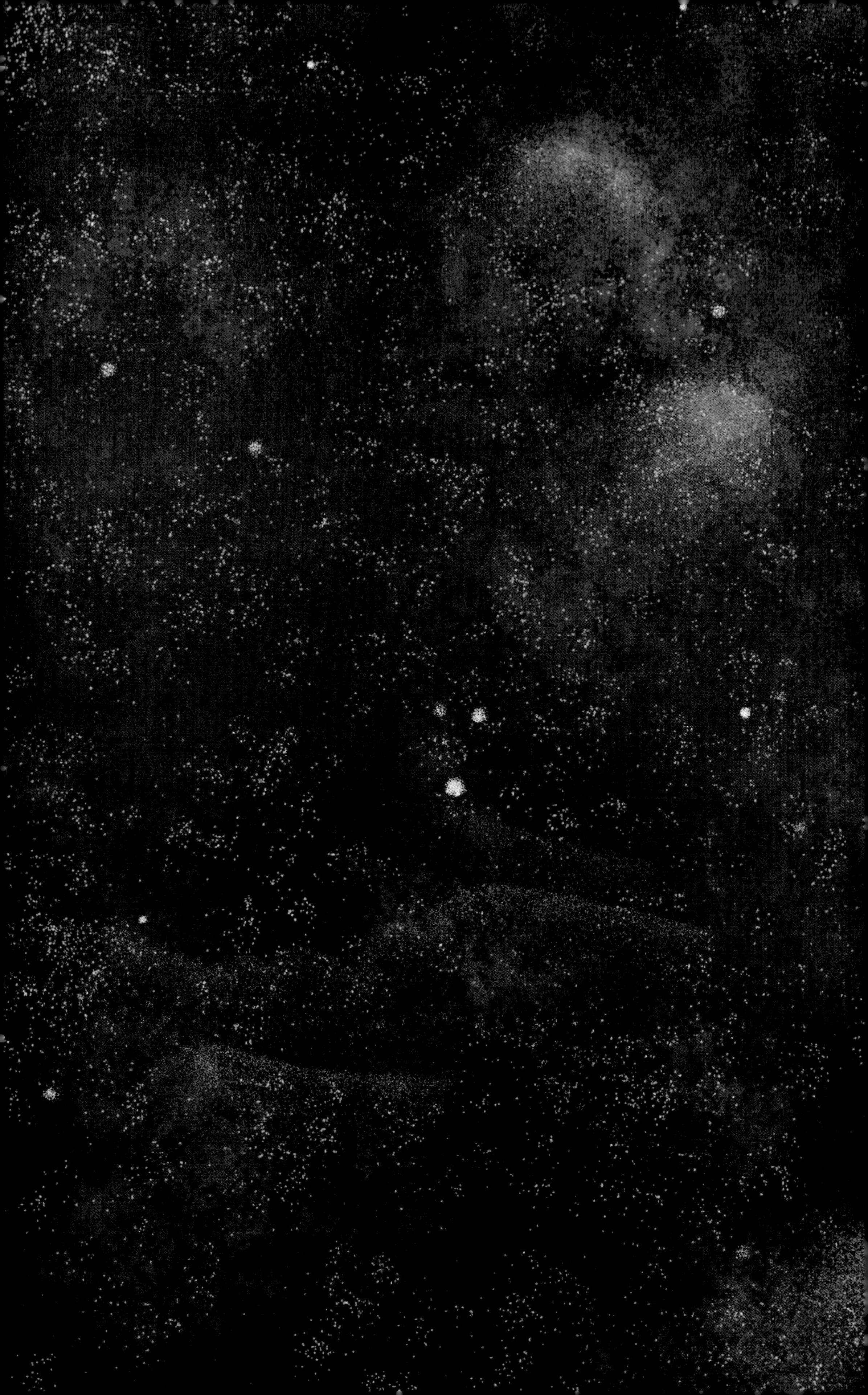

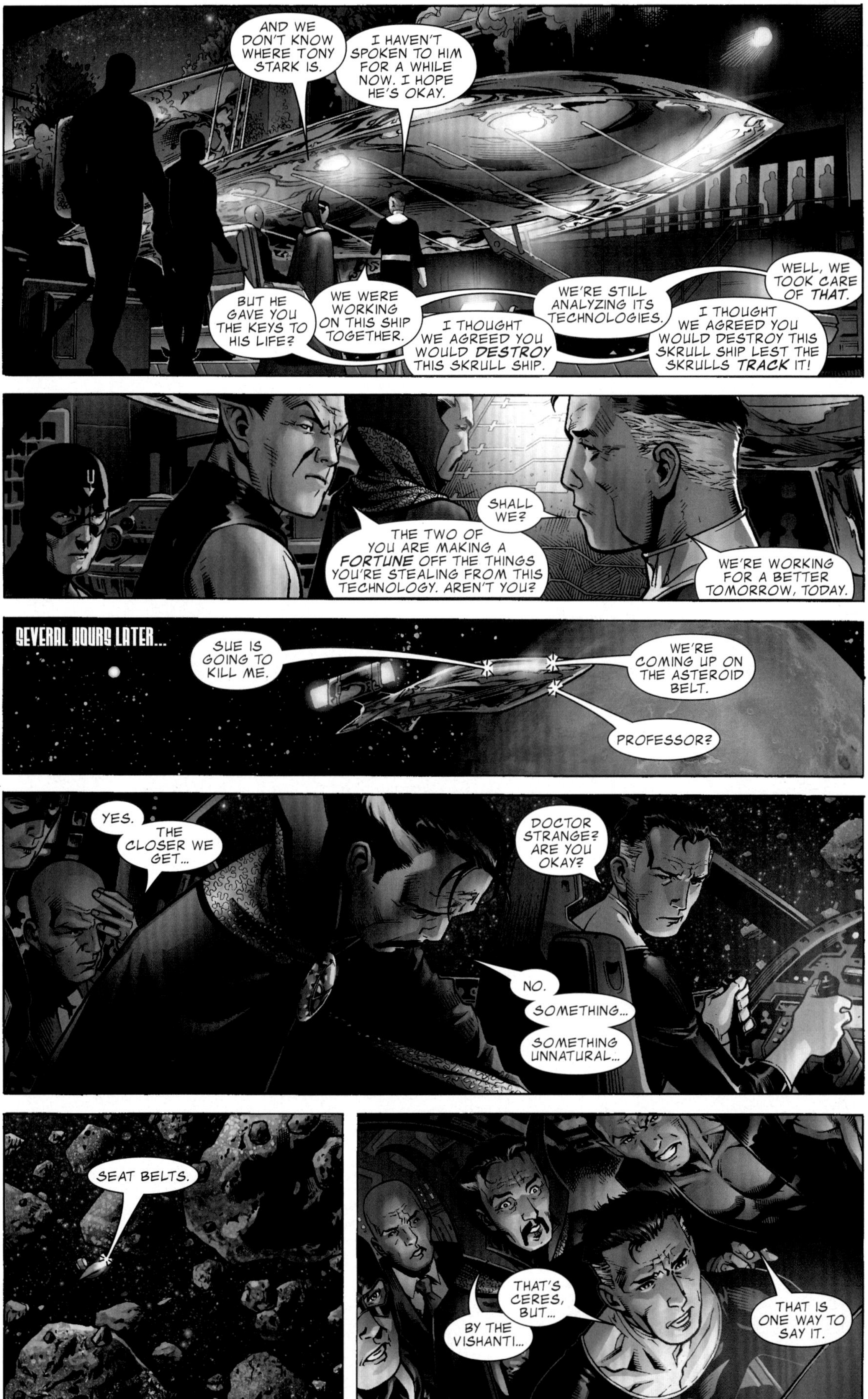
AND WE DON'T KNOW WHERE TONY STARK IS.
I HAVEN'T SPOKEN TO HIM FOR A WHILE NOW. I HOPE HE'S OKAY.
BUT HE GAVE YOU THE KEYS TO HIS LIFE?
WE WERE WORKING ON THIS SHIP TOGETHER.
I THOUGHT WE AGREED YOU WOULD DESTROY THIS SKRULL SHIP.
WE'RE STILL ANALYZING ITS TECHNOLOGIES.
I THOUGHT WE AGREED YOU WOULD DESTROY THIS SKRULL SHIP LEST THE SKRULLS TRACK IT!
WELL, WE TOOK CARE OF THAT.
THE TWO OF YOU ARE MAKING A FORTUNE OFF THE THINGS YOU'RE STEALING FROM THIS TECHNOLOGY. AREN'T YOU?
SHALL WE?
WE'RE WORKING FOR A BETTER TOMORROW, TODAY.
SEVERAL HOURS LATER...
SUE IS GOING TO KILL ME.
WE'RE COMING UP ON THE ASTEROID BELT.
PROFESSOR?
YES.
THE CLOSER WE GET...
DOCTOR STRANGE? ARE YOU OKAY?
NO.
SOMETHING...
SOMETHING UNNATURAL...
SEAT BELTS.
THAT'S CERES, BUT...
BY THE VISHANTI...
THAT IS ONE WAY TO SAY IT.

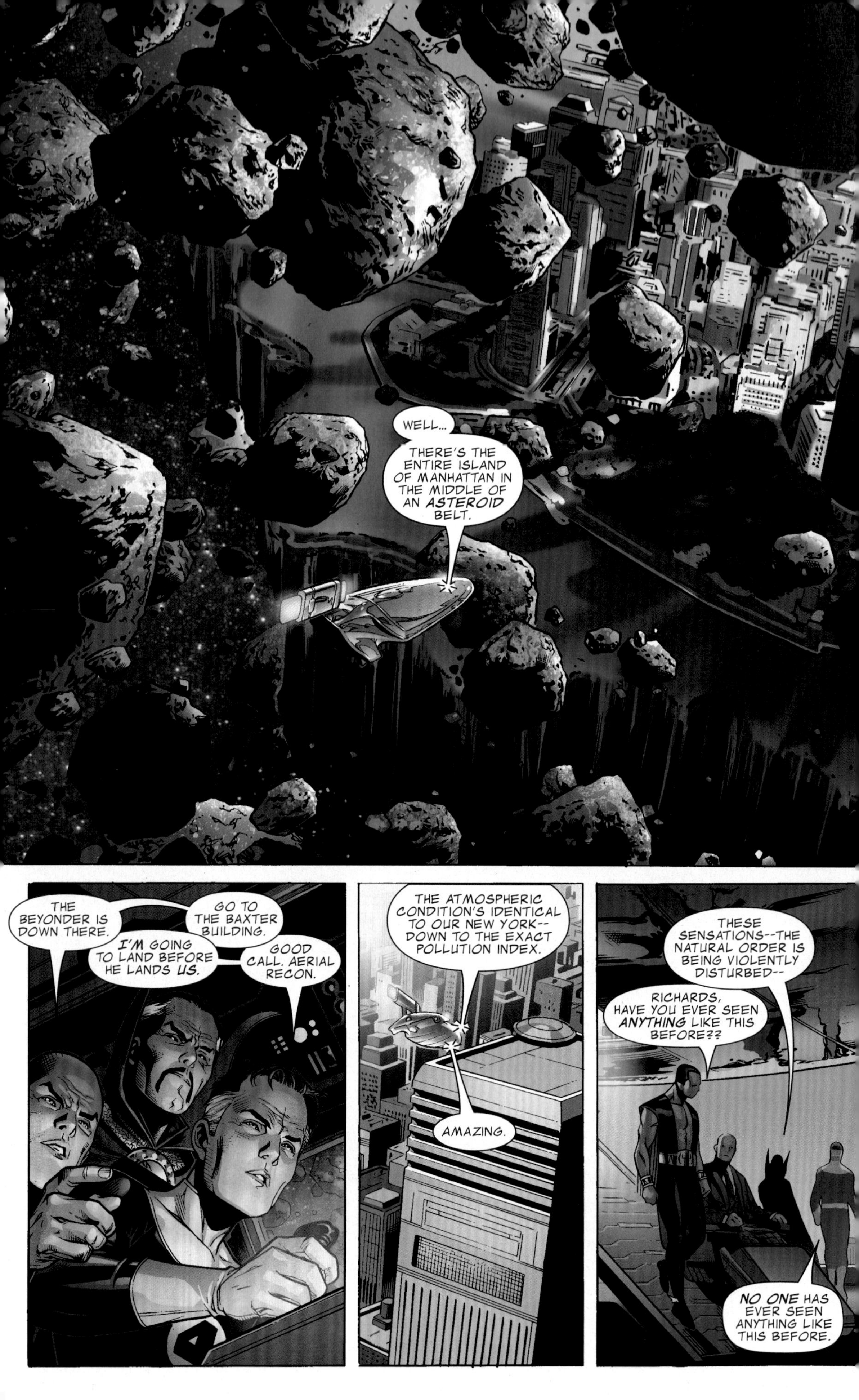
WELL...
THERE'S THE ENTIRE ISLAND OF MANHATTAN IN THE MIDDLE OF AN ASTEROID BELT.
THE BEYONDER IS DOWN THERE.
GO TO THE BAXTER BUILDING.
I'M GOING TO LAND BEFORE HE LANDS US.
GOOD CALL. AERIAL RECON.
THE ATMOSPHERIC CONDITION'S IDENTICAL TO OUR NEW YORK--DOWN TO THE EXACT POLLUTION INDEX.
AMAZING.
THESE SENSATIONS--THE NATURAL ORDER IS BEING VIOLENTLY DISTURBED--
RICHARDS, HAVE YOU EVER SEEN ANYTHING LIKE THIS BEFORE??
NO ONE HAS EVER SEEN ANYTHING LIKE THIS BEFORE.

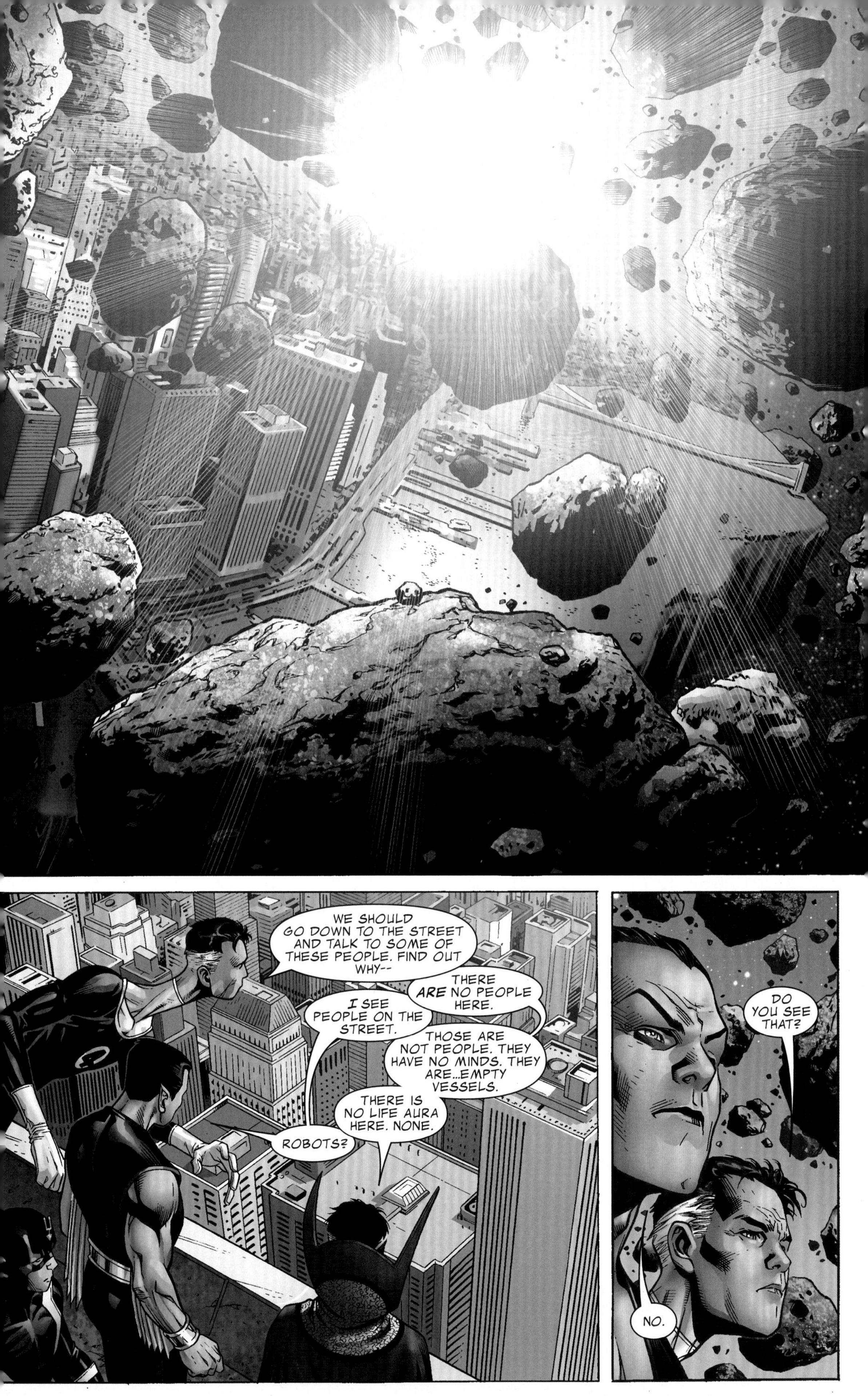
WE SHOULD GO DOWN TO THE STREET AND TALK TO SOME OF THESE PEOPLE. FIND OUT WHY--
THERE *ARE* NO PEOPLE HERE.
I SEE PEOPLE ON THE STREET.
THOSE ARE NOT PEOPLE. THEY HAVE NO MINDS. THEY ARE...EMPTY VESSELS.
ROBOTS?
THERE IS NO LIFE AURA HERE. NONE.
DO YOU SEE THAT?
NO.

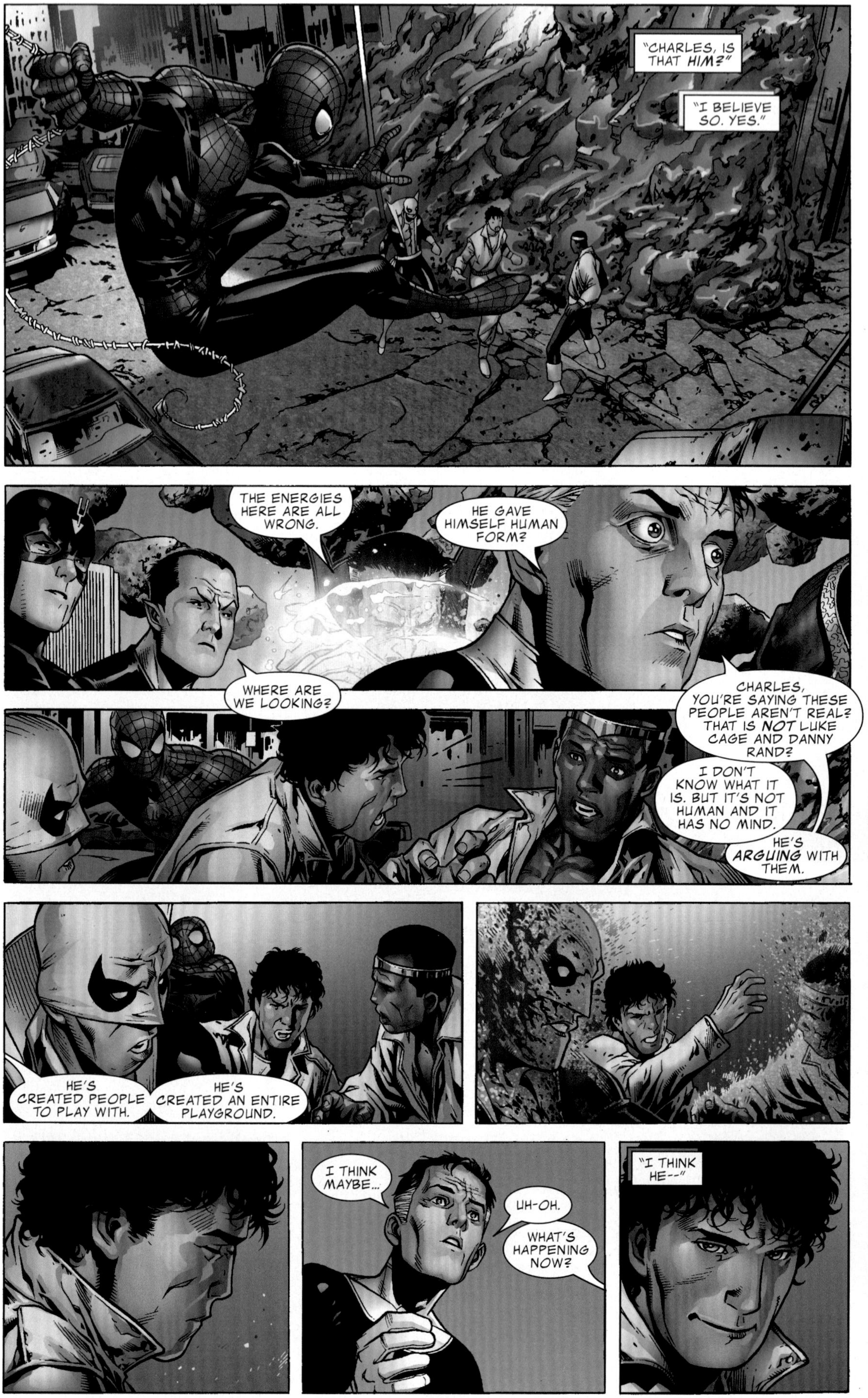

"CHARLES, IS THAT HIM?"
"I BELIEVE SO. YES."
THE ENERGIES HERE ARE ALL WRONG.
HE GAVE HIMSELF HUMAN FORM?
WHERE ARE WE LOOKING?
CHARLES, YOU'RE SAYING THESE PEOPLE AREN'T REAL? THAT IS NOT LUKE CAGE AND DANNY RAND?
I DON'T KNOW WHAT IT IS. BUT IT'S NOT HUMAN AND IT HAS NO MIND.
HE'S ARGUING WITH THEM.
HE'S CREATED PEOPLE TO PLAY WITH.
HE'S CREATED AN ENTIRE PLAYGROUND.
I THINK MAYBE...
UH-OH.
WHAT'S HAPPENING NOW?
"I THINK HE--"

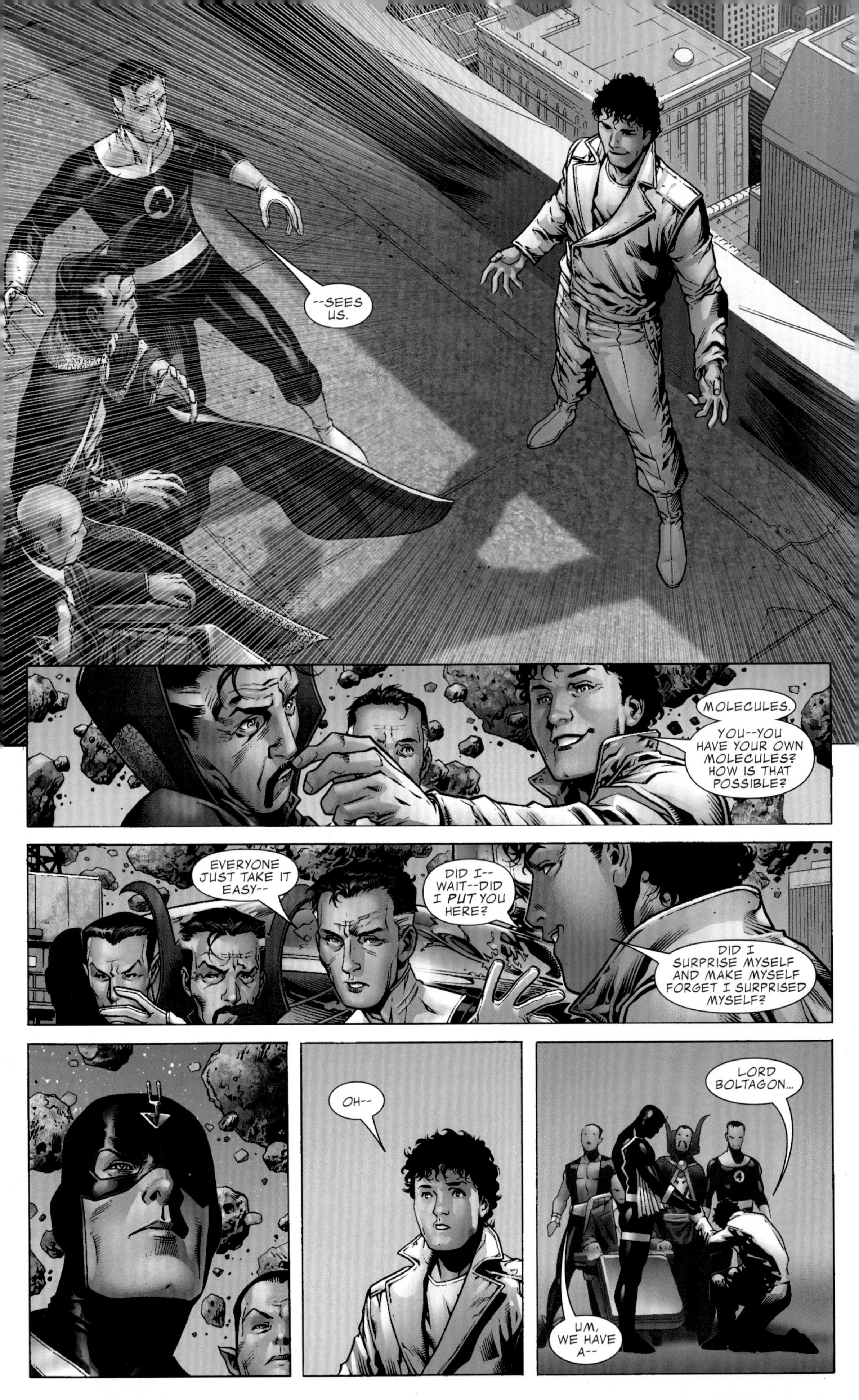
--SEES US.
MOLECULES.
YOU--YOU HAVE YOUR OWN MOLECULES? HOW IS THAT POSSIBLE?
EVERYONE JUST TAKE IT EASY--
DID I-- WAIT--DID I PUT YOU HERE?
DID I SURPRISE MYSELF AND MAKE MYSELF FORGET I SURPRISED MYSELF?
OH--
LORD BOLTAGON...
UM, WE HAVE A--

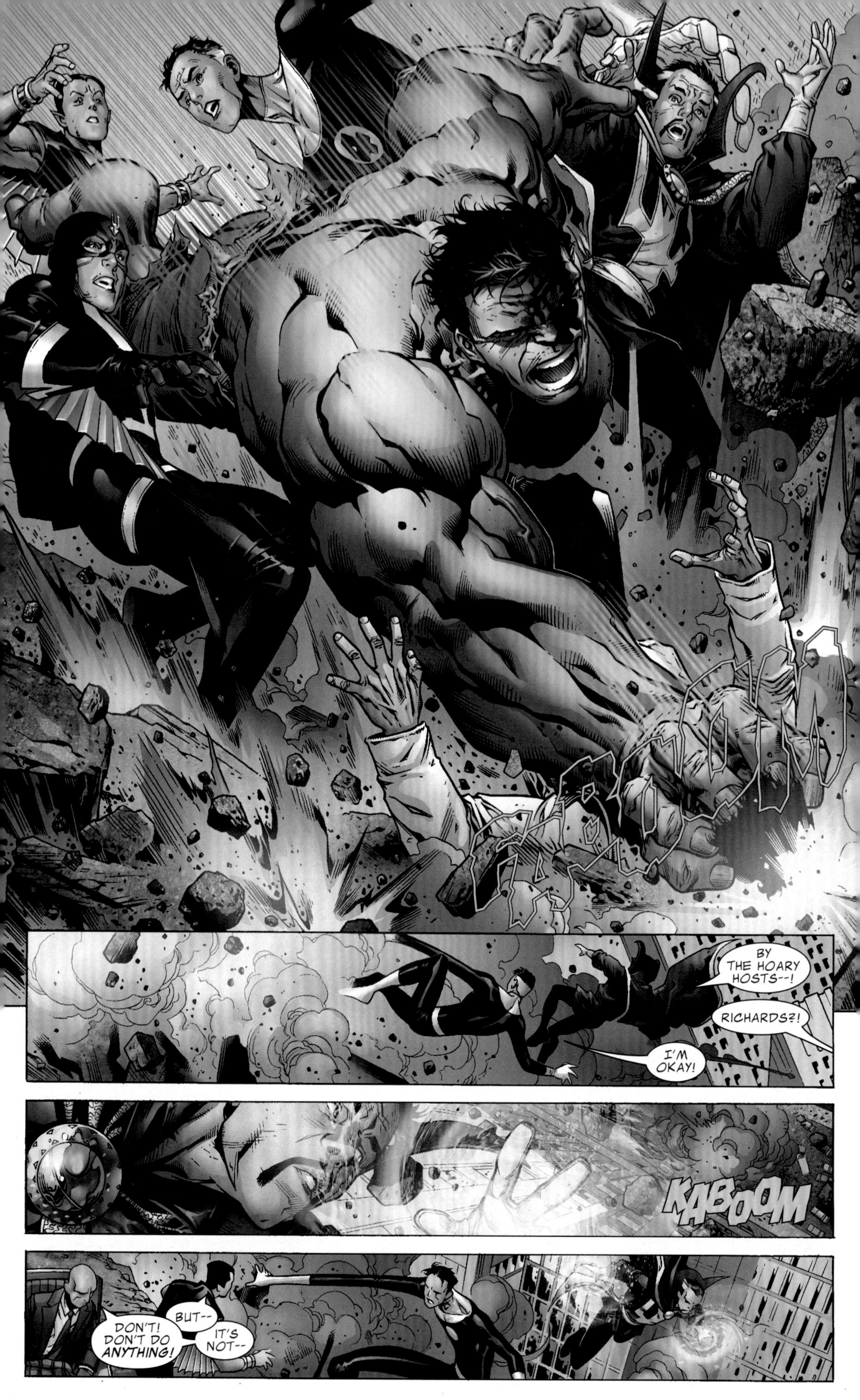

BY THE HOARY HOSTS--!
RICHARDS?!
I'M OKAY!
KABOOM
DON'T! DON'T DO ANYTHING!
BUT--
IT'S NOT--

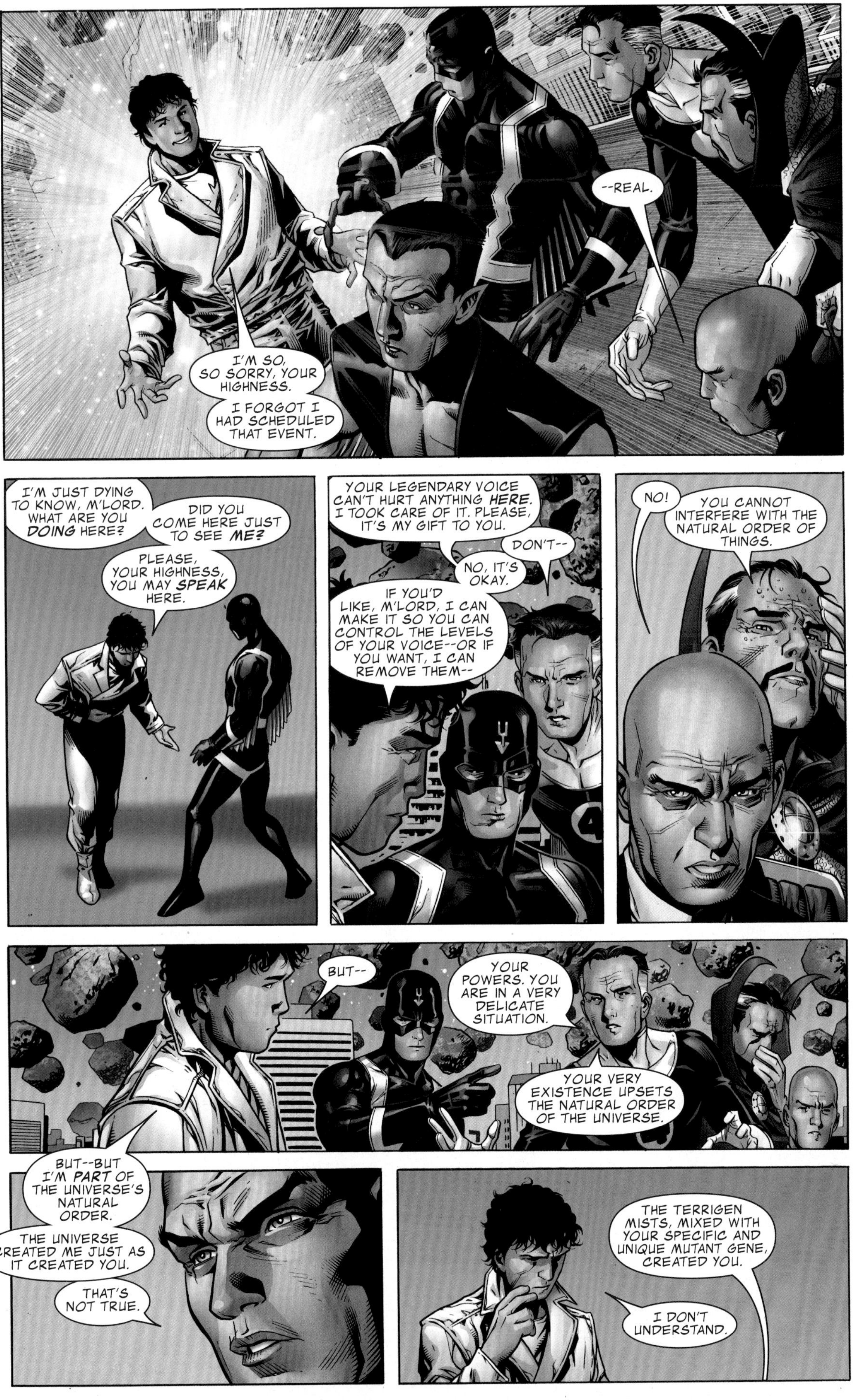
--REAL.
I'M SO, SO SORRY, YOUR HIGHNESS.
I FORGOT I HAD SCHEDULED THAT EVENT.
I'M JUST DYING TO KNOW, M'LORD. WHAT ARE YOU DOING HERE?
DID YOU COME HERE JUST TO SEE ME?
PLEASE, YOUR HIGHNESS, YOU MAY SPEAK HERE.
YOUR LEGENDARY VOICE CAN'T HURT ANYTHING HERE. I TOOK CARE OF IT. PLEASE, IT'S MY GIFT TO YOU.
DON'T--
NO, IT'S OKAY.
IF YOU'D LIKE, M'LORD, I CAN MAKE IT SO YOU CAN CONTROL THE LEVELS OF YOUR VOICE--OR IF YOU WANT, I CAN REMOVE THEM--
NO!
YOU CANNOT INTERFERE WITH THE NATURAL ORDER OF THINGS.
BUT--
YOUR POWERS. YOU ARE IN A VERY DELICATE SITUATION.
YOUR VERY EXISTENCE UPSETS THE NATURAL ORDER OF THE UNIVERSE.
BUT--BUT I'M PART OF THE UNIVERSE'S NATURAL ORDER.
THE UNIVERSE CREATED ME JUST AS IT CREATED YOU.
THAT'S NOT TRUE.
THE TERRIGEN MISTS, MIXED WITH YOUR SPECIFIC AND UNIQUE MUTANT GENE, CREATED YOU.
I DON'T UNDERSTAND.

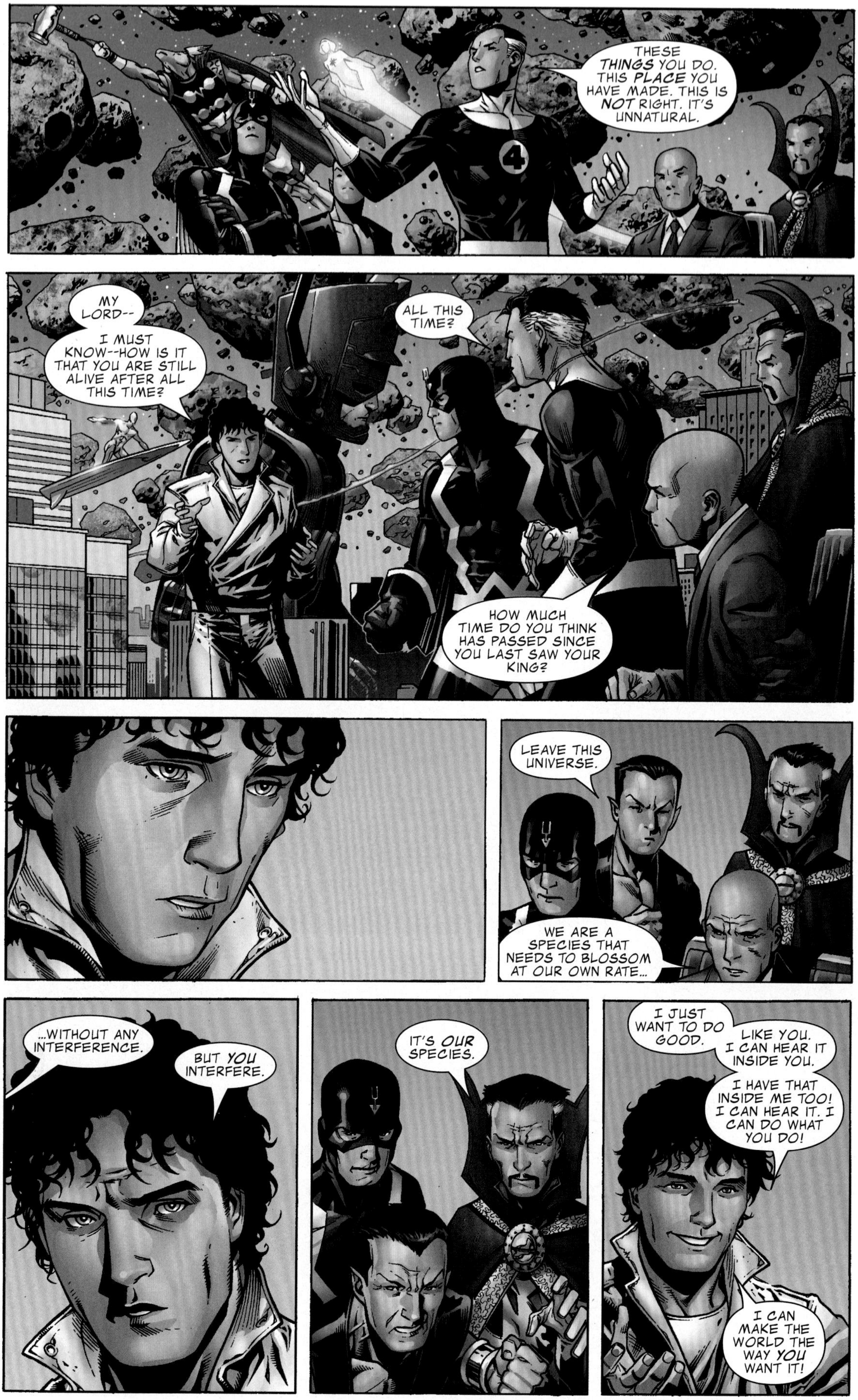
THESE THINGS YOU DO. THIS PLACE YOU HAVE MADE. THIS IS NOT RIGHT. IT'S UNNATURAL.
MY LORD--
I MUST KNOW--HOW IS IT THAT YOU ARE STILL ALIVE AFTER ALL THIS TIME?
ALL THIS TIME?
HOW MUCH TIME DO YOU THINK HAS PASSED SINCE YOU LAST SAW YOUR KING?
LEAVE THIS UNIVERSE.
WE ARE A SPECIES THAT NEEDS TO BLOSSOM AT OUR OWN RATE...
...WITHOUT ANY INTERFERENCE.
BUT YOU INTERFERE.
IT'S OUR SPECIES.
I JUST WANT TO DO GOOD.
LIKE YOU. I CAN HEAR IT INSIDE YOU.
I HAVE THAT INSIDE ME TOO! I CAN HEAR IT. I CAN DO WHAT YOU DO!
I CAN MAKE THE WORLD THE WAY YOU WANT IT!

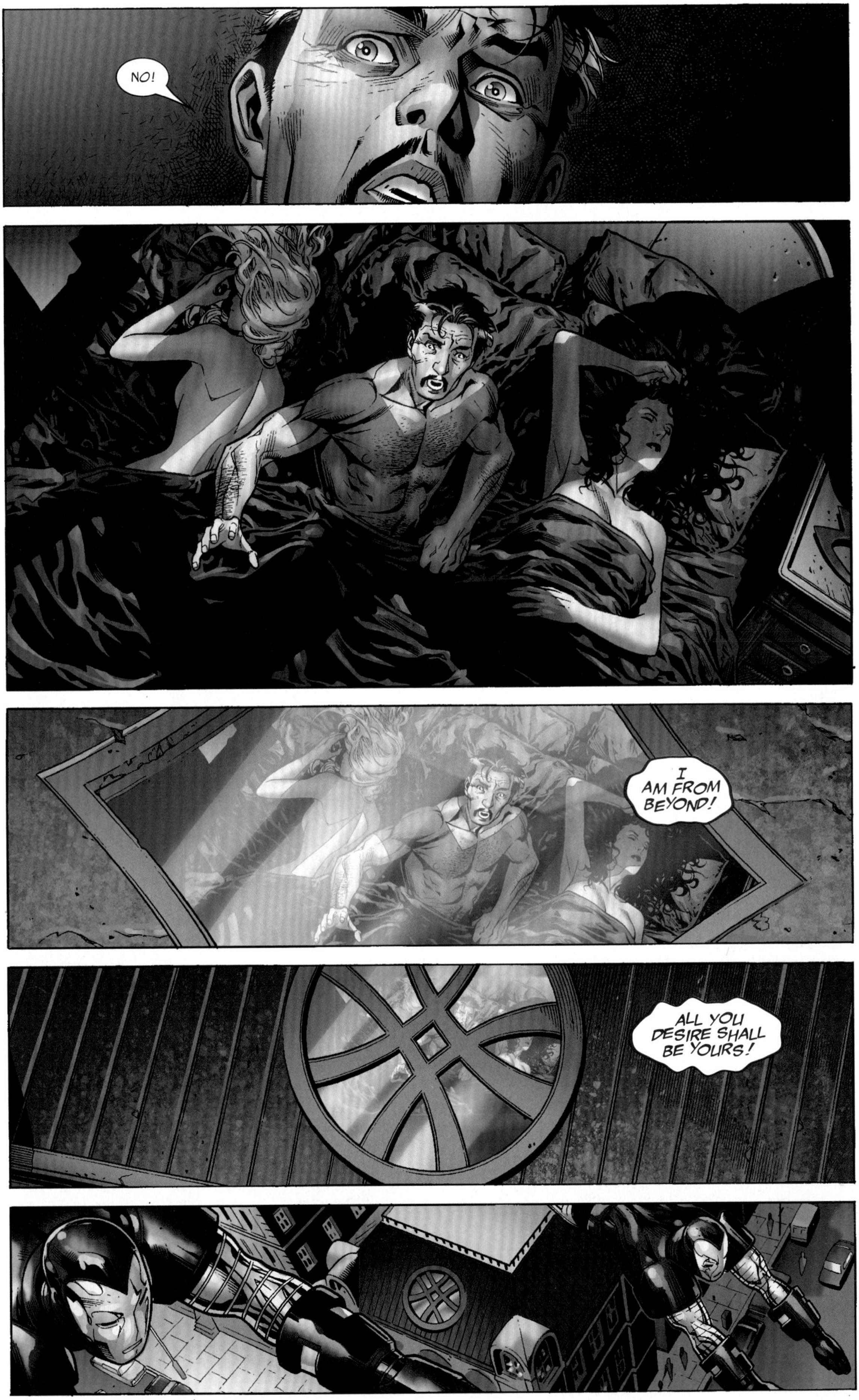
NO!
I AM FROM BEYOND!
ALL YOU DESIRE SHALL BE YOURS!

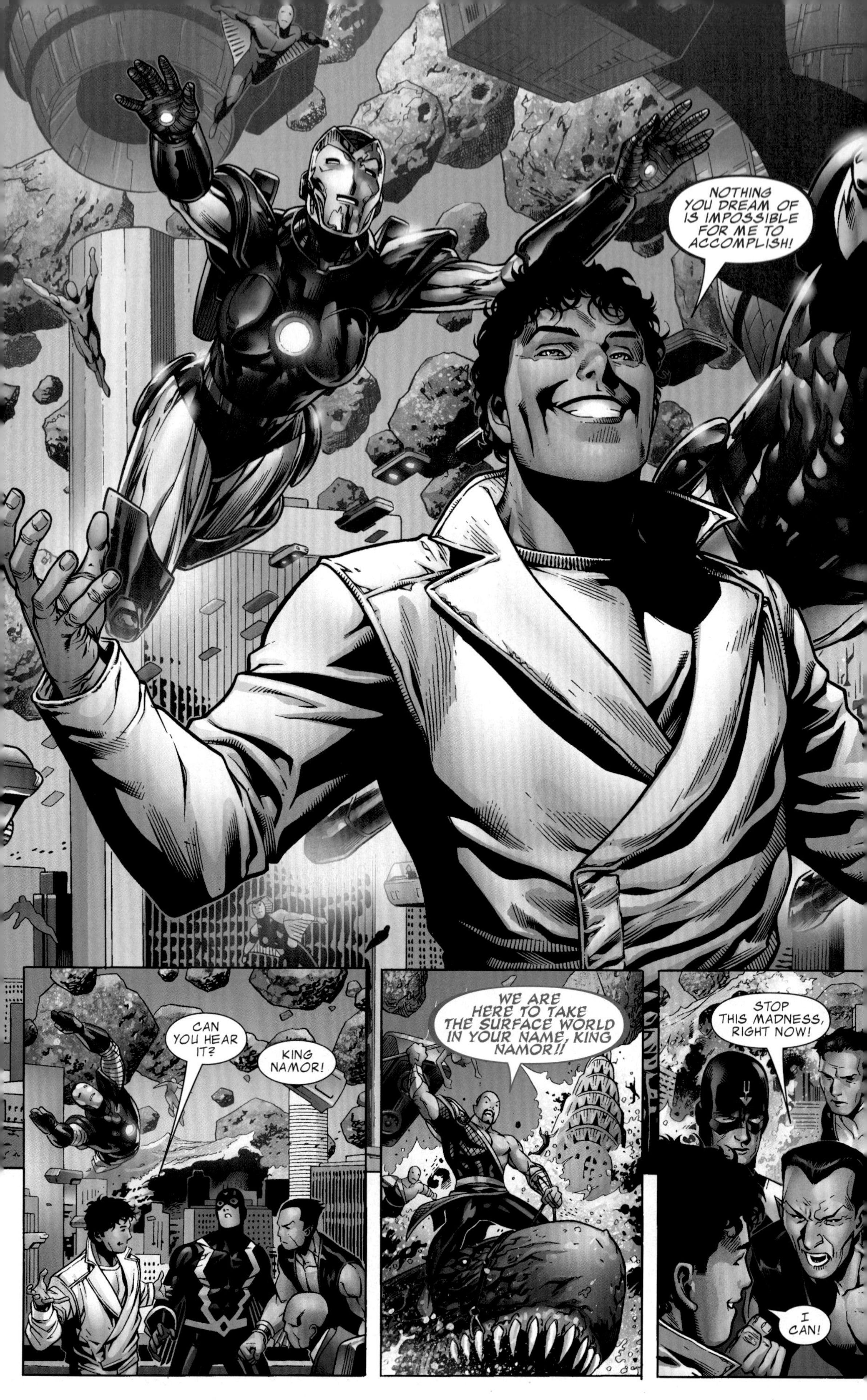
NOTHING YOU DREAM OF IS IMPOSSIBLE FOR ME TO ACCOMPLISH!
CAN YOU HEAR IT?
KING NAMOR!
WE ARE HERE TO TAKE THE SURFACE WORLD IN YOUR NAME, KING NAMOR!!
STOP THIS MADNESS, RIGHT NOW!
I CAN!

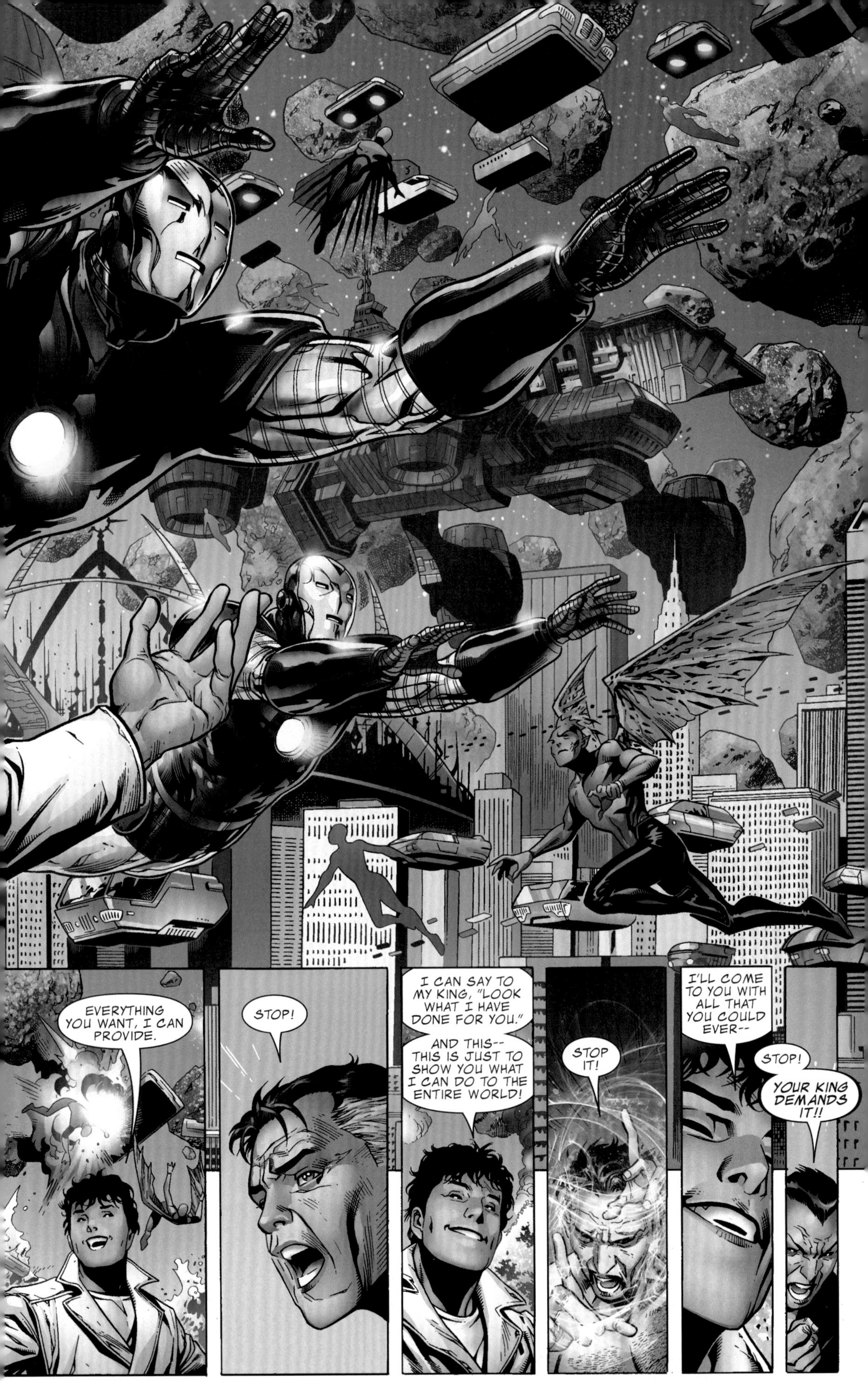
EVERYTHING YOU WANT, I CAN PROVIDE.
STOP!
I CAN SAY TO MY KING, "LOOK WHAT I HAVE DONE FOR YOU."
AND THIS-- THIS IS JUST TO SHOW YOU WHAT I CAN DO TO THE ENTIRE WORLD!
STOP IT!
I'LL COME TO YOU WITH ALL THAT YOU COULD EVER--
STOP!
YOUR KING DEMANDS IT!!

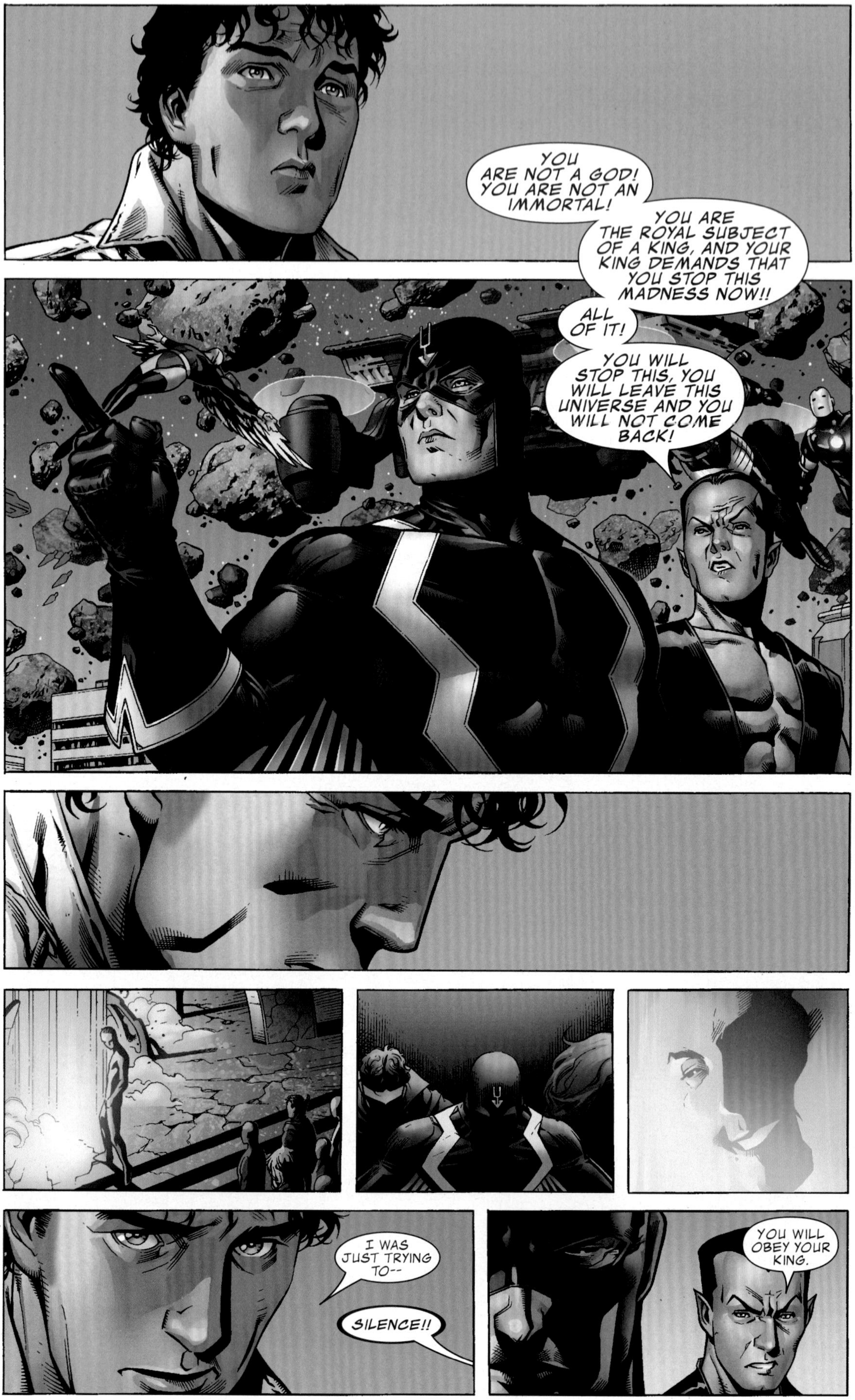
YOU ARE NOT A GOD! YOU ARE NOT AN IMMORTAL!
YOU ARE THE ROYAL SUBJECT OF A KING, AND YOUR KING DEMANDS THAT YOU STOP THIS MADNESS NOW!!
ALL OF IT!
YOU WILL STOP THIS, YOU WILL LEAVE THIS UNIVERSE AND YOU WILL NOT COME BACK!
I WAS JUST TRYING TO--
SILENCE!!
YOU WILL OBEY YOUR KING.

UM...

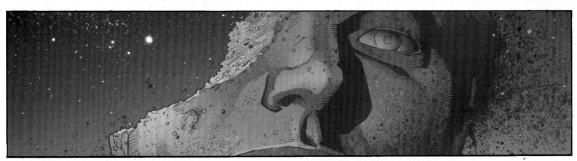

THOSE ASTEROIDS SEEM TO BE GETTING CLOSER.

I BELIEVE IT'S TIME TO GO.

I WOULD AGREE.

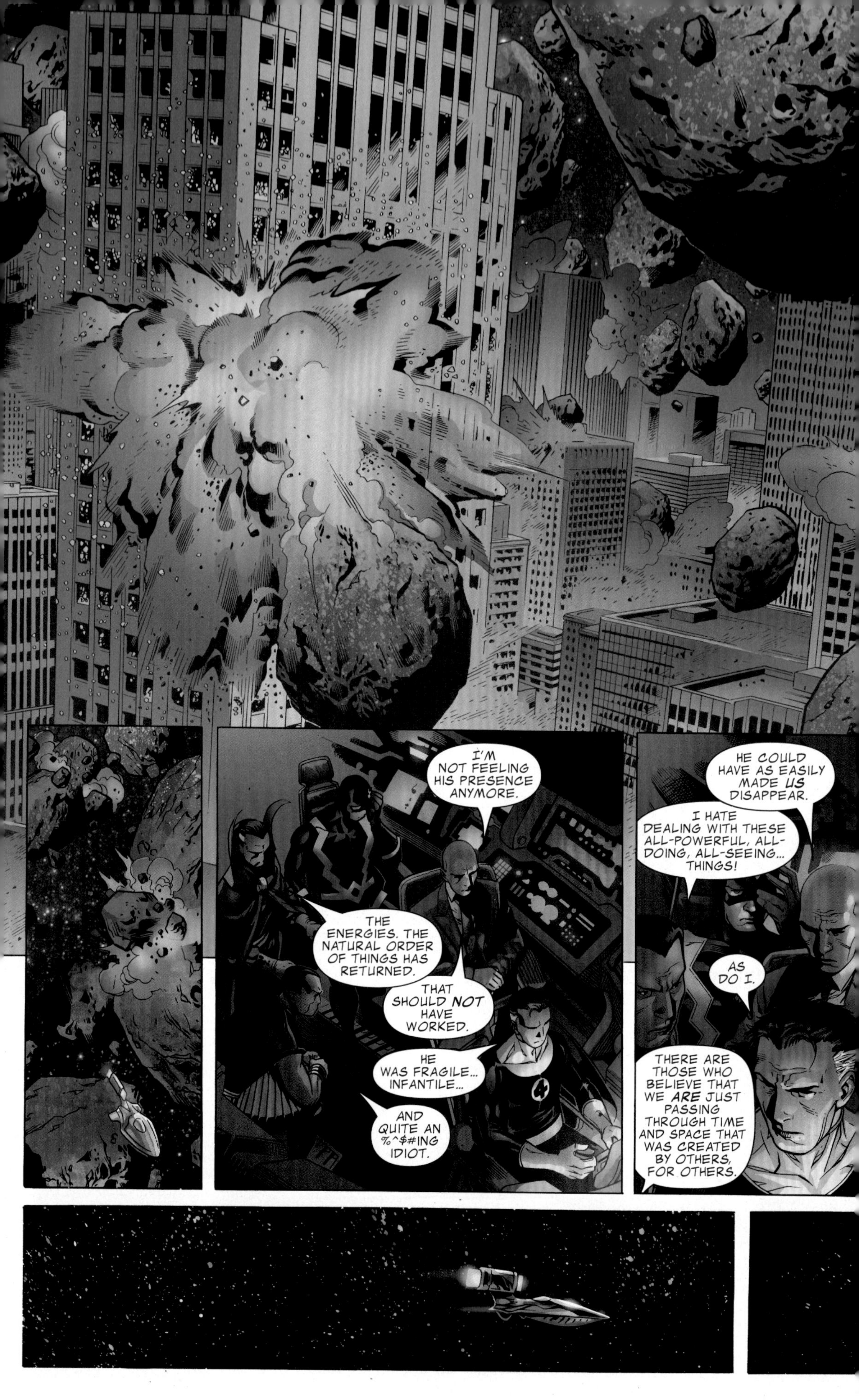
I'M NOT FEELING HIS PRESENCE ANYMORE.
THE ENERGIES. THE NATURAL ORDER OF THINGS HAS RETURNED.
THAT SHOULD NOT HAVE WORKED.
HE WAS FRAGILE... INFANTILE...
AND QUITE AN %^$#ING IDIOT.
HE COULD HAVE AS EASILY MADE US DISAPPEAR.
I HATE DEALING WITH THESE ALL-POWERFUL, ALL-DOING, ALL-SEEING... THINGS!
AS DO I.
THERE ARE THOSE WHO BELIEVE THAT WE ARE JUST PASSING THROUGH TIME AND SPACE THAT WAS CREATED BY OTHERS, FOR OTHERS.

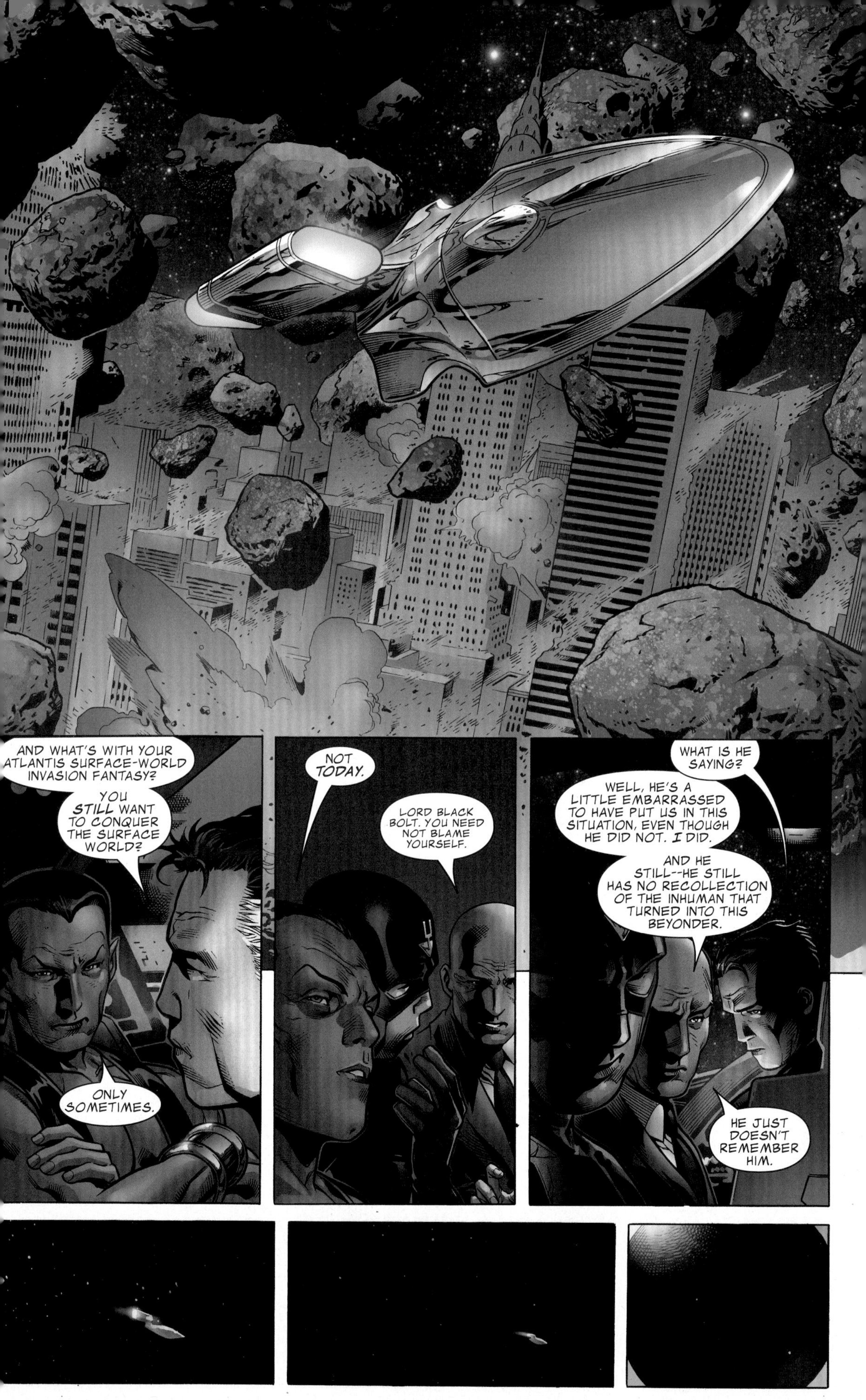
AND WHAT'S WITH YOUR ATLANTIS SURFACE-WORLD INVASION FANTASY?
YOU STILL WANT TO CONQUER THE SURFACE WORLD?
ONLY SOMETIMES.
NOT TODAY.
LORD BLACK BOLT. YOU NEED NOT BLAME YOURSELF.
WHAT IS HE SAYING?
WELL, HE'S A LITTLE EMBARRASSED TO HAVE PUT US IN THIS SITUATION, EVEN THOUGH HE DID NOT. I DID.
AND HE STILL--HE STILL HAS NO RECOLLECTION OF THE INHUMAN THAT TURNED INTO THIS BEYONDER.
HE JUST DOESN'T REMEMBER HIM.

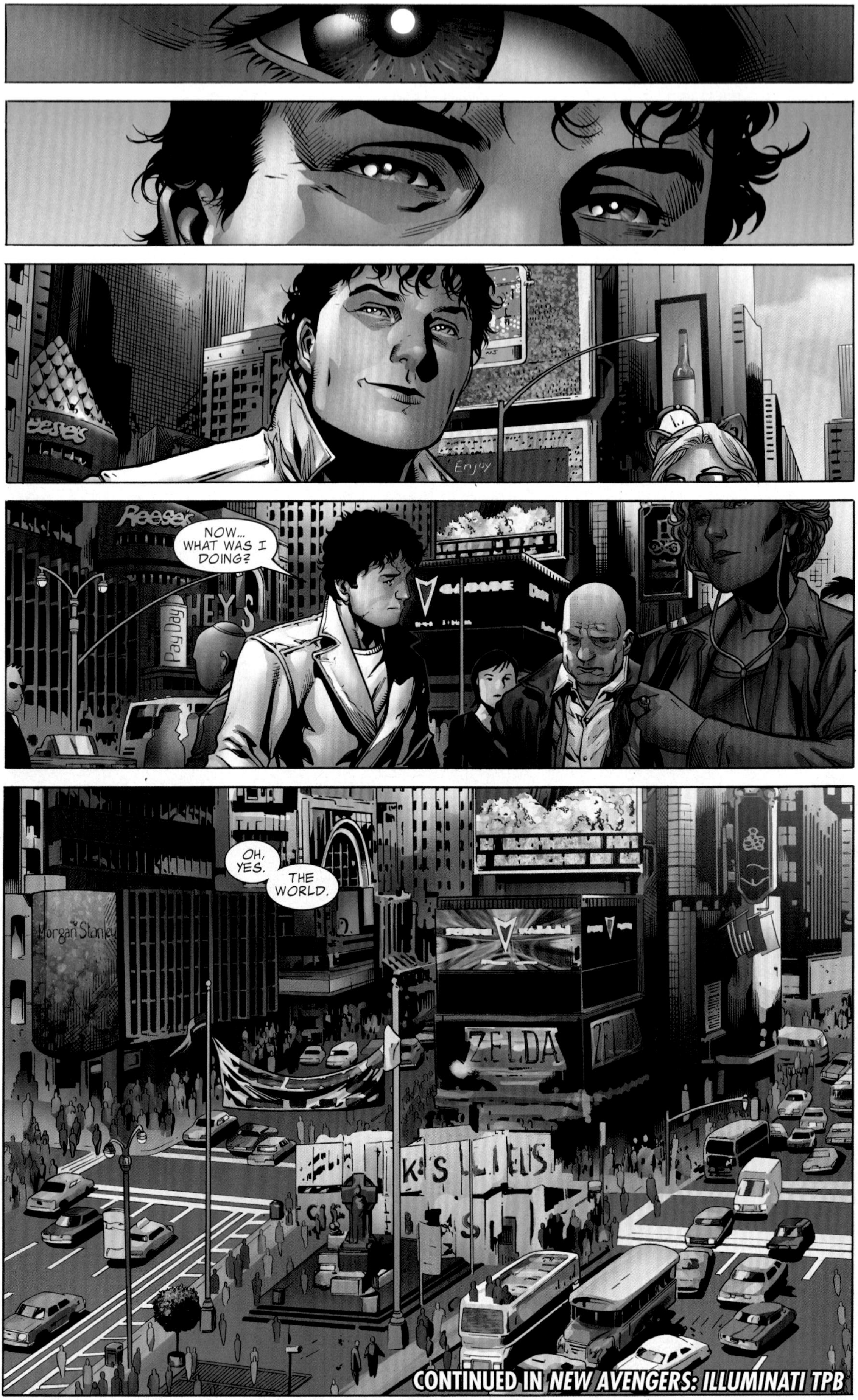
Reese's
Enjoy
NOW... WHAT WAS I DOING?
Reese's
PayDay
HEY'S
OH, YES.
THE WORLD.
Morgan Stanley
ZELDA

CONTINUED IN *NEW AVENGERS: ILLUMINATI TPB*

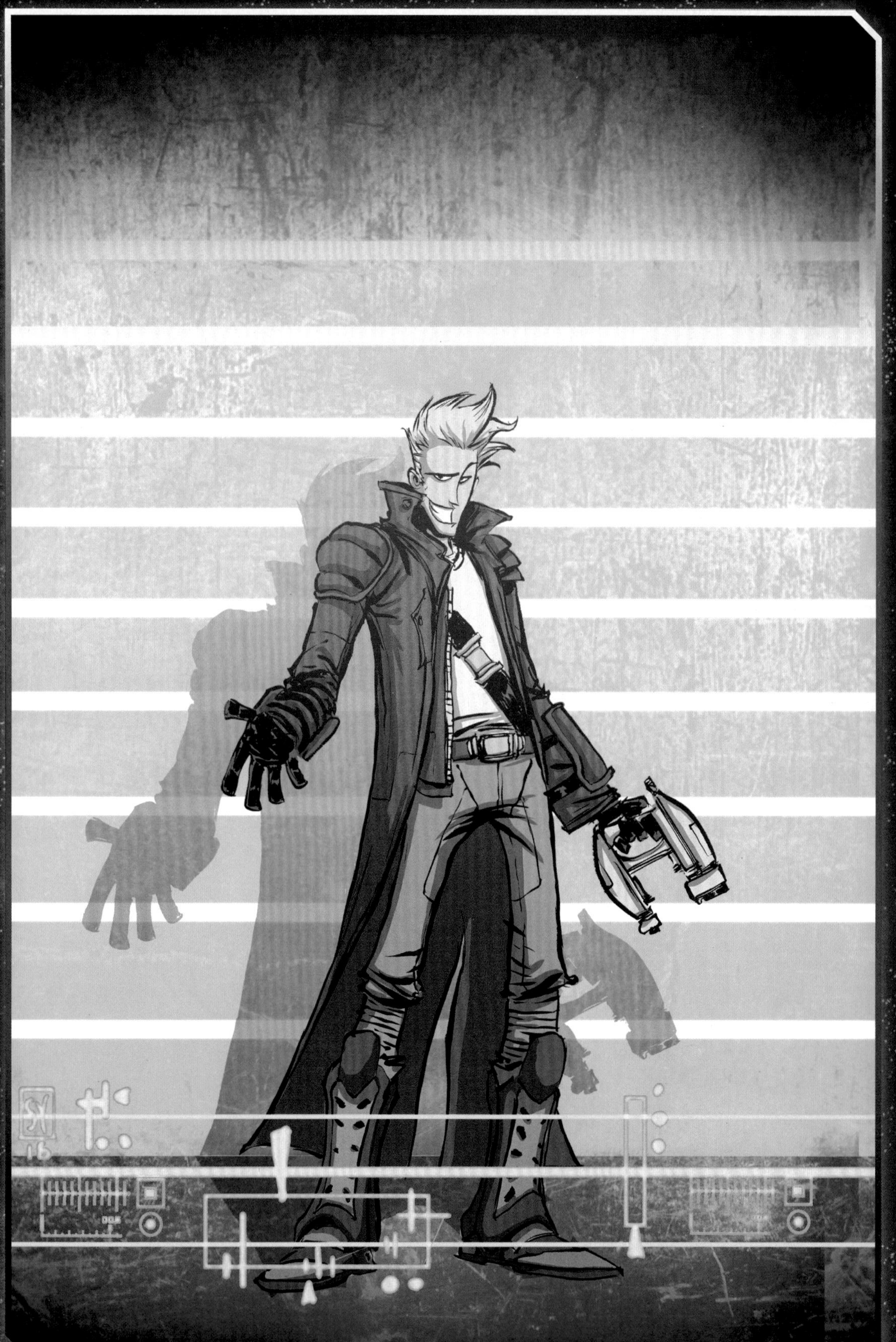

GUARDIANS OF KNOWHERE #1
VARIANT BY SKOTTIE YOUNG

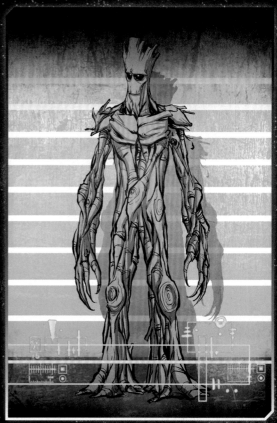

GUARDIANS OF KNOWHERE #1-4
VARIANTS BY SKOTTIE YOUNG